D1244168

Commonsense Computer Security

Titles in the IBM McGraw-Hill Series

Open Systems and IBM: Integration and Convergence
Pamela Gray   ISBN 0-07-707750-4

OS/2 Presentation Manager Programming: Hints and Tips
Bryan Goodyer   ISBN 0-07-707776-8

IBM RISC System/6000
Clive Harris   ISBN 0-07-707668-0

IBM RISC System/6000 User Guide
Mike Leaver and Hardev Sanghera   ISBN 0-07-707687-7

PC User's Guide: Simple Steps to Powerful Personal Computing
Peter Turner   ISBN 0-07-707421-1

Dynamic Factory Automation: Creating Flexible Systems for
Competitive Manufacturing
Alastair Ross   ISBN 0-07-707440-8

MVS Systems Programming
Dave Elder-Vass   ISBN 0-07-707767-9

The New Organization: Growing the Culture of Organizational
Networking
Colin Hastings   ISBN 0-07-707784-9

Commonsense Computer Security Second Edition: Your Practical
Guide to Information Protection
Martin Smith   ISBN 0-07-707805-5

CICS Concepts and Uses: A Management Guide
Jim Geraghty   ISBN 0-07-707751-2

Risk Management for Software Projects
Alex Down, Michael Coleman and Peter Absolon ISBN 0-07-707816-0

Investing in Information Technology: Managing the decision-making
process
Geoff Hogbin and David Thomas   ISBN 0-07-707957-1

The Advanced Programmer's Guide to AIX 3.x
Phil Colledge   ISBN 0-07-707663-X

Details of these titles in the series are available from:

The Product Manager, Professional Books
McGraw-Hill Book Company Europe
Shoppenhangers Road, Maidenhead, Berkshire, SL6 2QL
Telephone: 0628 23432 Fax: 0628 770224

Martin Smith
MBE, BSc, MIMgt

Commonsense Computer Security

Your practical guide to information protection
Second Edition

McGRAW-HILL BOOK COMPANY

London · New York · St Louis · San Francisco · Auckland
Bogotá · Caracas · Lisbon · Madrid · Mexico · Milan
Montreal · New Delhi · Panama · Paris · San Juan
São Paulo · Singapore · Sydney · Tokyo · Toronto

Published by
McGRAW-HILL Book Company Europe
Shoppenhangers Road, Maidenhead, Berkshire, SL6 2QL, England
Tel 0628 23432; Fax 0628 770224

British Library Cataloguing in Publication Data
Smith, Martin R.
  Commonsense Computer Security: Your
  Practical Guide to Information
  Protection. – 2Rev. ed. – (IBM
  McGraw-Hill Series)
  I. Title II. Series
  005.8

  ISBN 0-07-707805-5

Library of Congress Cataloging-in-Publication Data
Smith, Martin R.
  Commonsense computer security: your practical guide to
  information protection/Martin R. Smith. – 2nd ed. p. cm.
  Includes bibliographical references and index.
  ISBN 0-07-707805-5
  1. Computer security. 2. Data protection. I. Title.
  QA76.9.A25S64   1993   93–9060
  658.4'78—dc20   CIP

1234 CUP 9543

Typeset by Datix International Limited, Bungay, Suffolk
and printed in England by the University Press, Cambridge.

Contents

Foreword

The IBM McGraw-Hill Series

IBM UK and McGraw-Hill Europe have worked together to publish this series of books about information technology and its use in business, industry and the public sector.

The series provides an up-to-date and authoritative insight into the wide range of products and services available, and offers strategic business advice. Some of the books have a technical bias, others are written from a broader business perspective. What they have in common is that their authors—some from IBM, some independent consultants—are experts in their field.

Apart from assisting where possible with the accuracy of the writing, IBM UK has not sought to inhibit the editorial freedom of the series, and therefore the views expressed in the books are those of the authors, and not necessarily those of IBM.

Where IBM has lent its expertise is in assisting McGraw-Hill to identify potential titles whose publication would help advance knowledge and increase awareness of computing topics. Hopefully these titles will also serve to widen the debate about the important information technology issues of today and of the future—such as open systems, networking, and the use of technology to give companies a competitive edge in their market.

IBM UK is pleased to be associated with McGraw-Hill in this series.

Sir Anthony Cleaver
Chairman
IBM United Kingdom Limited

Acknowledgements

I should like to thank my friends at McGraw-Hill and at IBM (UK) for their support and encouragement towards the preparation of this second edition of *Commonsense Computer Security*. Of course, I remain grateful to those who were involved in the original production, but this time I must also acknowledge the contributions of my colleagues, especially Stephen Daniels and Mark Tantam. Rod Parkin and John Sherwood have also been of great assistance, for which I am indebted. I owe you all a beer.

In particular, though, I should like to express my gratitude to Ken Slater, for his kind permission to reproduce the details in Chapter 24 on computer legislation, first contained in his excellent book *Information Security in Financial Services* (1991) which I recommend without hesitation to those of my readers who wish to delve further into the fascinating subject of computer security.

I have included a bibliography of my other major sources of reference, but there were many other books and articles painfully and sleepily digested and absorbed during the bumpy ride on the 7.15 each morning from Bedford, and a variety of late trains on the return journey each evening. Now that it is finished, perhaps I might join my fellow commuters in their studied slumbers. Until, perhaps, the third edition. . . .

Preface

Many things have changed since I began writing the first edition of this book some five years ago. Of course, like us all, I'm a little older, greyer and, hopefully, wiser. I have retired from the Royal Air Force and I am now working as Director of Corporate Security for Kroll Associates in London. Oh, and there's a new little Smith.

During this time too, previously unimaginable political changes have brought down the barriers between the East and West and the Cold War has ended. But to my mind an economic war has already replaced it, with information an even more valuable currency to be fought over with increasing cunning, determination and boldness. While state and military espionage activity involving government classified information may have become less significant as old enmities end, increased industrial espionage operations now affect most sectors of our international economies. Once, spies targeted the latest weapons systems; now that effort has been turned towards more mundane items vital to the growing nations.

Information is, even more now, the key resource of industry and business; it is the new currency. Growth and success follow from good information; failure follows from its loss, corruption or unavailability. Possession of information has become a goal in itself, and the methods the opposition use to acquire it vary from the ingenious through the improper to the downright dishonest. Like capital and people, information is an essential corporate asset. Yet this vital resource now resides in vast quantities within the new technology that today has become part of our everyday lives—the computer—and the perils associated with the loss, corruption or non-availability of such electronic data await the unwary, unwise or careless.

Computer security has become the subject of much discussion and a whole industry of books, seminars, conferences and courses has emerged. But still not enough is being done about introducing it practically. Most believe they have no need for it, or insist that disasters and security breaches only happen to others; some learn the hard way that this is not so. It need not be, as many claim it is, either complicated or expensive, nor is it an impossible task. The solutions are straightforward, and need not be highly technical. Low-tech insider crimes and operator errors are the greatest threats, not highly sophisticated attacks; the countermeasures need to be similarly uncomplicated. Computer security is a people problem, not a machine one, and should be dealt with accordingly.

Yet computer security still tends to be dismissed too easily from the business equation. Management is often only interested in results with the minimum overheads, and has no time for the new-fangled machines provided they do their job; computer personnel will nurse their charges with all the fervour of young mothers, with total faith in them and complete blindness to their faults and weaknesses; and security staff regularly display ignorance, and a suspicion and distrust of this new technology verging on the phobic. But encouragingly I have seen a positive change over the last five years. Where once I felt I was a voice in the wilderness, I have now been joined by many others from each of these disciplines emphasizing the importance of management involvement and promoting the use of old-fashioned and reliable security techniques. There is still a long way to go and progress is too slow for my liking, but at last the movement is all in the right direction. That this book has been endorsed by IBM speaks volumes for the approach I am advocating.

Positive efforts by all concerned are needed if progress is to be made towards improving the safety and security of computers, their operations and their data. The importance of this increases as we are driven towards greater networking, more distributed resources pushed downwards to the desk of the lowliest worker, and with open systems interconnection (OSI) a more open and therefore inherently more insecure computing environment. However, the beginning of this process is an understanding of the dangers and available defences, in terms comprehensible to all parties involved. This book aims to provide just that. In simple language, free from the misconceptions, prejudices and suspicions of managers, computer experts and security staffs alike, the threats to computers are described and their vulnerabilities defined. Countermeasures are listed to allow a cost-effective security policy to be developed. No simple answers are offered, but armed with a basis of common knowledge the corporate team may then consider the options available, if not to eliminate the risk, then at least to reduce it to an acceptable level. Further, armed with such knowledge, management will once more be in charge to dictate its security requirements to the computer suppliers and not, as is the case now, the reverse.

My background is not in computing but within the diverse world of security, and I bring with me into the world of information technology the lessons I have learned in traditional security methodology. Defence in depth is offered as the most effective counter to the many weaknesses inherent in computer systems, and I discuss each element of security in detail but in non-technical terms—I know no other way. It is hoped my small contribution to the 'great debate' will reach all staff, whatever their role, training and background, and enable everyone to meet on the common ground of understanding. The views expressed in the book are obviously my own and not to be taken as representative of any organization.

One final word of encouragement: I believe the vast majority of those involved in any way with the computing world, like their colleagues in almost every other walk of life, to be honest and conscientious. If they are failing in their duties it is probably due to over-enthusiasm or ignorance rather than from malice aforethought. During the time I have worked within the field of computer security I have encountered a most positive reception from computer, security and executive staff alike. They are uneasy in their minds anyway, without really knowing why, but once the dangers have been explained to them there is an almost frantic willingness to learn about and improve computer security standards. It seems the only barrier to a massive step forward is the current lack of awareness. In 1960, following his study of security in government departments, Lord Radcliffe stated that then the biggest single risk to security was probably a general lack of conviction that any substantial threat exists. Thirty years on, this has become so true today of computer security, but as noted in the Radcliffe Commission report this attitude of mind can be overcome by a 'sustained and skilfully directed educational effort in the right quarters'. This, then, must be the way forward.

Martin Smith
Hillands Farm
1993

How to use this book

Commonsense Computer Security has been written as a story, with a beginning, a middle and an end. I advise you to read it as such, since while we all have to fire-fight problems in our everyday professional lives, I would prefer that my story prepared you for the war rather than armed you for a particular battle. You can dip into it if you wish, but you will miss a great deal of my tale.

There is another reason, though, why I have told a story. It is because, like all solid structures, information protection is made up of interdependent component parts fitting together with a beautiful symmetry. The absence of each weakens the whole, and a minimum number need to be present before any strength is apparent. I hope, then, more than anything, that this book reveals to you this wonderful mosaic of information protection that never fails to fascinate me.

In this second edition, I have used the term 'information protection' to describe a more comprehensive approach to the taking care of data. While most information is associated with computer systems and networks, there is also a host of other forms of information held within any organisation. In the main, though, the term is interchangeable with the more familiar term 'computer security' used in my first edition.

Part 1
The nature of the problem

1
The nature of computer security

1.1   What is a computer?

Computer—automatic electronic apparatus for making calculations that are expressible in numerical or logical terms; reckoner, calculator. . . .

(Concise Oxford Dictionary of Current English)

It's a sort of electric brain, daddy.

(Madeleine Rose Smith)

We all know what a computer is, at least until we have to define one precisely. Certainly, information technology has entered our everyday lives to an extent most of us have yet to fully realize, and as such applications become increasingly diverse and widespread, our dependence on them grows accordingly. Indeed, we are already at a stage where the loss of computer facilities in a host of areas would endanger our lives, our well-being and our businesses. There are few functions in our modern society that are not becoming computer-dependent.

But what is a computer? It is nothing more than a machine for the manipulation of information in electronic form. It is no more important in itself than any other tool, except that its fuel is the modern currency of information, and its speed, accuracy and memory provide considerable attractions to all areas of commerce, industry and the Government. And because it is such an efficient and helpful tool, it makes itself indispensable in a very short time. Its principles of operation are unseen; its functioning is silent and mysterious. Many people are ignorant and fearful of this still modern invention, and this prejudice is self-perpetuating. Understandably, computer personnel do little to dispel their unsought status and strength as masters of these awesome machines; their specialist language further isolates them from others. Many of us 'outsiders' do nothing to come to terms with the inevitable march of progress towards a computerized society. Instead of education, there is polarization, especially between the young and the old; and as information technology becomes more advanced and its applications more specialized, this gap between computer people and non-computer people can only widen. Yet the fact remains that computers are only tools for the manipulation of data, and are basically extremely simple and remarkably stupid machines. They are nothing to be frightened of.

It is the information within the computer which is the essential resource. Possession of accurate, up-to-date and comprehensive information is now the key to growth and success, when once it was perhaps the ability to manufacture, or harvest crops, or trade overseas. The City of London, for example, is nothing more than a giant information factory. The capacity to manipulate data, to model forecasts of events, to store, channel and transmit information as required—these are the modern measures of success or failure. The computer myth has masked information as the real hero of the modern age, and our attentions must not be diverted from the need to protect and preserve that vital data by an obsession with its container, the computer. It is the data which we must keep confidential, free from corruption, safe from the elements, the thief, and the saboteur, and available when needed, literally at the touch of a button.

A computer, then, is a data processor which permits arithmetic and logical operations without the intervention of a human operator and working to a set of stored instructions (the program). Computers are unintelligent, although they appear to be more clever than they actually are because their programs can be written to take account of previous data and results.

The main characteristics of a computer are:

1 *Speed* The speed with which computers, in particular the latest models, can process and manipulate data is almost beyond comprehension, with millions of calculations taking place each second.
2 *Accuracy* Computers will perform a given task exactly as instructed, as many times as required, with an error rate a fraction of that of humans. The operators, the programmers and the users are responsible for the greatest part of any computer's failings.
3 *Memory* Computers can store data in vast amounts, compacted into minute areas within microchips, or on magnetic tapes or fixed and floppy magnetic disks.

Processes may thus be complex to a degree previously beyond the normal realms of human ability. Not only can tasks now be performed with ease and speed, which before would have required an inordinate effort or simply have been beyond sensible or manageable human resources, but also human effort can be eliminated entirely in many areas. Such savings can be used to release staff from drudgery and improve efficiency; often though, they have simply resulted in staff reductions which in turn have contributed to the fear of, and resentment towards, computers.

The refinement of computers has raced ahead since the invention of the earliest device. Several generations of computers have come and gone, and the progress continues with ever-increasing pace. As this evolution has continued, the computer has moved away from the enormous, environmentally controlled frame rooms, in centralized locations and with specialist staff tending to their every whim, to the personal computer taking massive processing power to the office desk, typing pool and factory floor and placing it in the hands of the ordinary worker. It is as if the mainframe has burst like a ripe fruit, scattering its seeds throughout all parts of the organization to germinate as personal computers (PCs), which in turn have spread their network connections like the threads of a spider's web.

Whatever its form, though, the computer remains essentially a simple device, and while its internal workings will be necessarily complex, the actual operation remains straightforward. While the modern road vehicle can be a highly sophisticated piece of machinery, most of us can, with only a little training and some practice, drive one. There is no real need to understand how a car works, merely how to work it, and once mastered it is then a relatively straightforward progression to the juggernaut. It is thus with computers. (Nevertheless, a basic understanding of the principles of any machine must improve one's performance on it.)

1.2   What is security?

Keeping me safe, and keeping people out.

(Peter Henry Smith)

We live in an unsafe world, in which every day we encounter threats against our safety and security. There are, too, our own weaknesses and vulnerabilities, those of our families, and those in the physical defences we have built around us to defend our lifestyles. These threats and vulnerabilities to our well-being are often inevitable: sometimes they can be reduced or avoided, or they can be transferred to an insurer, or we can accept and ignore them. The actions we take will depend on the impact upon our lives should the worst happen. Our lifestyles, then, are a balance between the threats and vulnerabilities, the impacts and the countermeasures, or else we would all either be dead or nervous wrecks. We can never hope to protect ourselves entirely: risk taking is an essential ingredient of our make-up, and a level of stress is necessary for us to achieve a balanced state. Too little stress can be as harmful for us as too much—the racing car driver or mountaineer will testify to the benefits and pleasures of controlled stress.

We build up our homes over a considerable period. Our endeavours over many years can be most clearly seen in our possessions, our homes, cars, gardens. These valuable and sentimental assets, and our loved ones, are subjected to the threats of fire, flood, theft, damage, and a host of nightmarish dangers which we cannot entirely eliminate but which we can accept within reasonable limits. We develop, often subconsciously, our personal risk assessments to produce unique security policies within which we live our lives. We spend a certain amount on insurance; we spend so much money on locks and anti-burglar devices; we drive at certain speeds and in a way which makes us feel safe; we empty ashtrays in the lounge last thing at night; we don't allow our daughters to walk home from the disco on their own at night. Most of us discover an acceptable position in the centre ground which, in the main, avoids the unfortunate experiences, or at least softens the results, while allowing us to continue normal lives and avoid the traps of obsession or paranoia.

Good security, then, both at home and at work, consists of the identification of all the threats and vulnerabilities, an assessment of the likelihood of a particular misfortune afflicting us, and a reasonable and personally acceptable combination of countermeasures to protect our families, ourselves and our possessions accordingly. The effort applied will, of course, depend on the impact of the threat and the value of the asset concerned; we will take more care of our personal safety than we will of our possessions, or at least a reasonable person will, but of those possessions we are likely to take more care of our expensive jewellery, or the deeds to our houses, than we are less valuable or important objects. But, human nature being what it is, stable doors will be bolted too late, our efforts being redoubled after a threat materializes; homes, once burgled, will sprout alarms, and driving will be far more cautious after an accident—for a while!

1.3   What is computer security?

It's what my daddy does when he goes to work

(Grace-Marie Smith)

Within the specific environment of the computer, security entails:

1   Identification and valuation of the assets to be protected, so that none is overlooked and the more valuable can be looked after better.
2   Recognition of the peculiar vulnerabilities and weaknesses of computers in general, and the system in question in particular.
3   Identification of all the threats against computers in general, and the system in question in particular.
4   An assessment of the likelihood—the risk—of a particular threat occurring or weakness emerging, and the consequences that would result.
5   The development, implementation, and enforcement of a cost-effective security policy to reduce as necessary the risks against the system, and hence its data, to an acceptable minimum while allowing the system to perform its task. This minimum will, of course, be determined by the nature and importance of the system.
6   The preparation of suitable plans to recover from any disaster that befalls the computer system.
7   Monitoring and reviewing periodically the effectiveness of the security arrangements.

The importance of a particular computer and its data, its significance in the overall operations of the enterprise, and the effect of its loss on the survival of the enterprise, will dictate the security effort which is appropriate. Any computer will attract some degree of protection; if it has no importance whatsoever to the enterprise, and if its data is valueless, then get rid of it—no one needs electronic paperweights!

Computer security has a considerable range; it extends from the corruption of a single item of data to the total destruction of an entire computer centre, from the careless act of a junior member of staff to the determined efforts of the industrial spy or saboteur.

We must be clear about what is meant by the term computer system. Only a few years ago it would have been possible to define in simple terms a particular computer and the physical bounds within which it was contained. The computer personnel were limited in number, and the public contact with computers was almost non-existent. Nowadays, such clarity is rare, as the computing function is dissipated around the enterprise and networks abound. We must consider all these following parts if there is to be no weak link in the protective shield we hope to create:

1   Software and hardware, including communications equipment and other associated specialized devices.
2   All manual processes associated with the computer operations.
3   All associated documentation, in whatever form and of whatever nature.
4   The people associated with the system—those who operate it, use it, are responsible for it, maintain and service it, or come in any way into contact with it.
5   The environment of any component of the computer—buildings, utilities (electricity and water supplies, air conditioning, etc.), communications links and their physical housing.

But this tells only part of the story. We can describe computer security, but more importantly we must get senior management to recognize just how vital it is. In a recent survey, two out of every three companies questioned said their businesses would be 'seriously affected' after just a few days without their computers. At the same time, nearly half had experienced some sort of computer security incident, though this figure must be much less than the truth since most companies are notoriously reluctant to admit to significant or embarrassing security incidents of any sort, and those companies that have gone out of existence because of a computer security failing will not have been included.

Yet, while most managers recognize the importance of their computer systems, and many will have already encountered the results of poor computer security, precious little is being done. Despite much talk on the subject, and a whole growth industry of books, conferences and courses, the truth is that the basic requirements of sound computer security are largely unrecognized and ignored. It is in this context, then, that we shall consider in detail the vulnerabilities of computers and electronic data, the threats directed against computers, and the countermeasures available to protect those systems. We shall also bring together all these aspects to describe how a cost-effective computer security policy can be prepared and sold to management and staff alike.

All members of an enterprise, but in particular the management, computer, security and internal audit personnel, have a clear duty to ensure that computers and their data are protected to a standard at least as good as for any existing or superseded traditional procedures and records. The security measures for electronic data must be durable at all times. Security should be most reliable under the most adverse of conditions, especially those extremes encountered during emergencies and disasters. But a sense of proportion must also be maintained, and there is no need to overreact. In the pre-computer days there were insecurities and weaknesses, and there will be with computers. Impossible standards should not be demanded—if the entire paper registry is destroyed by fire, it is not expected that its staff re-create it by start of work on Monday.

Computer security is common sense. Computer security is straightforward. Computer security may be involved, but it is certainly not difficult. Computer security is within the reach of everyone, and not necessarily at great expense. This book will show all this to be true.

2
Threats and vulnerabilities

2.1   Qualities of information

The ultimate aim of computer security must be to protect the electronic data held within the computer system. Information has three qualities that must be preserved in any medium:

1   *Integrity*   The information must be preserved in its original form. It must not be altered overtly or covertly, either accidentally or for malicious reasons. It must not be unintentionally destroyed. Integrity is a measure of the information's accuracy and reliability.
2   *Continuity*   The information must always be available when required.
3   *Confidentiality*   The information must be kept as private as its owner wishes. Only those authorized by the owner should see it. Its unauthorized disclosure must be prevented.

It is these features of information that will be the cornerstone of any computer security policy and we will keep returning to them as we progress through this book.

Computers must provide a level of security at least as good as the protection afforded to information in non-electronic form. However, since electronic data is more at risk than other forms of information, computer security will probably have to be more stringent just to maintain this *status quo*. Whatever security measures are applied to electronic information, they must take into account the particular vulnerabilities of computers and the data they hold and process, recognize the threats directed against computers, and acknowledge the disproportionate impact any computer security breaches can have on an enterprise's well-being and survival.

2.2   Threats to computers

Those menaces which threaten any computer system can be grouped into three main categories.

2.2.1   Accidental threats to computer security

There are a number of threats to computers from accidental causes:

1 *The delicate equipment may malfunction*   Simple faults, especially intermittent ones, are often more difficult to detect and repair than catastrophic failures, and the consequences can be far-reaching. Often such faults only become apparent long after they have begun affecting the data, when integrity, availability and confidentiality may already have been seriously damaged, and when it may be too late to recover.

2 *Human errors will inevitably occur*   It is a sobering thought, but for maximum efficiency and reliability, manual procedures within the installation should be reduced to a minimum and human intervention avoided wherever possible. Carelessness, lack of training, excessive enthusiasm and misunderstandings can create operator and programmer errors which, once introduced, will by their very nature be difficult to detect, contain or remove, and will tend to be perpetuated. Often the in-built checks within the computer's software, designed to pick up human errors, will be deliberately overridden by staff in order to speed up their work or otherwise make their lives easier.

3 *The software may malfunction*   Software is impossible to test completely. Modern programs can extend to millions of lines of computer code, with countless permutations of sequences. While some testing is carried out during the preparation of the programs and the development of the system there will always remain some in-built 'bugs' which will emerge when least expected or wanted, and with unpredictable results.

4 *Power supplies may be interrupted, or may fluctuate outside the computer's design limits*   Other public utilities, such as telephone links and water supplies, together with essential disposables, such as stationery, necessary for the operation of the computer, may be subjected to unavoidable interruption.

2.2.2   Natural hazards to computers

Computers are fragile beasts, and their delicate nature means that many natural hazards exist. Any extreme of temperature (particularly fire) or humidity (especially direct contact with water) will affect the computer. Dirt, dust and smoke particles, even those from a cigarette, can damage the intricate workings of the circuitry or disk drives, or spoil the data held on the magnetic storage media. Insects and vermin can also be a grave danger to computer installations. Finally, earthquakes, hurricanes, electrical storms and unforeseen acts of God are never far away, even in the United Kingdom.

2.2.3   *The threat to computers from human action*

There is always some group that would wish to exploit any weakness, and computers are not immune from such attentions. Espionage, either military or industrial, is one obvious motive, but ignorance, nuisance, greed, revenge and seeking to embarrass are other causes of human action against a computer installation. Such attacks may be deliberate or accidental, overt or covert:

1   *Intelligence services*   Within the military environment any attack of espionage will come from hostile intelligence services. Friendly forces are those agencies sympathetic with the aims of the Government. They are treated as allies, and a controlled and limited mutual interchange of intelligence and other information may take place. In the industrial or commercial sector, any competitor must be regarded as hostile until declared a friendly force, and defences must be arranged accordingly. Industrial espionage is a growth industry in its own right, especially with the end of the Cold War. Possession of information about a rival's research, performance, forecasts and plans is invaluable, and the resources and effort applied to the acquisition of this information can be immense if the stakes are sufficiently high. The methods used can vary from the simple—a phone call to an unsuspecting unwary employee—to highly sophisticated technical eavesdropping devices implanted covertly.

2   *Disenchanted, disaffected and dishonest employees*   The greatest threat to any computer system is not from sophisticated attacks mounted from without, but from low-tech insider crimes committed by those already allowed access to the system. After operator errors, the next greatest threat to the safety and security of any computer system comes from disenchanted, disaffected and dishonest employees and those with an eye for the main chance. They may be seeking personal gain or they may simply be acting out grievances or frustrations. They may even be acting on behalf of some malevolent third party lacking that vital authorized access needed to mount a successful attack. There is no doubt, though, from all the surveys and case histories over recent years, that insiders (defined as those with authorized access to the computer system though not necessarily employees of the enterprise) are by far the most likely to attack that system and are able to inflict the greatest damage. As we give increasing computing power to the more computer-literate user, using PCs in the relaxed atmosphere of the modern office, with software tools which enable those users to construct with relative ease their own tailor-made programs, the equivalent of which would have taken in the past a team of experts many months to develop, we must not be surprised if they become tempted. Finally, industrial action can be disastrous to computer operations, especially if the installation's key workers go on strike, but also if some third party or supplier fails to provide an essential service.

3 *Vandals and hooligans*   The modern vandal can create havoc and cause
   unknown damage without recourse to the stick or the stone. Viruses and
   vindictive hacking are but two examples of computer vandalism. Once more,
   the insider intent on such vandalism will be able to cause the greatest damage.

4 *Users*   Malpractice by users can have damaging effects. Non-standard and
   unauthorized working practices, often adopted for the very best of reasons,
   can have both direct and knock-on effects on the system and its data. Games
   and other system diversions—football pools permutations, for example, or
   the chess club membership list—not only use valuable system time and
   resources but could confuse the system's security features; their use should be
   banned, or if thought to have a useful training function then at least tightly
   controlled and supervised.

5 *Subversive/terrorist organizations*   There are a growing number of subversive
   and terrorist groups which recognize the importance of computers as sources
   of information to aid their activities. There is even an organization dedicated
   to the abolition of computers! Subverted employees aiding such groups will
   have insider access. Political extremists, from the left or the right, may fall
   into this class of attacker, and while their ideologies will be different their
   methods may be just as violent and determined.

6 *The media/newspapers*   Reporters are ingenious investigators and will use a
   variety of ruses to ensure they get their story. The computer represents a
   wealth of information and is thus an attractive target for their attentions.

7 *Members of the public*   To some, the computer is a focus for fears and
   frustration about unemployment, authoritarianism, impersonality and a host
   of other grievances. Others may have a genuine complaint—how many of us
   have had gas bills for £10 million? With the change in our society's standards
   and values over the past years, action against a mere computer, when set
   beside ghastly crimes of violence and cruelty, can appear harmless and almost
   justifiable.

8 *The criminal*   Computer crime is big business, even though accurate estimates
   of the totals involved are difficult to come by. Most enterprises are understandably reluctant firstly to report their losses or then to press charges against the
   computer criminals. Computer crime can produce massive profits with little
   chance of detection, and then the possibilities of either successful prosecution
   or significant punishment are slim. It still represents the 'perfect' crime and
   the trends must be towards it and away from the more direct robberies which
   involve a greater degree of risk to the criminals themselves. There is also a
   degree of glamour associated with computer crime—nobody really gets hurt,
   and it serves the computer right!—which mitigates in favour of the computer
   criminals. Finally, the criminal will be more highly motivated than the
   defender and will probably invest more money in attacking than the victim
   will invest in defending.

A gloomy picture must not necessarily be drawn from this depressing list of potential enemies. In truth, the majority of computer incidents involving loss, corruption or unavailability of data are caused by the actions of careless or incompetent employees with no criminal motive. Even malicious action is restricted in the main to insiders who would already have access to the system. In 1984, a survey by the Government's Audit Commission revealed that over 80 per cent of reported frauds had been committed by staff of the enterprise concerned, and that over 70 per cent of these crimes arose from input frauds rather than any specialized computer skills and facilities. In 1987, a follow-up survey added that computer disasters have had a greater impact than computer crime. The UK's National Centre for Computer Security confirmed all this in a major survey in 1991 into computer security failures and breaches. While this should not encourage complacency, it does narrow down the nature of the computer security problem and thus points towards the solution.

2.3   Vulnerabilities of computers

Computer systems display particular vulnerabilities and weaknesses which allow the threats to occur more easily. These must be countered if the electronic information is not to be placed at even greater risk than its traditional form:

1 *Data can be stored in very compact form*   The contents of a single storage disk or tape can equal the contents of an entire registry of files and documents. A floppy disk placed in the pocket and taken away from the office, or damaged by spilt coffee, could contain vast amounts of information.

2 *Data is invisible*   Electronic data stored on a magnetic disk or tape cannot be seen. It cannot be visually inspected for alteration, as it could be if written on a piece of paper, and it is extremely difficult to account for and trace.

3 *Data can leak*   Electromagnetic radiations can leak from a computer to be intercepted and analysed by unauthorized persons. Such compromising emanations are present in any electrical device: those from a computer, however, are in a form that can be deciphered to betray their contents. This phenomenon, sometimes referred to as TEMPEST, has been overstated in the past. It remains, however, a very real consideration for the security of very sensitive installations where it may be worth an attacker resorting to this difficult and expensive way of capturing data.

4 *Data is accessible*   Electronic data can be easily copied without trace and without authority, rather like a pirate copy can be made of a musical cassette tape. Remote terminals away from the computer can tap straight into the heart of the system and retrieve data back to the remote site. Often the operators who perform these processes can remain anonymous. Once access to a computer has been obtained, generally speaking all the data on it is then available. There are ways of constructing privacy barriers within the

software, but a good knowledge of the system and some patience will often suffice for these to be subverted. Privacy will therefore be difficult to impose.

5 *Data can be inadvertently retained on storage media* The data, held on the magnetic storage media as minute electrical charges, can permanently magnetize the media so that even when erased it will leave readable traces of its existence which can be subsequently deciphered, rather like pencil marks on paper. Commercial programs, which can go back over many overwrites and re-format an original message with remarkable clarity, are becoming increasingly available. More significant, however, is that on most computer systems, deletion of electronic files merely deletes the label at the front of the packet of data—its name and address. The contents of the file will still be there, and available with only a little effort to unauthorized persons.

6 *Aggregation of data* Once collected together, data can attain a higher value than its component parts. Sales figures, which on their own are unimportant, once merged could reveal the performance of the company. The computer is able to bring together vast amounts of information, and so this principle of aggregation is particularly relevant to computer security. Furthermore, computers can derive conclusions from that data automatically and very efficiently, so much so that whole new manipulations are now possible.

7 *The mystique of computers* The computer is still, to many of us, and certainly amongst the senior generations who still run industry and commerce today, a complete mystery. Those to whom we entrust computers are often able to operate unsupervised by their bosses and the opportunity for corrupt practices to abound is proportionately greater.

8 *Technological advancements* Information technology is racing ahead. Seemingly each day new products appear, conceptual breakthroughs are announced, and gadgets become smaller and cleverer. At the same time, though, the unsexy subject of computer security is finding it hard even to hold its own ground. The gap grows with every passing day between the security standards we ought to achieve and those we have to settle for.

9 *Communications and networking* Increasingly, computers are linked with one another to form networks. Modern computers themselves often comprise several smaller, distributed processors linked together. The data links connecting the systems are vulnerable from a variety of threats: physical disruption to the links, either deliberate or accidental; line tapping to allow eavesdropping of the signals traffic along the link; line diversion to a pirate terminal; unauthorized access to the system by outsiders through an unprotected external line (so-called 'hacking'); overlooking of restricted sections of the database by unauthorized insiders; all these and more are possible through the communications links of a networked system. In addition, it is vital that each computer is certain exactly which other computer it is sending to and receiving from, and there must be a method of authenticating the link.

10 *System integration* Allied to networking is the increasing trend towards

system integration with many different types of information on a single communications channel. Other developments such as smart cards and electronic points of sale (EPOS) will also mix different sorts of data on a common medium.

11 *Distributed data processing*   As we move away from the mainframe environment to the informal office environment the dangers to data increase alarmingly. At the same time there has been a growth in computer literacy—from those now with sufficient knowledge to make a real mess of things to those with enough knowledge to subvert systems for a variety of dishonest reasons.

12 *Security standards*   Despite much talk there are still no common standards for either computer security practices or products. Until such standards appear and are universally accepted and enforced it will be extremely difficult to achieve truly satisfactory levels of computer security.

These many and varied vulnerabilities place in jeopardy the safety and security of the electronic data in a number of ways—physical damage to the installation, unauthorized access by outsiders or unauthorized activities by authorized users, and computer crime (mainly fraud and theft), to name but a few.

2.4   Methods of exploitation

Study of the methods of exploitation, either deliberate or accidental, may help us in our work in improving the security of our computers.

2.4.1   Temporary removal and copying of stored information

As we know, magnetic storage media are compact, and easily transported under cover to be copied away from the site without affecting the original. Further, security features held in code on the tape (usually at the beginning and end) can also be copied, analysed carefully and subsequently circumvented for unimpeded access to the rest of the system. Such illicit copying need not be performed elsewhere; it can be carried out on site and in a manner that would not necessarily raise suspicions. It need not be technical—a discarded printer ribbon could contain all the information printed out on it, in one long stream of clear strikes on an otherwise unmarked inking. Additional copies of computer files can be created ostensibly for back-up files; moved from classified to unclassified tapes which will be less stringently controlled; scrambled and stored elsewhere in the system for subsequent recovery; and removed as part of a fault-tracing process, either spurious or genuine, or under the guise of program testing, maintenance and repair. Neglect or abuse of accounting procedures would help to hide such nefarious activity, though many system managers would probably never notice anyway.

2.4.2 Deliberate misrouting of information

Deliberate misrouting of information to unauthorized recipients is another method of gaining data. While computers which are part of a network or have remote terminals are most easily accessed and therefore most at risk from this attack, no computer acts entirely in isolation. Misrouting of such information, either in printed form or on magnetic media of some sort, would compromise the data as completely as interception of that data in its electronic form within the system. Even unauthorized overlooking of the printed output could be a source of compromise, especially if untrusted staff—cleaners, or maintenance engineers, for example—can gain access to an active printer.

2.4.3 Modifications to the equipment

With sufficient access, changes to the system's hardware or amendments to the programs can be made, so that integral security controls and monitoring procedures can be avoided. Devices can be placed surreptitiously which will intercept to record or divert communications traffic. Links can be tapped to create rogue terminals, giving complete access to the system. Such methods of attack are complicated and not without some risk to the perpetrator of detection during or subsequent to the attack, but there are occasions with highly valuable or sensitive data when the benefits of access would justify the effort. The ingenuity of such attackers will possibly outstrip even that of the system's own creators and operators.

2.4.4 Sabotage/criminal damage

The results of sabotage are immediate and catastrophic when directed against a computer installation or its support facilities. Sabotage is the deliberate destruction or damage of equipment by disaffected employees or other persons, acting against the interests of the enterprise. Criminal damage has the same effects, but is more a case of wanton disruption and destruction. Fire, explosives, or other physical attacks are reported daily in the news, though not often in the context of computers. An attack of this nature may come from within, and may not be directed primarily against the computer itself; an attack against a telephone junction box some distance from the installation, or the interruption of the mains water supply which feeds a computer's air conditioning plant, will also bring down the system. Whatever, and however, though, sabotage and criminal damage are certain to work, and remain major threats against the delicate computer system.

3
Assessing the risks

An old navigator sat next to the young, brash pilot straight from flying school.

'Two degrees to starboard', instructed the navigator to keep them on course.

'We do not need to fly that accurately', replied the pilot. 'We can sort ourselves out nearer our destination.'

The old navigator sucked on his pencil, then persisted.

'Believe me, we need to turn two degrees to starboard'.

'In any case', rejoined the pilot, 'this old crate can't fly that well. I can't alter course less than ten degrees. We will be all right. Trust me'.

The old navigator sucked on his pencil again. He was naturally reluctant to trust anyone. He did not intend to trust this man.

'OK. Give me ten degrees to port.'

Now the pilot was happy. He could see the point of such a major change to course, and he could manage it. The plane banked gracefully onto the new heading.

After a few moments, the navigator said, 'Now give me twelve degrees to starboard'.

The morals to this story are as follows. Firstly, always listen to those older and wiser than yourself: they are probably right. Next, old age and cunning will always overcome youth and enthusiasm. But most importantly, wherever you are going, your heading must be as spot on as you can make it, and the old navigator knew this. He had got lost on many trips before.

Those human activities we call everyday life must also be run on the correct heading. Any slight deviations from course will eventually become massive diversions from which it will not always be possible to recover and which could leave us totally lost.

Preparing a security policy to protect electronic data is no different. The computer security policy must set out on the correct heading if it is to stand any chance of success, and to do that it must be based above all else on a sound and accurate assessment of the risks. There is no simple way to avoid this initial effort, and the quality of all subsequent work depends on it.

3.1   The importance of computer security

The new information technology methods allow the storage, retrieval, manipulation and dissemination of vast amounts of data. With increasing networking between systems, the capacity to interchange information is now almost limitless. But we must not allow ourselves to become blinded to the infallibility of this apparent panacea; the more of our operations that we trust to its insatiable grasp, the greater our dilemma if that technology fails us in any way. The need for sound computer security has never been greater, and it is growing all the time.

While there is no room for complacency, encouragingly there seems to be a growing recognition of at least the *need* to care for electronic data within computer systems. A recent poll showed clearly that, above all others, the greatest worry to senior managers was indeed the security of their computer data. Nearly half of those questioned recognized the fundamental part that computer systems now play in the running of their businesses, and accepted the need for computer security.

Worryingly, though, of those who expressed their concern in the poll, most were in general quite satisfied with their existing measures to control the risks. This is in spite of a host of reports, surveys and investigations over a number of years by a variety of learned and independent authorities which have highlighted the poor state of computer security standards in industry and commerce today. While there has been some store placed in the technical aspects of the solution— TEMPEST, software and hardware security, encryption, virus vaccines—and while stereotyped but scant attention is sometimes paid to disaster recovery, there remains a long way to go before the general standards of computer security can be thought of as satisfactory. The management issues remain largely unaddressed and little thought seems to have been given to the problems that lie ahead.

There is then a dichotomy between perception and reality. On the one hand, business managers are rightly worried about the safety and security of their computing facilities. At the same time, though, they are doing little to defend themselves and seem content that all is well in the garden. This epidemic of complacency is in itself perhaps the greatest danger of all to computers.

It is likely that many of those asked in the survey were unaware of the true extent of the risks to computers. The importance of, the threats against, and the weaknesses and vulnerabilities of, computers are many and varied and often far from obvious. Breaches of security are far more prevalent than commonly realized, and disasters are not infrequent, but only recently have these received wider publicity, and then only when the victims have been prepared to disclose their misfortunes. The nature and extent of the danger is thus, mostly, shielded from public view.

Other managers will be computer-illiterate and ignorant of the real consequences to the well-being of their enterprises following any loss, corruption

Figure 3.1. Risk.

or unavailability of their electronic data, for whatever reason. Some will sincerely but foolishly believe that 'it will never happen to me', and others will simply bury their heads in the sand. A great number will be unaware of the proper countermeasures, or will have been frightened into believing that the only remedies will be expensive, or highly technical, or both. Sadly, few will recognize the true dangers and take adequate steps to counter the risks.

It is quite without parallel that otherwise cautious and competent managers will have recognized a huge business risk but then failed to take sensible and adequate precautions, yet this is what is happening too often with computer security today.

3.2   What is risk?

Risk in any context is the sum of threats (those events which cause harm), vulnerabilities (the openness of an enterprise to the threats) and asset value (the worth of the asset in danger)(Fig. 3.1). Increase any of these factors and the risk increases; decrease any, and the risk decreases. Our efforts to reduce in various ways the risks to the safety and security of a computer system and its electronic data is what we call computer security.

3.3   What is risk analysis?

Computer security involves reducing the risk to our electronic data. We must find ways of protecting the confidentiality, integrity and continuity of that information from the threats and vulnerabilities ranged against it, in proportion to the information's value.

But what exactly are the threats against, and vulnerabilities of, a particular computer system, and exactly how valuable to the enterprise is that system, its role and its data? It is possible to describe the range of risks faced by computers in general, but every enterprise is unique and changing all the time. Indeed, every computer system is unique. There will be those systems essential to operations or those holding highly sensitive data, while other systems will be of relatively lesser import. There will be those to which access is strictly limited to a few trusted workers, and those open to all, including outsiders. The relevance of a computer system may change with time, or depend on whichever role it is performing. Thus for each system at a given location at a given time performing a given function, the overall risk to the electronic data will differ and the countermeasures need to be tailored accordingly if we are to achieve efficient, adequate protection at the most effective cost. To do otherwise is to be on the incorrect heading.

So, in order to determine the appropriate defences, we need to analyse the risk to a given computer system—and every time, since each system, each enterprise, is unique. This is fundamental if the solution is to be correct. The needs and plans of any dynamic enterprise will naturally change with time, and the security policy must adapt accordingly. Any risk analysis and associated defence must be able to accommodate such changes, but this is not to detract from the importance of original accuracy.

Risk analysis is an art, not a science. It is a finger in the wind, a feel for events. It uses intuition and depends on a deep and comprehensive study of the enterprise concerned, its aims, its culture, its direction and its history. It depends, too, on a thorough understanding not only of the risks to computers but also the risks to the enterprise. It requires a knowledge of the available defences, and thus a background in security methodology is useful, perhaps more so than computing skills.

Risk analysis is best performed standing back a distance—to see the wood, not just the trees. Some say it is best performed by an outsider, but perhaps only those intimate with an enterprise can best assess its vulnerabilities and needs. A team may be the answer, with outside experience advising and guiding the enterprise's management staff.

Risk analysis is not just about computers. It is as much, perhaps more, about the people who surround them. Such people are less predictable than a piece of hardware, which complicates the issue further.

The risk analyst can best be likened to the medical practitioner. Our doctors sometimes call us forward for regular checks, but more often we go to see them when we feel or suspect a problem. The doctor will talk to us, study our history and lifestyle, and apply standard tests before making a diagnosis based on experience and observations. The doctor will recommend a treatment and monitor our progress back to health.

There is no standardized or foolproof method of risk analysis. There are techniques which can be adopted to assist in the process, but ultimately it comes down to the skill of the practitioner. Those skills are not easily learned, nor are they easily taught. But a good risk analyst will know when he or she has a workable method, and it is likely that the method will be unique to that person. It is unlikely, however, to be quick or easy. Good risk analysis requires careful consideration of all the pressures on, and resources offered by, the enterprise in question, and will begin at the fence and end at the source code of the operating system. It may even start further out, in the enterprise's sphere of influence, to include rivals and peers in the same business.

All I can say, though, is that I have my own method. It involves much talking, and even more listening. It requires me to draw on my experience in the field of security, incorporating all facets of security. I need to understand the enterprise concerned, and I must have sufficient knowledge of information technology in all its guises to draw on the greater knowledge of the enterprise's own staff about their system. I need to use the best tools available and these are discussed later in this chapter. In harness with the 'home team', together we need to explore the wealth of experience and knowledge we are able to pool. In most cases, the resident staff themselves have all the answers, but which may not be crystallized into a cogent assessment of the risk. That will naturally fall out from what is, in effect, an investigation, a diagnosis, a review. The simple act of thinking will usually produce the answers, and it is important that the effort is willingly and conscientiously applied and the time is set aside.

With the business pressures we all feel in the modern market place, it is inevitable that security falls to the bottom of the list. There is no measure of successful security other than that nothing untoward has happened. Thus, management is often loath to commit resources to such an intangible, and even less likely to continue an expensive effort. We are often willing to drive more carefully only after a traffic accident, and then only until the memory dims. We are none of us keen before the event, only afterwards when it might be too late. But then, ironically, a good risk analysis will make clear the dangers and the extra effort may follow. This is the continuing conundrum of security—which comes first, the precautions or the cure?

An important role of the manager is to ensure that the enterprise takes steps to prevent disaster rather than have to respond with a cure. Since security is a form of insurance, it does not contribute directly to, but instead (at least in the short term) takes from, the profits of the enterprise. Senior management will have to be convinced of the need for appropriate defences against the risks to the computing function, and this will include illustrations of the consequences to the enterprise should system security be breached in any way. But a major part must be to explain those risks and to suggest a suitable policy of defences to counter them. Risk analysis will allow us to do this. Thus risk analysis is fundamental to corporate computer security wherever in the story you choose to start.

Risk analysis should be repeated on a regular basis, or earlier than planned when something happens to change the situation. Risk analysis should allow you to do the best you can with the resources at your disposal by minimizing the likeliest and most immediately harmful dangers.

3.4   Risk analysis techniques

The least precise, most time-consuming but possibly ultimately the most satisfying method of analysing the risks faced by an organization and its information technology, is to view them subjectively within the environment of the computer operations themselves. All those involved would be included in the deliberations —those staff familiar with the (intended) role of the computer system, the nature of the business and the organization, its security, its competition and the market place in which it operates, and the history of problems encountered (or not) over the years will make an invaluable contribution to any risk analysis.

Subjective risk analysis is no longer good enough on its own, though. It lacks vigour, and is not formal in that it does not involve the professional application of defined and recognized standards, procedures and/or guidelines in a manner which is documented, recorded, consistent and repeatable. Unfortunately it depends *entirely* on the skill of the practitioner and there is no safety net to ensure that aspects not included in the review are picked up.

While it is still vital that risk analysis is performed in a mature way by staff who understand fully the nature of the problem and the solution available, it is now necessary to provide appropriate tools to aid them in this process. To return to our medical simile, the doctor now needs the full range of medical techniques, equipment and drugs, since the laying-on of hands is not quite enough for today's demanding patient.

Risk analysis tools to assist the practitioner fall into two groups: quantitative analysis and automated high analysis methodologies.

3.4.1   Quantitative analysis

In order to calculate how much effort should go into computer security, expressed in the crude terms of how much should be spent annually, the expected loss for that period is calculated in monetary terms. This value is derived from the following:

1   the likely frequency of each threat occurring, expressed in number of times each year. For example, if it is expected that a major fire will occur once every 30 years, then the frequency per year is 0.03. If operator error is expected 10 times each working day, then the frequency per year is 3000;

2   the impact in round figures of such an event. A price is awarded to each and every system asset, from the hardware to the software and data, and to a degree any consequential losses. For example, the major fire would destroy the computer centre worth perhaps £1 million; lost business and the extra costs of operating from standby facilities would add another £0.5 million. The total impact is £1.5 million. On the other hand, each and every operator error on average is calculated to cost the company £10 to note and correct.

The product of these two factors – frequency and impact – is a statement of the expected annual loss. For the fire, this annual loss expenditure (ALE) would be 0.03 (the frequency) × £1.5 million (the impact), or £45 000. The organization can expect to lose this amount each year over the given 30 years between fires, and any expenditure on fire precautions should reflect this annual sum. For the operator errors, the ALE will be £30 000, and so up to this amount could be spent before it stops being economical to detect them and cheaper to let them slip through.

The limitations of this methodology are clear. Fires do not work to timetables, and your turn could be tomorrow. Operator errors are not all the same, and do not cost an 'average' amount; it is bound to be the one you let through that causes the lawsuit, or orders 10 million paper clips by mistake. Accurate figures for consequential losses cannot be assessed; for, say, a military defence system how much is the invasion of the country worth – £1 million, £100 000 million –

and how often will it happen—once a decade, once a century? Quantitative analysis techniques are, fortunately, going out of fashion.

3.4.2 Automated risk analysis methodologies

There are a number of computer-based investigation tools that can be used to support any risk analysis. Their mindless use as bludgeons in the hands of the ignorant or careless will do more harm than good, but employed sensibly they are of enormous help and should be used on all but the simplest of systems.

Of all, in the UK the most popular and accepted automated tool is the government approved CRAMM. In the late 1980s central government attempted to identify the need for the limitations on computer security. Its extensive assessment of available tools found that none of them provided a comprehensive answer or could be applied by an 'aware' IT user. This review also set out a specification of the 'dream candidate' computer-security assurance procedure. The specification demanded that it should be able to:

- deal with operational and administrative systems of all sizes;
- encompass all technical (e.g. software, communications) and non-technical (e.g. physical and personnel) aspects of IT security;
- be used during the development of a system, as well as within existing installations;
- be used by staff with general IT experience;
- be integrated into a speedy review;
- be implemented by an automated support tool;
- present results in a form readily understood by management.

In response, an internal agency within government, the Central Computer Telecommunications Agency (CCTA), developed CRAMM (the acronym's full title is CCTA Risk Analysis and Management Method). The authorities then approved it as the 'preferred' method for the identifying of countermeasures to threats to government IT systems. The method, and its PC-based support tool, are now in use in all government departments and in many other agencies.

In late 1988, the method was made available on a commercial basis. A number of leading businesses, councils and health authorities now use it. International interest and commitment to CRAMM is strong and an independent CRAMM user group has recently been formed. The CCTA remain committed to the method and a strategy for ongoing development is in place. This support and large client base is leading towards CRAMM becoming a *de facto* industry standard.

The CRAMM method consists of three stages, each supported by question-naires and guidelines. Each stage aims to answer one or two significant questions, as follows:

- *Stage 1:* Is the value of assets (consisting of hardware, software and data)

high enough to warrant security procedures more stringent than the use of a general 'code of good practice'?
- *Stage 2:* What and where is the security need? The answers can be found by identifying the vulnerabilities of the system;
- *Stage 3:* How can the need be met?

Stage One

The CRAMM approach starts by identifying the system's assets by type, location and role. This knowledge will later drive the introduction of appropriate controls.

Physical assets such as terminals, CPUs and printers are valued in replacement-cost terms. Each data asset is valued according to the user's perception of the likely damage suffered by the organization and the public if the asset is:

- unavailable (over three variable time periods),
- destroyed,
- disclosed (either to staff or outsiders),
- modified (accidentally or deliberately).

The impacts described by the user are translated into qualitative measures drawn on predefined 1–10 scales.

Software assets are identified and categorized as systems software or application software. Thereafter they are divided into packages, utilities and programs. Where the software is unique and vital, its value to the organization can be defined in the same way used for assessing the value of data.

After these initial assessments of value have been made, individual assets are then related together to identify their interdependence. For instance, the CRAMM user will try to determine the dependence of an application on the existence of a certain software utility. Such dependent assets thereafter take on the value of the data they support.

Stage Two

Once the asset values have been agreed by management, CRAMM seeks out the vulnerabilities of the system. This task can be supported by software which identifies relevant threat types and can, when the occasion demands it, group assets to simplify data collection.

CRAMM recognizes a total of 31 threat-types. These range from building fires and user error through to network failure. Questionnaires are used to interview the appropriate members of the management team. These are comprehensive documents which allow client-specific considerations to be included. Manager's answers are used to calculate a score which identifies low, medium or high states of risk.

At the end of Stage Two the assets values calculated during Stage One and these vulnerability scores are compared with a standard table. This enables the CRAMM user to identify 'security requirements' (more often known as measures of risk) which are expressed on an ascending scale from 1 to 5.

Stage Three

During Stage Three, CRAMM uses the measures of risk calculated in Stage Two to make practical recommendations according to given threats to the system. The tool recommends countermeasures from appropriate groups (e.g. fire protection for building fire) with the appropriate or lower measure of risk. In this way the right 'cost-justified' countermeasures are earmarked from over 1000 total measures covering every aspect of security.

The countermeasures themselves were originally identified by a large number of experts. They are collected into 52 different groups. The CRAMM user finds out from the appropriate system and security staff which of the recommended controls are already in place or are being met by some other means. Then reports are distributed to management with the aim of prompting discussion. CRAMM will kick off the implementation process by putting suggested countermeasures into priority order, based upon cost-effectiveness and coverage. This list can be reviewed in the light of management input.

During the course of the review, the CRAMM tool will have constructed a model which the user can interrogate to gain alternative approaches or to identify the impact of different scores. Furthermore, the tool contains a range of documents (such as a recommended security policy and management report) that can be used to document the review and to formalize security. The accumulated CRAMM model can be used later on to assess the impact of changes and as an information resource for other reviews.

CRAMM achieves IT security by giving management a clear understanding of assets' vulnerability to security threats, the adequacy of existing countermeasures and further countermeasures that should be installed. CRAMM acknowledges that IT security is a management problem and gives management the means to take objective, informed decisions to address that problem. Most importantly of all, though, CRAMM enforces vigour over the risk analysis process.

4
Countering the dangers

Perfect security can never be achieved or guaranteed, and no single counter-measure will ever be completely effective. At best, the risks to any asset can only be reduced to an acceptable level by reducing some or all of the threats, vulnerabilities and impact.

The unstable and delicate nature of electronic data means that its recovery in the event of damage, loss or compromise is bound to be difficult and unlikely to be completely effective. Further, detection of unauthorized human intervention can prove virtually impossible (especially if the perpetrator intends such an attack to be covert). Thus, prevention must be the watchword of computer security. Nevertheless, and since no security can ever be total, provision must be made for recovery from an accident or attack against the installation which may have lost or compromised the data, altered its accuracy or damaged the system so that service is no longer available.

Security features should be introduced into the system from the very earliest stages of design and procurement. No effective or efficient defences can ever be successfully implanted into an existing system, and any such retrospective measures will inevitably be limited, expensive and more inconvenient to introduce.

The security and safety features of a computer system are vital to its long-term effectiveness: it is this simple fact which, even now, managers, computer staff and security officers seem unwilling or unable to grasp.

4.1   The nature of the security features

The security features of a computer must protect the information within it to at least the level of its manual predecessor or alternative. To this end, the security measures must:

1   Operate in conjunction with the corporate way of life, its aims, methods and culture, and whatever task the computer is performing. Any security measures which cut across these boundaries will at best be ignored, and at worst deliberately circumvented. Security, to be effective, must be accepted by those whom it affects and those (the same) people who will have to make it work.

2   Not depend on a potential attacker's lack of knowledge about the system as a defence.
3   Be simple. The best security is usually the simplest, simply because there is less to go wrong and, of course, it is cheaper.
4   Be durable and efficient (with few false alarms). They must be resistant to attempts to deceive or tamper with them, and in the unfortunate event of failure in any way they should default to the most secure form until any problem has been resolved. In the worst case this should be a controlled (graceful) shut-down of the system, preserving as much recent data as possible.
5   Be as complete as possible, and capable of adaptation as the system or the prevailing risks change.
6   Present a cost-effective form of defence. Security resources will always be limited, and they must be used to the maximum benefit.
7   Be achievable and feasible.
8   Few companies will be prepared to change overnight, and even fewer will be able to. Security measures will by necessity need to be introduced over a period, progressively improving the safety and security of computer operations. The sense of the security measures should be clear to everyone within the organization.

4.2   Defence in depth

It must be accepted that there is no single security measure which, on its own, will be able to eliminate the risks to a computer, or which can ever be totally reliable. We should never rely on a single element for the preservation of our safety or security in whatever context. The most effective defence must therefore comprise several interlocking layers. In this way, each weakness in a security feature will be balanced by at least one other countermeasure. This policy of defence in depth has been used for countless centuries; its application to computer security is in no way novel. Castles throughout the ages have been built with numerous defensive rings, each of which would need to be breached before access to the heart of the fortifications is achieved and the castle overrun.

A sound computer security policy employs defence in depth, with interlocking and complementary layers of security which provide an effective overall countermeasure to the prevailing risks against the system. It is the elements of each of these separate layers which are described in detail in later chapters as a catalogue; they should be selected as necessary, moulded together and applied to the system in a comprehensive, practical and appropriate manner which merges into the overall security policy of the company. Each layer will, inevitably, be incomplete, but if such weaknesses are prevented from aligning with those of other layers then any gap should be met by at least one more defensive mechanism.

4.2.1   Organization

Sound organization is fundamental to secure and safe operations in any field, especially computer security. Essential elements of organization, without which computer security can never be made to work, include the following (though the list is not exhaustive):

1   Sensibly assigned and properly laid-down security responsibilities.
2   Clearly written orders or instructions so that staff are informed of the computer security policy and know how they are supposed to achieve their security tasks.
3   Realistic assessment of the risks to the system.
4   Registration of company computer assets.
5   Appropriate and adequate computer insurance.

4.2.2   Physical security

Physical security measures should be applied to a computer installation in the normal way, but there will be those elements specific to computer security. Physical security must be applied throughout; for example, it is folly to protect a remote terminal to a lower standard than the heart of the system to which it is connected.

4.2.3   Document security

Computer documents (including VDU displays, magnetic media, printouts, and even the manuals detailing how the system and its security mechanisms work) need to be protected from unauthorized access, copying, alteration, removal, destruction or overlooking. These document security procedures should as much as possible mirror the enterprise's existing traditional methods of protecting ordinary documents.

4.2.4   Personnel security

The greatest threat to any computer system lies with the people operating or using the system. Whatever the nature of the safety measures enforced, eventually the people involved must be trusted; it is this trust that they can betray. Measures should be taken to bar those of doubtful character from sensitive operations or access, and to ensure that those employees who have been invested with responsibility are of the highest integrity. Honest people should be kept honest; dishonest people should be kept away! Ironically, though, those same people, if trained properly and made fully aware of the threats to their computer system, can become the system's greatest assets in the fight to improve data safety and security.

4.2.5   Hardware security

Steps must be taken to protect the computer hardware—the mechanical and electrical/electronic components of the system. Such hardware can be physically damaged, but more insidiously it could be modified to harm the data or reveal the secrets of the system to unauthorized parties. At the same time, though, the hardware can be designed so that it contributes to overall system safety and security. Finally, but very importantly, maintenance procedures must be strict, and purchase/maintenance contracts must be watertight.

4.2.6   Software security

Steps must be taken to care for the system's software—the precious programs which allow it to perform its desired manipulation and processing of the data, and vital to safe and secure functioning. At the same time, however, those very programs can be designed to incorporate security features to protect themselves and the data from unauthorized access. They can be used to record details of system use, showing for example who has performed what functions on the system, where and when. They can also segregate the data into privacy groupings. In short, the system's programs can be designed with an in-built ability to protect themselves and the data being stored and processed, by access, audit and separation. Software security comprises these two elements—protection of the software itself, and protection afforded by that same software.

4.2.7   Tempest

Compromising electronic emanations from equipment can be intercepted, and after analysis reveal to an unauthorized party the data within the system. Radiation security, or TEMPEST, aims either to reduce the strength/clarity of these compromising emanations, or to increase the difficulties of intercepting any leakage that does occur.

4.2.8   Communications (network) security

Increasingly, computer systems are becoming both widely dispersed and are being linked into other systems and networks. The communications lines between computer systems, or to local or remote terminals or other separate parts of a dispersed or networked system, are particularly vulnerable because they extend unavoidably beyond the immediate confines of the working environment. They also tend to be forgotten—'out of sight, out of mind'. Communications, or network, security is concerned with safeguarding these links and the data messages they carry.

4.2.9   *Business continuity planning and disaster recovery*

Plans for the recovery from the materialization of any of the threats or system weaknesses, including disasters, are vital. Since there is no such thing as total security, someone somewhere is about to suffer a computer failure, disaster or breach of data security or safety. Unless there are plans made for what to do in such dire circumstances, and if the business has come to depend on the computer system (which most do very shortly after 'computerization'), then it is likely that that business may die. Plans must be made in advance to get the business going again, with or without the computer system that has failed. And disasters do not always happen during the working day or come in recognizable form, so it is important to think of all the possible ways in which your computer system could fail you.

4.2.10   *Security awareness*

There is a need to improve staff awareness before general standards of computer security can improve significantly among the general user population. But bringing computer security plans to life during an effective training campaign will produce significant improvements in computer security standards far out of proportion to the effort involved. Raising awareness and educating a wide audience in the basic countermeasures will generate, pound for pound, a far more profound and longer lasting improvement than any purely technical solution could ever hope to achieve.

A combination of all these security measures, to varying degrees depending on the system, should be employed to wrap around the vital resource—the data—and protect it from corruption and compromise and ensure its continued availability. The security policy of the computer system defines the manner in which these measures ensure data integrity, continuity and confidentiality—who can do what to which information, when, and what is to be protected from whom and how. The degree of protection to be afforded the computer and its data will depend on the value of that data, the nature and role of the system, and the risks against it and the data, and must be defined by senior management.

Security and computer personnel, under the direction of management and in line with the aims of the enterprise, must devise a balanced, cost-effective security solution appropriate to the computer system while maintaining its efficiency. Since the risk is the sum of the threats, the vulnerabilities and the impact, any reduction in these by the employment of a combination of the security measures described above will reduce the risk. The four factors are inextricably linked, though, and must be considered as a whole. There is, for example, no point in spending vast sums of time and effort in reducing vulnerabilities on a computer system of little value for which the threat is either minimal or not reduced by the particular precautions taken; nor is it wise to ignore certain threats or misjudge the risks against the system. This process of risk analysis, in order to determine the appropriate security policy, is the final piece in the jigsaw of computer security.

5
Valuing data

Information is made up of items of data. The need to protect the data and the information is the same, and so in the context of this book the terms are considered interchangeable.

In order to decide how much effort should be applied to protect a particular computer, the overall worth of its data must be sensibly assessed. There is little to be achieved from looking after something with no value, but there is much to be lost from not caring for that which is of great importance or which is extremely sensitive. The values of hardware and support facilities such as buildings are easily expressed in terms of replacement costs; there will also be a measurable cost to the enterprise incurred by the lack of computer facilities during the replacement period. But the worth of information is more difficult to determine. Within a single system, data will have a variety of qualities; some will be more valuable, some less. For a cost-effective security programme, we need to be able to identify the worth of each item of data and concentrate the security resources on those which are the most valuable or critical. By identifying and labelling those assets which require protection, and if then those assets are ranked in order of importance, we can see clearly where attention should be paid, and so set and adjust the security level accordingly.

Consequential losses are also difficult to determine, but they are an important aspect of this valuing process. Loss of data, for example, or loss of the computing facility will result in consequential effects such as loss of market share or damage to reputation or market confidence. While at first sight certain data may appear to be of little worth, do not forget its hidden, and often more significant, value.

5.1   Ownership

The individual best qualified to value the particular worth of a specific piece of information is its owner, who should be in a position to evaluate potential risks to that information and to know its value to the enterprise. Thus, the owner can be defined as 'that individual manager or representative of management who has responsibility for making and communicating judgements and decisions on behalf of the enterprise with regard to the use, identification, classification and protec-

32

tion of a specific information asset'. Ownership, though, is only a role; legally, the actual owners of the information are the shareholders, proprietors, taxpayers etc. Ownership flows through the hierarchy of the enterprise to, ultimately, its Head Officer, but it should be pushed down to the lowest reasonable level possible and assigned to a named individual.

Ownership of information should reside with appropriate business areas, not the computing function. Simply because information is held within and processed by a computer system, there are no more grounds to pass ownership of that information to the computer staff than there are to pass ownership of one's money to one's bank manager. Computer staff are custodians of business information with a duty to protect it. Similarly, users with authorized access to information have a duty to protect it, but no rights of ownership exist.

The classification/privacy grading should not be changed without the authority of the owner, but suspected over- or under-classification should be challenged to avoid over- or under-protection. Further, to hype the grading of material or information 'just to make sure it is looked after properly' will rapidly degrade the higher grading levels and reduce confidence in the whole process. As with the typing pool, where every document has to be marked priority for it ever to reach the top of the pile, without strict control and discipline over the classification process all documents will gravitate towards TOP SECRET to earn even basic protection.

5.2   Classification

Classifying information involves the award of a level of worth, and with such a label will come a predetermined set of security controls giving a recognized standard of protection. Information with a greater worth will require a greater level of protection. Classification is no more than a simple and easily enforced way of informing everyone just how sensitive and valuable information is, and thus what protection it needs. It is, inevitably, a subjective process made less so by a structured and strictly enforced classification scheme.

Information should be classified according to its *confidentiality* (sensitivity to disclosure), its *integrity* (sensitivity to modification), or its *continuity* (sensitivity to unavailability). Such classifications should be made separately—for example, information can be sensitive to unavailability but not to unauthorized disclosure.

The quantity of information—aggregation—can affect its value, as can the context within which it is found. How up-to-date and current information is, and how much it is worth to your competitors, will be other important aspects of its value—annual performance figures which do not contain the latest inputs will be of less worth than the latest versions, and they will be less valuable after publication than just before they are announced.

The way in which information is valued will vary between enterprises. Within the military services, confidentiality of information is perhaps the most important issue. In other fields there may be different priorities: integrity of data is often more immediately important within the commercial and industrial sectors, but data continuity may be the critical factor.

5.2.1   Confidentiality

Confidentiality within government departments

Her Majesty's Government uses a system of confidentiality classification which has existed for many years, and is well known throughout the UK public and private sectors. The damage resulting from loss or compromise of the information is used as the yardstick to 'price' the information's need for protection.

Superimposed on such a primary classification of confidentiality can be a further privacy classification so that access to data of whatever confidentiality classification can be further restricted to named groups or individuals. Two examples of such privacy markings are:

1 *In confidence*   Such markings as Staff-in-Confidence, Medical-in-Confidence, Police-in-Confidence dictate the distribution of the material, whatever its confidentiality. It is quite common to see a combination, such as Confidential/Staff-in-Confidence.
2 *Personal for . . .*   Such material is intended to be seen by the named person(s) only.

Confidentiality in non-government enterprises

In non-government enterprises, there are no accepted standards for grading confidentiality. The definitions of each level, and the associated arrangements for protection, are dictated by the enterprise's structure and needs; however, following the Government's baseline, the effect upon the business's success or profit of the loss or compromise of the information would be a suitable measure of confidentiality. Such gradings could then be:

1 *Unclassified*   Information and material to which access may be granted to any other person or enterprise.
2 *Internal use only*   Information which, because of its personal, technical or business sensitivity, should be confined to use only within the enterprise for purposes related to its business. Such information could include internal personnel listings or telephone directories, organizational charts, or unsensitive procedures.
3 *Confidential*   Information, the unauthorized disclosure of which would:
   • adversely affect the business;
   • blunt the enterprise's competitive edge;
   • reveal operational direction over a short term;
   • reduce the technical or financial success of a product or service.

Such information could include summaries of financial data, business results for part of the enterprise, technical characteristics of a particular product, or personnel's career, salary or other details. It should be available only to those with a business need to know.

4   *Confidential restricted*   Information, the unauthorized disclosure of which would:

- prejudice the success of the business;
- significantly blunt the enterprise's competitive edge;
- reveal operational direction over an extended period of time;
- seriously affect the technical or financial success of a product or service.

Such information could include business results for significant portions of the enterprise's business, consolidated summaries of financial data, forecast assumptions, or concentrations of information of lower classifications. It should be disseminated only to those with a prearranged need to know.

5   *Registered confidential*   Information the unauthorized disclosure of which would:

- injure or kill the business;
- remove the enterprise's competitive edge;
- reveal operational strategies and major direction;
- terminate the technical or financial success of a product or service.

Such information could include business operating plans and strategies, details of unannounced products or services, results for the overall enterprise's business, or concentrations of information of lower classifications. It should be available only to those with a confirmed need to know.

Additional descriptive terms could be added to define more clearly the information, for example 'FORECASTS CONFIDENTIAL' or 'RESEARCH REGISTERED CONFIDENTIAL'. Privacy markings can also be used to restrict access to certain groups or individuals—'For Board Members Only', or 'Personal for. . .'. Control statements can be added, too—'Do Not Copy', or 'Encrypt for Storage', or 'For Development Use Only'. In this way, a hierarchy of labels can be built up. Whatever the system adopted, however, and as with the government system, the gradings should be simple, and be clearly stated to all staff so that they can be properly applied to information and the appropriate countermeasures enforced. Most importantly, whatever its form, the system should be properly managed and policed so that the enterprise can have confidence in its effectiveness and enforcement. It is vital that, when forfeiting possession of valued information to the custody of another, one is entirely happy that the receiver will look after it at least as well as oneself, and that everyone is working to a common standard.

5.2.2   Integrity

Classification by degree of integrity should also be considered where data integrity has a value to the enterprise:

1 *High integrity*   High integrity is required. No errors should occur.
2 *Medium integrity*   A moderate level of integrity is required. There should be no errors that would seriously affect operations.
3 *Low integrity*   Integrity is not important. Errors can be accepted.

Systems such as air traffic control computers will require high integrity, while confidentiality is relatively unimportant: heavy investment in comprehensive software testing will be necessary. Computers used for training purposes, on the other hand, may well be able to manage without a high degree of data integrity.

5.2.3   Continuity

A continuity classification will indicate the effect upon operations of loss of the computing facilities:

1 *Essential*   No interruption of service is acceptable. This grading may be further refined with the caveat '. . . for more than . . . [time]'.
2 *Desirable*   Interruption of service should be avoided if possible.
3 *Unimportant*   Interruption of service will be inconvenient, but will not significantly affect operations.

Again, our air traffic control computer will have an essential continuity classification, necessitating such facilities as back-up systems, uninterrupted power supplies and 24-hour staffing by support engineers as well as system operators, all at significant extra cost.

We have returned to those three essential qualities of information—confidentiality, integrity and continuity. Computer systems will have differing roles and importance, and their data will attract differing emphasis on each of these qualities. Where confidentiality has traditionally, because of its importance within the Government sector, received the greatest attention, continuity and integrity are likely to be just as important in the commercial and industrial environments.

6
Developing a computer security policy

The enterprise should already have clear policies about the nature of its business (the business policy), how and with what resources it is to achieve its aims (the technical policy), and how it intends to protect both its assets and its continued ability to function (the security policy). Such policies should be formal, documented and agreed by senior management. Within each there may be further policies; within the security policy, for example, there could be described the enterprise's physical, personnel and document security policies. Now, too, there should be a clear statement of enterprise computer security policy. Ultimately, there should also be a system security policy for each and every computer system, unique to that system and describing the ways in which its electronic data is to be protected.

This book will provide us in Part Three with a shopping list, a catalogue of available defences against those potential threats and vulnerabilities which we feel are relevant to our particular enterprise and which place its computers at risk. We must identify and analyse the risks, deciding which are most likely to occur, which will affect us most and how, and which of the risks we are most worried about and would most like to avoid. We must then select from the list of all the possible countermeasures those which, for each system in its given environment, carrying out a particular task and operated by certain personnel, will provide the best acceptable level of security at an affordable price. Finally, we must define how we intend to spend those funds we have devoted to security in order to get the best value for money.

There will always remain a degree of risk to the safety and security of our computers and their data, since there is no such thing as total security. It is important that we are happy and can live with this risk, and have prepared in advance contingency plans for the disasters which may befall.

6.1 Defining the computer security policy

In the past, security has evolved in reaction to events and in order to reduce the effects of disasters and breaches, aided by a combination of tradition, meddling and stop-gapping. Every manager must at some time have been tempted to do

without expensive security advice, since at first sight it must appear a luxury and
'anyway there is nothing complicated about putting out a few guards'. However,
the achievement of sound security is as difficult and specialized a job as any
other. All too often though, in order to save time and money it is either ignored
or made the responsibility of everyone, when it becomes the responsibility of no
one. At best, cosmetic and face-saving solutions may be put into place. Security
will, in most enterprises, be forced to the back of the queue of priorities. In the
context of computer security this must not be allowed to happen—the stakes are
too high.

The enterprise must consider how it intends to ensure the confidentiality,
integrity and continuity of its electronic data and associated information
technology—senior management must prepare a corporate computer security
policy.

6.2   The security charter

Many enterprises, when asked, will claim to have a computer security policy, but
on examination such a policy will often turn out to be a couple of pages in length
and contain little except an acknowledgement of the danger and a statement of
intent to become secure. Such a 'security charter' is an essential starting point for
any corporate plan for computer security, but it will not indicate exactly how the
problem is to be tackled. Enterprises should not be lulled into a false sense of
security by believing such a charter will do anything practical or positive towards
improving computer security; its purpose is to highlight to senior management
that the issue of computer security needs to be addressed and to assert that—as a
matter of policy—action will be taken. The security charter can be regarded as
the fuse which should detonate the security effort. Any existing 'policies' which
simply fulfil this role should be viewed only as a starting point for the production
of a security policy.

6.3   The corporate computer security policy

Moving on from any security charter, the corporate computer security policy will
comprise those rules, regulations and practices which make up the way in which
electronic data is to be protected from loss, corruption or unavailability. It must
address all forms of that data and all aspects of its control, and will not
necessarily be limited to the immediate environs and operations of computer
systems. More sensitive or valuable information will clearly attract more security
effort, but the policy should not be limited to such data.

The corporate computer security policy's rules will normally be high level and
of a general nature. Specific techniques or procedures should not be detailed in
this document, but it should define the range of countermeasures that management intends to be used, and in what way and to what extent, in order to counter
the general risks faced by the enterprise.

6.4   System security policies

Further refining of the corporate computer security policy will then be necessary for each major system or network in order to produce a range of system security policies. It is likely that such subsidiary policies will bear much common resemblance, but they will be tailored to each system in its unique role and will describe the specific countermeasures to be used.

6.5   Technical security policies

Within very sensitive environments where great reliance is placed upon the defences provided by the system itself, it may be necessary, in addition to the system security policy, to produce a technical security policy that specifies the hardware and software security aspects of the system security policy in more detail.

6.6   Security operating procedures

Before our new computer is brought into service, and indeed for any existing computer, the staff must be told in detail the manner in which they should operate it to ensure data safety and security—they must be provided with security operating procedures. In any aspect of our working lives, in order to achieve set goals we must be told what it is that is required of us and exactly how our masters want us to get there. Without such orders, instructions and formalized guidance, employees will either set out on their own route towards the objectives, or not bother setting out at all. Either way, chaos will ensue, and when things go wrong, which in this context is when data security is breached or safety measures break down, if we have not explained ourselves properly to the culprits then it is unreasonable to hold them entirely to blame.

There are those who will fail in their duties no matter how carefully they are briefed. Nevertheless, most people want to do a good job, both for reasons of self-respect and in order to earn the praise of their superiors, subordinates and peers. There will always be the lazy and dishonest, but the majority of any workforce will try to turn in a good day's work for a good day's pay. If mistakes are made, as inevitably they will be, usually they will be unintentional and caused by lack of training, lack of knowledge, or lack of incentive and motivation. Management, computer and security personnel must do all in their power to reduce these factors. A satisfactory training and awareness campaign must be one such way, but clear orders are the other essential.

Security operating procedures must explain in detail the security arrangements for a computer system and list the responsibilities, duties and procedures for those staff involved in any way with its safe and secure operation. Such orders, if followed, will ensure that the data is protected to the standard specified in the system's security policy, and they must be:

- easy to understand, or they will not be implemented;
- explained where the purpose is not clear, or they will be ignored;
- enforced with vigour, or they will be evaded. Breaching the security rules has to be seen to be an offence.

The security operating procedures should include, in a similar format, all those aspects of computer security addressed in the detailed policy statement (already prepared?) for that system. As with the system security policies from which they are derived, security operating procedures will be system-specific and will vary in format and detail from a couple of pages to a thick volume, depending on the nature and importance of the system. They must be clear, concise, relevant and understandable. They should be prepared by project management staff at the end of the procurement and development cycle prior to the commissioning of the system, but for computers already in existence they should be produced by the system manager; either way, they should be approved by departmental and corporate security officers to ensure that they receive appropriate support from all staff.

There are some important differences between the procedures and the policy:

- Not all system staff will need to see all parts of the security operating procedures. Distribution should be arranged so that individual departments and users are issued only with those parts relevant to them. In this way, what can be a daunting document appears not so lengthy that staff are reluctant to read or refer to its contents. There could be a separate section containing general operating procedures and guidance to users; this ready-reference 'Novice's Guide' would summarize the duties of the users, and should be able to stand on its own.
- Unlike the policy, the security operating procedures should receive the widest possible distribution so that all personnel have access to them.
- Security operating procedures must be written as a series of unambiguous directives. The policy can be less abrupt, but it is important that these associated orders define clearly exactly what is and is not to be done, and do not leave individuals in any doubt as to their responsibilities. The procedures must be capable of both attributing blame when they are not followed, and protecting those let down by the failings and omissions of others.

6.7   The importance of the corporate computer security policy

The corporate computer security policy is the major foundation from which subsequent system security policies should derive (Fig. 6.1). It, and system security policies, must be based above all else on a sound and accurate assessment of the threats against the computer systems and host enterprise, together with a proper and sensible analysis of the risks. There is no simple way to avoid this initial effort and the quality of all subsequent work depends on it.

Following a corporate risk analysis, which should aim to identify the generic

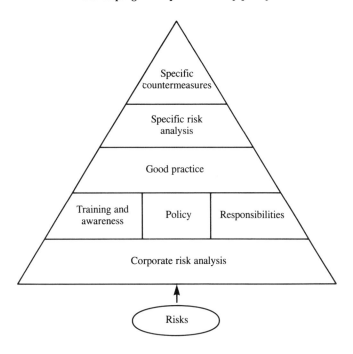

Figure 6.1.   Computer security policies.

threats, vulnerabilities and asset values of the enterprise's information technology, the corporate security policy may be prepared. It should be complemented with a clear allocation of security responsibilities and a comprehensive training and awareness campaign. It should describe those general countermeasures which together form a code of good security practice. For major systems, specific risk analyses will then identify particular threats, vulnerabilities and asset values to allow specific countermeasures to be applied on a system by system basis and from which security operating procedures can be evolved.

6.8   Policy decisions

The risk analysis will have produced an assessment of the likelihood of a harmful event occurring and its impact upon the enterprise (Fig. 6.2). The security policy (and hence the countermeasures to be employed) must reflect this analysis or there was no point in performing it.

6.8.1   Accept risk

If a risk is unlikely to occur and will have little adverse impact, it is reasonable to accept it and suffer the consequences. The cure might be more trouble than the disease. The policy for such a risk should be that no countermeasures are put in place. It is the 'so what?' category!

Figure 6.2.   Policy decisions.

6.8.2   *Plan*

If a risk is unlikely but will have a high impact, the policy should be to plan what to do should it ever be realized.

6.8.3   *Avoid/escape*

Risks that are harmful and likely to occur must be avoided, or there must be some way to escape from their effects. Countermeasures should be devised accordingly.

6.8.4   *Control*

Risks that are likely but will have little impact should be controlled by the countermeasures in force.

   Clearly there will be interaction between the host of risks and it will not be possible to compartmentalize them or their appropriate countermeasures as neatly as described above. Nevertheless, the security policy should reflect the implications of the risk analysis, so that countermeasures are sensibly and cost-effectively applied.

6.9   **Format of computer security policies**

The corporate computer security policy should remain static since its assertions are high level and are likely to be affected only by the most dramatic changes to the enterprise, its business, its information technology strategy, or its risks.
   While essentially remaining the same, inevitably a system security policy will

evolve alongside the evolution of the project, growing in depth, range and detail and changing subtly its form and function. During its early life, the system security policy will be brief and wide-ranging, but as the system's design, development, procurement and installation proceeds, more detail will be added to cover all the necessary matters. The system security policy should finally be issued as a series of sections covering the main elements of computer security. In the early days of project development it will guide the manufacturers of the hardware and the designers of the software, and allow the computer and security staff to prepare and practise the other measures which go to make up the complete set of security features for that system. When the computer is introduced into service, the security policy will provide a benchmark for the data's safety, privacy, integrity and continuity. It will provide terms of reference for all involved with the system's operations and will allow the actual security in force to be compared with the required level set in advance by management.

There is no set or recommended format for a computer security policy. No two enterprises, no two computer systems, will ever be the same, and a security policy must uniquely interpret the risks and the appropriate countermeasures for a given enterprise or system, in a given role, in a given place, and operated by nominated staff.

- It must always be written in clear, concise and comprehensible terms, defining its aims, and describing the principles and methods of accomplishing those standards of data safety, security and integrity set by the company. It must be well documented and authoritative, issued on behalf of, and carrying the signature of, the highest levels of management.
- It should be drawn up by those charged with the use, operation and security of the system. It is these staff who will have the most intimate knowledge of, and skills upon, the computer to be protected. They will have to make the policy come to life, and so their support is vital.
- It must achieve a level of security at least equal to, but not necessarily greater than, the security of similar information held in traditional form. It must be positive, and not rely upon a potential attacker's knowledge as a defence. It must be as simple as possible. It must be reliable at all times, and it must be comprehensive, addressing all the computer system assets and all aspects of their work.
- It should fit in with the corporate way of life, and must take into account the aims, culture and methods of the enterprise. It must cooperate with the company's ideas and uses for, and methods of, computing, and should protect the computing function to an extent commensurate with the importance of that function to the company's survival and growth. It is no good imposing strict regimes of security upon systems that are of little import and at no great risk, nor is it wise to enforce low levels of control over highly attractive computers which hold and handle data vital to the well-being of the enterprise. In the first case, time and effort have been wasted and the

efficiency of the computing function reduced, while in the latter case the data is at inordinate risk. The policy should encourage rather than threaten.

- It must not be set in concrete. As the business's aims and technical abilities change, so too will the computer security requirements, and there has also to be flexibility to allow constraints or business needs to override, if necessary, the security features. It must be regularly reviewed and updated to meet any changes to the threats, vulnerabilities or importance of the system. This task must be assigned to a named individual. No computer will remain static in its form or role; the very qualities of computers cause dynamic change, and it is only right that this is so. The policy can quickly become out of date. Staff must be told of any changes to the policy, and how such changes will affect them. The reviews must be comprehensive and repeated at appropriate intervals (not too often, not too few).

- It must include only feasible objectives. Unrealistic or unattainable demands bring a policy into disrepute and disuse. It must contain only appropriate objectives given the nature and aims of the enterprise. Unnecessary security arrangements are wasteful. It must be phased in, and should avoid all-or-nothing statements.

- Adequate resources must be provided for it, but at the same time it must remain cost-effective. Having accepted the security objectives, management must then be prepared to devote the necessary effort to their achievement. On the other hand, the resources available will inevitably be set at a certain limit by management, since there will not be a bottomless purse of security funding, and so the policy must be set to this level also. Grandiose plans will be destined to stay as such and never be put into practice.

- It must provide for adequate training of all staff concerned with the computer's operations. The best-laid plans will be of no value if the staff are either unaware of them or not taught how to enforce and work with them.

- It must allow for the worst case. In the event that the security protection afforded by the policy fails in some way, contingency plans to deal with such a situation must be outlined in order to recover to normal service as soon as possible.

6.10   Contents of a system security policy

Sensibly, a system security policy will fall into discrete sections within three main parts. Although the following is a description of a system security policy, the overall corporate computer security policy from which it has been derived should have been designed along the same lines, but at a higher level. All of the issues described below are discussed in this book.

6.10.1   Part one: Overview of the system

This part will set the scene. It should:

- Begin with a statement from senior management, ideally the Chief Executive or equivalent, emphasizing the policy's importance and senior support for it.
- Describe the system, its name, what its purpose is to be, why it was needed, and who will be using it. It should give its intended location, and exactly what it will comprise, including peripherals and connections to networks.
- Specify the nature of the data to be stored and processed, including its (maximum permitted) sensitivity and value, and the mode of secure processing to be enforced.
- Identify the operational and security responsibilities, ensuring that all such aspects are assigned to a named individual or appointment and that such nominees are made aware of these duties. In particular, responsibilities for supervision should be clearly stated.
- Provide the terms of reference for system staff and describe the composition and terms of reference of the system security committee.
- Outline the incident reporting procedures.
- Describe the administrative procedures for the review and testing of, and changes to, the security policy and its enforcement and implementation. This task in particular should be assigned to a named individual.
- Describe the development of the project and the agencies and manufacturers concerned, their responsibilities before and after delivery and commissioning, and any deadlines.
- Refer to the contracts and terms agreed, together with penalty clauses (if any) that apply to either side.
- Outline planned future developments, uses and refinements of the system.

6.10.2   Part two: The risks to the system

As a result of the risk analysis it should be possible to describe those risks to the computer which are considered to be relevant, and their order of priority. The dangers from deliberate attack should be defined, together with some indications about potential enemies, their resources and the attractiveness of the system to them. Accidental and natural hazards should also be detailed. A brief description of the strategy intended to counter these risks, as a balance of separate but merging defences in depth, should be included so that the third and most lengthy part of the policy can be viewed within the context of an overall plan. Finally, business continuity plans and disaster recovery strategies should be outlined.

6.10.3 Part three: Specific countermeasures

The major part of the policy document will describe the specific countermeasures to be invoked. It will describe in detail the various measures to be adopted in order to wrap around and protect the system's information from loss, corruption or unavailability. The following points should be considered for inclusion:

- *Physical security* A brief description of the principles of defence in depth, and the aims of physical security, should be followed by details about:
  - the location, general design and layout of the computer's accommodation, and the principal features of its physical security;
  - arrangements for controlling entry to the data centre and specified rooms therein, including the checking of all incoming and outgoing baggage, equipment and supplies;
  - the protection of computer system services and utilities, including lighting, heating, air conditioning, and water and electricity supplies;
  - fire protection.
- *Document security* Details about handling, marking, accounting for, backing up, purging and destroying all forms of computer documents. It might be useful to list and describe those documents included within this section, and any associated and 'as if' documents.
- *Personnel security* The elements of personnel security should be described in outline, before providing details about:
  - the need-to-know principle;
  - the need-to-go principle;
  - the two-person principle;
  - rotation of duties;
  - authorized users of the system, by name against post. Administrative procedures for the regular review of this list;
  - sensitive duties and key posts;
  - key personnel and the terms and conditions of their employment to ensure that no single individual is entrusted with an inordinate amount of authority, importance or unsupervised access;
  - the recruitment of personnel, and their screening;
  - security clearances, and their administration;
  - the prohibition of tampering and browsing, and the penalties to be imposed on staff performing such unauthorized acts. It will be this policy statement which may be cited subsequently in any disciplinary proceedings against an offender;
  - joining and termination of employment procedures, in particular non-disclosure agreements;
  - security awareness and education arrangements;
  - the supervision of computer staff.
- *Hardware security* This may be a suitable place to list (in more detail than

in Part One of the policy) the hardware components of the computer system. Then give details about:

- securing hardware from tampering;
- hardware identification devices;
- hardware integrity checks;
- maintenance procedures. Inevitably, this will be a long and detailed section if it is to receive appropriate attention within the system security policy;
- fault tolerance;
- the contracts for the procurement and maintenance of the system, again in more detail than in Part One of the policy.

● *Software security*   Since it is important to put software security in context, it would be appropriate to outline the aims and capabilities of software security and its limitations. Then give details about:
   - general measures which should be taken to protect software (in particular the operating system and other system programs) from damage or subversion;
   - access controls provided by the system software. The control and issue of passwords and tokens will feature significantly at this point;
   - separation, and the mode of secure processing to be employed;
   - audit;
   - the procedures which should be established to control the design and development of, and changes to, system software in general and security software in particular;
   - the procedures to guard against, detect and treat any viruses;

● *Compromising emanations* (*TEMPEST*)   Details about:
   - simple precautions used to reduce any compromising emanations;
   - use of TEMPEST-proofed equipment.

● *Business continuity and disaster recovery plans*   Broad reference to the business continuity and disaster recovery strategy should be made, and the disaster recovery plan itself may be included as an annex. Plans for dealing with utilities or equipment failures should be included.

● *Insurance*   Details of those risks which are to be transferred by insurance elsewhere should be included. Arrangements with any insurance companies should be explained, and copies of agreements and policies could be attached. Any risks deliberately accepted without either precautions or insurance should be identified.

● *Personal Computer Security*   Special arrangements or specific countermeasures for the protection of data handled or stored by personal computers (PCs).

6.11   Uses for the system security policy

The computer security policy is vital to any computer of any real significance to the enterprise's well-being, since without it no cohesive and cost-effective computer security can ever be achieved. The policy should be present from the earliest stages of the project, and as the system development progresses and crystallizes, so too should the security plans and procedures. By the time the system is introduced into service, the security policy should be complete, comprehensive and workable, and should be capable of providing the best possible security for the available money and resources.

For a large mainframe of some significance to the enterprise's operations, the security policy document will inevitably and necessarily be of considerable length and contain much detail; it will emerge in its final form only after much hard work and careful planning by all those involved with the development of the project from its inception. There is no simple or easy way to any security solution; there are no short cuts, and this is no exception. It is necessary, though, that the security implications are addressed:

- For a small system, or PC, with little significance to the actual survival or growth of the enterprise, there will be less of a need for extensive security, and the associated security policy will be easier to prepare and may be less formal.
- Existing systems, with their inherent and incurable security weaknesses and vulnerabilities, will demand differing policies which accept these constraints and produce appropriate solutions with compensatory security features.
- There may be, within an enterprise, commonality of computer operations. For example, many models of the same PC may be in use throughout, and so many of the security measures will apply to them all. Staff screening procedures will be common to all departments. Physical security of large buildings applies to all parts of them. There may also, then, be scope for standard policies, 'topped and tailed' for each specific computer, or for policies which refer to a set of systems, such as PCs.

The permutations are numerous, and the design of system security policies should be adapted to the needs and structure of the enterprise. The aim must remain constant, though, and that is to define the ways in which an enterprise intends to safeguard the electronic data within a specified computer.

The production of corporate and system computer security policy documents may become an alternative to any real action towards improving the security of computer operations. Nevertheless, any such policy, over the ensuing period of a computer's existence, will repay its costs, and many times over if it saves a single security breach or disaster.

Part 2
Responsibilities for computer security

7
Computer staff versus security staff?

Computer security is a discipline that comprises two very separate elements: on the one side the computer scientists and technicians are trained to improve the efficiency of the enterprise; while on the other hand the security managers and administrators are required to contain the risks against the enterprise. At first sight there seems little to draw these groups together. Their training, attitudes and methods differ fundamentally, yet it is essential, if effective information protection is ever to be achieved, that they work in harmony towards the common goal. But for too long computer personnel have been left to their own devices, and for too long security personnel have buried their heads in the sand. To improve the relationship between these two groups it will be useful to consider the qualities and limitations of them both, and their interactions with management. In particular:

- security staff must accept the challenges offered by information technology;
- computer staff must accept the advice and competence of others in areas where perhaps they have never before been questioned, and recognize that the solution to computer security does not lie solely within the technical arena.

While traditional security policies and practices may well be established within an enterprise to protect and defend against the familiar threats of espionage, sabotage, subversion, terrorism and criminal acts of theft and damage, no such defences can remain complete if the major new asset—the computer—remains the unprotected weak link in the chain. We have discussed the need for a cost-effective computer security policy attuned to the business needs and operations of the enterprise, and this must involve the close cooperation of both computer and security staff if it is to be totally successful.

To this end, computer personnel need to be educated in the ways of security, and security personnel need to be aware of the principles and problems of information technology. The two groups must work in harmony if information protection is to be achieved. Most important of all, though, is the winning of the vital support of top management, without which not only is it unlikely that the necessary resources will be made available in the first place, but the incentive to continue with initial efforts and to maintain vigilance will be lost; a concerted campaign by security and computer personnel together will stand a better chance of gaining this support.

The responsibility for computer security therefore falls upon the shoulders of these two broad groups—the computer personnel (including users, programmers and operators) and the security personnel (including guards and managers)—working together for management in order to secure data integrity, confidentiality and continuity by addressing risks to computers and their data. Each group has its strengths and weaknesses, each has differing knowledge and skills, and neither is a perfect beast. But recognition of each one's limitations is the first step towards improvement and, in addition, there are particular and shared problems that each and both need to address.

7.1   The interdisciplinary approach

Computer security must dovetail into the overall security policy of the enterprise. It must fit into the enterprise's structure and culture, and must be compatible with existing operational and security practices. It must not be developed in isolation, it must not impinge unacceptably on efficiency and it must be flexible enough to absorb changes to circumstances or business direction. Computer security therefore requires an interdisciplinary approach, so that all parties involved with the use, operation, supervision and security of the computing function can inject their contributions to all aspects of system development, including safety and security.

Information technology changes so fast that computer and security personnel must have a sound working relationship to allow the rapid and effective incorporation of such changes into the security policy. As in all walks of life, the best time to prepare, by understanding others' problems and methods and by building friendships with one's colleagues, is in advance and over a longer period to ensure thoroughness, and not while the sky is falling.

7.2   Mutual problems

There are problems mutual to the two main groups of players in this game:

1 *The language problem*   In common with any new area of development, the pioneers of computing necessarily developed a strange and specialized language to describe the elements of their work. Who, for example, in the early years of this century, would have easily understood the terms used to describe the working parts of that new-fangled invention the motor car—'half-shaft', 'big end', 'differential gearing'—or could have even visualized the wonder of a television set (in colour) in everyone's front room? This existence of unfamiliar terminology and of, to the lay person, incomprehensible but marvellous achievements, isolates the computer world and increases the

ignorance and fear of the outsider. But, in its way, the security world has its own special language and its own peculiar ways, seemingly inhabited only by fierce dogs and frightening people in uniform who come awake only in the dark hours, and to an outsider it too appears a confusing and closed world. This language barrier is real, and must be recognized by all involved. Effort must be applied to overcome it, and it should not be used as an excuse for further prolonging the differences between the two groups, or as a reason for failing to understand another's problems or points of view.

2 *The culture difference* Computer staff are designed for efficiency. Their tool of trade is the computer, which is there simply to speed things up. Security staff, on the other hand, are there to ensure the secure performance of the enterprise's work, and their very presence, even before they have done anything, inevitably slows things down. Security, by its very nature, causes restrictions which impede efficiency. It introduces cost and time constraints which, in the short term, seem to block the progress of the workforce. Control of entry, physical security, screening of personnel, recording and controlling documents, and implementing software and hardware security features, all involve overheads which must be included in the final 'price' of whatever the product is. Within data processing, these two cultures need not be mutually exclusive, but both computer and security staff must recognize each other's motives and work together to achieve a sensible compromise between security and operations.

7.3 The problems with being a computer person

Computer personnel are ill-equipped to tackle computer security issues on their own for a number of reasons:

1 Computer personnel are technicians with great knowledge of, enthusiasm for, and familiarity with computers. Their judgement may be clouded by all this, and they may not recognize the importance of their data or the weaknesses in their operations and practices. They may not see a problem which exists in others' eyes; experts cannot see problems because they have the expertise to overcome them, but they remain for the non-expert to stumble over or the criminal to subvert. Parents are the last people to see the faults in their children; the trusted friend and confidante is best able and willing to point them out. The same is true for security in general, but for computer security in particular, when an independent but competent third party must be employed to introduce an impartial security policy.

2 Programmers, systems analysts and the variety of other specialist computer personnel are the greatest threat to any installation, since they have privileged access to the system and the knowledge to subvert its defences to perform illegal or damaging acts on the system. The internal threat of poor personnel security is every security manager's nightmare. Theft, sabotage and espionage

are all made easier with insider knowledge or access, but could prove fatal if the powerful but vital computer is placed entirely in the hands of those responsible for its operation. The temptations are great to the disaffected or dishonest employee, who will probably encounter no real constraints upon his or her incorrect or illegal interference with the computer and its data. We are handing the sweet jar to the child if we give responsibility for computer security to the computer personnel alone, and yet within many enterprises this is exactly what has been allowed to happen.

3   The risks to a computer system from those charged with its operation are increased by the fact that the activities of computer personnel, especially those at sites away from the main centre, are often anonymous and certainly difficult to trace.

4   There is a high turnover rate among computer staff and a constant shortage of high quality, properly trained personnel. Good computer people are able to name their own price and work to their own terms, while their loyalty to the company is not always as strong as desired, for they are traditionally more loyal to their trade and machine than they are to their employer. The use of unknown and even less loyal contract staff, especially programmers, further decreases the trust management can place in their computer staff. The inherent risks from such a transient and fickle staff, upon whom the manager must depend, creates a major weakness in the company's defences.

5   For years, computer staff have presumed a considerable public ignorance of information technology. The mystique of computers has to a degree been reduced in recent years and the status held by computer staff has lessened accordingly. Resentment would be an understandable reaction to this.

6   Computer staff will, understandably, defend their territory and claim that only they are capable of properly looking after their systems. But throughout the ages and across all aspects of industry and government, responsibilities are assigned which do not require detailed technical skills. The general can win the war without being able to drive a tank, but the tank driver cannot necessarily be a general. This principle of every person to their trade is followed strongly in the police and security fields, where investigators call in doctors, accountants or engineers for specialist advice during the course of their work. Computer staff must accept this rationale.

7.4   The problems with being a security person

Security managers and their staff are also ill-equipped to tackle computer security for a number of different reasons:

1   We have discussed that the greatest threat to the modern business is to its information, and that protection of this vital asset in its electronic form within the computer is more important perhaps than any other aspect of security. Yet most security managers will admit to ignorance about computers

and the ways in which to protect them. Like most lay persons, they are afraid of computers and suspicious of anyone who does understand them, mainly, it must be acknowledged, owing to their lack of familiarity with the technology. They will deliberately avoid any involvement with computers, and are reluctant to learn about them. However, security managers cannot afford to be left behind in the march of progress. They must take all possible steps to gain competence in computer security, which must surely soon surpass in importance the more traditional aspects of security and policing. Unless they do this, they will not gain the trust of their computing colleagues, and they will miss any dishonest or unsafe actions of the computer staff. While some progress is surely being made to this end, the resistance is still considerable.

2   Security is still seen as an activity low down on the company's list of priorities, not directly concerned with the enterprise's mainstream operations. Any expertise that is required is bought in the form of retired military or police officers, or from specialist consultancies. There is little incentive therefore for ambitious and capable staff to make security their chosen long-term career within the enterprise. There is no point in gaining expertise in the field if there is no way from it to the upper reaches of the management structure. With junior management on the way up thus steered away from exposure to it, security is condemned to a life in the shadows. All this creates in the security workforce a sense of being second class, and must reduce the calibre of those who move into it. Yet an aggressive, intelligent and élitist approach to computer security is needed if this new subject is to be mastered and if the confident computer personnel are to be matched on their own ground.

3   As stated, many professional security personnel in industry have come from the military or police environments, and are used to a rigid and disciplined environment. Within the world of computers this style is inappropriate: it will not engender cooperation, and will undermine the security staff's credibility. Computer personnel are intelligent and discerning people, and the heavy hand and inflexible instruction will not be readily accepted. Computer security is not an exact science, and there will be times when security procedures must be determined on a case-by-case basis rather than as a result of reading a set of rules. In some instances it may not be technically possible to enforce certain required security features, and flexibility will be necessary. Finally, operational requirements must be borne in mind, and it may be that security advice is rejected in favour of completing the task in hand. These factors are alien to the traditional view of security, where tried and tested practices are written in tablets of stone, understood by all, and in the main complied with by all. In short, modern security managers and their staff must adjust their attitudes and methods if they are to be accepted into, and effective within, the modern computer culture.

4   Security personnel are automatically greeted with reserve, often with distrust and dislike, and sometimes with outright hostility, for we all have guilty

consciences. The sight of a police patrol car is always enough to slow us down, even though we may not be exceeding the speed limit. These barriers must be broken down between computer and security staff, to allow their close liaison to flourish. It is the responsibility of the security manager to overcome this problem and gain the trust of the computer personnel, who are, after all, already in their natural environment. For their part, the computer personnel must react positively to any such approaches, and accept that while security personnel will be ignorant of the minutiae of computers they (the computer personnel) will be ignorant of the detailed aspects of security.

5   Managers are risk takers, while security staff are risk avoiders. There is no such thing as total security, especially within the field of computers. In the interests of operational efficiency and costs there has always been the need to establish a balance of risks. Fire officers do just this when they recommend fire protection measures. The insurance agent quotes premiums based on the assessment of the risks. The managing director considers the risks and advantages of the new product launch. The general fights each battle with a consideration of the chances of victory and an idea of what the costs will be. While security managers have always assessed and then accepted a risk level in their traditional roles, as with everything associated with computers this process is magnified in the information environment. They must demonstrate the ability to manage the whole range of risks sensibly, and to bear in mind not just the immediate consequences of the loss or damage, but also the consequential, and often abstract or not easily recognizable, damage associated with computer security incidents.

6   Security managers must be seen by management as providers of solutions— '. . . if we do this, we shall prevent/save . . .'—rather than as problem givers— '. . . you cannot do that because. . .'. They must become respected members of the team that solves those problems encountered during the normal operations of a business. They must accept the faults and weaknesses of others and of the enterprise in the interests of the greater aim of growth, and if they do this they will narrow the credibility gap between themselves and the more obviously productive staff. It will also help management towards the view that security is paying its way. More of this is discussed later in this chapter.

7.5   The role of the internal auditor

There is a third party to be considered—the internal audit department—which at first sight could be seen as suitable for assuming the information system security role. On reflection, though, this is not necessarily the case.

Most large companies have developed the necessary ability to check all aspects of their operations and administration in order to ensure the proper and most efficient running of the enterprise. The role of the auditor is to appraise, evaluate and report on the effectiveness of management's internal controls. The internal auditors must be entirely independent of the rest of the workforce, and rightly so, since their task is to report directly to top management about their reviews of all aspects of the enterprise's affairs, and how quality of performance and effectiveness of such things as security are affecting the achievement of management's aims. There is a subtle but important difference, then, between security and internal audit; the former is a *part* of the overall effort of the enterprise, while audit reviews *all* aspects, including that vital security effort.

Security and audit staff have always been natural allies. Indeed, many of today's computer security specialists have their origins within the audit world. The advent of information technology has bred the specialist EDP (Electronic Data Processing) auditor with the particular skills needed to probe the integrity and reliability of large computer databases. Auditors refer to controls, while security managers talk of security countermeasures, but the game is the same.

The internal EDP auditor will concentrate attention on the preventive, detective and corrective controls within the information system in order to identify security gaps and to suggest remedies. The relationship between the auditor and the security manager is thus extremely close and each must benefit from the other, providing their mutual independence is not breached and each does not undercut the other's efforts:

- Each can make use of the other's independent reporting chain to senior management in order to bring greater impact and to speed up the implementation of sometimes unpalatable recommendations.
- Each can make use of the other's specialist and technical knowledge and assistance. For example, the auditor can monitor the effectiveness of existing security countermeasures and advise on their fine-tuning accordingly. The security manager can aid the introduction of new controls recommended by the auditor.

Together, the security manager and the internal auditor represent a formidable force for maintaining tight computer security standards.

The computer security function within a modern information-oriented company is, we have seen, essential to that company's success, and weaknesses or gaps in it could be catastrophic to the fortunes of the enterprise. It is perhaps one of the most important areas to check out, and if audit staff are to do this objectively and entirely independently it is vital that they have not been involved in the first place in the computer security effort.

7.6   The role of the external auditor

The external auditor, when providing independent evaluations, brings a broad knowledge of similar enterprises and a wealth of experience in the audit role. These external examiners, by fostering a cooperative and constructive relationship with their clients and by not assuming an overbearing and superior stance, can help enormously in improving security standards without necessarily compromising the proper discharge of their statutory duties. Any examination should fulfil a teaching role too. At the very least, external auditors should be sensitive to the many everyday internal constraints and pressures faced by security managers and internal audit staff, and show sympathy and support towards whatever efforts are being made to improve information system security standards.

7.7   The role of the external consultant

The employment of external specialist consultants is appropriate in a number of ways. Major studies, especially those where long-term and costly decisions need to be made, need careful and thorough reflection that might be beyond the resources or competence of local staff. There may be tasks which do not justify the full-time employment of another member of staff, especially with all the associated cost and administrative overheads and complications when the task is complete. Consultants can bring highly technical or specialized knowledge, and they are able to cross normal management lines and divert round local politics which might be clouding the issue. Finally, like external auditors, the external consultancies have a broad knowledge of their subject and can help avoid any re-invention of the wheel. Although apparently expensive, their cost can be justified provided their task is carefully defined and controlled.

1   The project requirements and expected results must be clearly stated. Specific and measurable way-points during the project must be described in advance, and met by the consultants. Fees must be agreed in advance, and all this must be wrapped up into a formal contract before work begins.
2   Projects will inevitably unfold in unpredictable ways, but changes to the project requirement or to the contracted work of the consultants must be agreed as soon as they are identified.
3   Consultants should work closely with local staff, and be supervised by someone with a competent knowledge of the enterprise and of the project under way. Any shortfall in ability or digression from agreed tasks should be referred to senior management immediately.
4   Select the consultancy, and the consultant(s) assigned, carefully. Do not be swayed by costs. Look to competence, qualification, experience and good standing. Stick with reputable consultancies, especially those recommended by either previous assignments within the enterprise or by word of mouth from trusted allies. As in all things, one gets what one pays for and corners cut in this area will continue to produce adverse effects long after the consultant has moved on.

7.8   Making security pay

Security must become part of the profit factor in the new information age. It is no longer sufficient for security to be at best benign but at worst obstructive, since any small impingement upon computer operations will have an effect far greater than any security control upon traditional working practices. A ten minute delay on a car production line will undoubtedly lose some of the valuable production; a similar delay on an essential computing facility could have massive effects reaching far beyond the immediate circumstances. Alternatively, a saving of ten minutes as the result of good security will produce far greater benefits in the computing function than the production line. The competitive edge in the market has never been keener than in this age of information technology, and at the end of the day security must be seen to have actually contributed to the final profit and loss figures. This can be achieved by the provision of an efficient and cost-effective solution to the computer security problem. Security must become an integral part of the business and management processes, reflecting the company's philosophies and blending with the company's practices. Security managers can afford even less to act in isolation, and must take steps to become even more involved in all aspects of their company's operations.

But how to prove that security is helping to give a competitive advantage? Security has always been a negative art: success is measured by the fact that nothing untoward has happened. There now need to be clear indications that security is not only working, but is actually paying its way. Security managers and their staff require a degree of business acumen which before was not quite as necessary.

1   Security has, and probably always will be, regarded by business managers as a necessary evil. But their lukewarm support for security is often caused by the security manager's inability or unwillingness to 'sell' his or her wares as other sector managers within an enterprise do. Once the security manager shows that security can provide value for money or can even turn in a profitable contribution towards the bottom line the support enjoyed will be far greater.

2   Allied to this, security managers must recognize the importance of selling themselves to senior management. An enterprise's personality largely reflects the character of its senior management. Security managers need to become the trusted allies of these top leaders, gaining their respect and confidence. At the same time they should seek to establish a power base of support amongst the middle layer of management, where they will likely be sitting themselves and which wields greater power and influence than its status would suggest.

3   Security managers often neglect to understand the primary business aims of their organization, or to familiarize themselves with the business climate in which they must operate. Security must merge into the environment which it protects and propose controls appropriate to the company ethos. To operate in a vacuum regardless of business needs or culture is to court rejection, contempt and eventually failure. Provided security managers get in step with the rest of the enterprise and start working with rather than against the rest of the business they will be accepted into the fold, gaining that support vital to the success of the security programme.

4   The selling—of the individual and of the security programme—must continue; the process must be fuelled the whole time. Persistence is essential. Success must be publicized, and those who have helped improve security standards praised. Those who transgress should have their misdemeanours and punishments similarly broadcast as a deterrent to others. Security managers must, above all, carry out the approved plan through to completion, and they should keep their senior management informed at all times on:
- the nature and number of security incidents and breaches, together with the actions taken to resolve them and prevent reoccurences;
- the progress towards implementing the security policy. Senior management will have approved that policy and will therefore have personal and professional stakes in its successful implementation;
- changes—hopefully improvements!—in trends of security incidents and breaches. There will always be such events, for there can never be total security, but it is important to show reductions in rates being achieved by the enforcement of the security programme. It is no good at all doing a good job if no one knows about it! Demonstrate good results; every other business function does.

Keep management on your side, and while killing the alligators never forget that your objective is to drain the swamp.

5   Information system security is often only one of several allied functions. Physical security, guarding, audit, risk management and quality assurance all work towards similar goals. Unless these various functions are working in harmony, management will become even more disenchanted at the waste and conflict that are bound to occur. When these functions are not coordinated, or worse, when rivalries and hostility are allowed to develop, security standards and public support will decline rapidly.
6   It is too easy for the security manager to lose a sense of proportion, becoming blinkered to the operational needs of the business and overreacting to security incidents or breaches. Such an evident lack of balance and judgement combined with that faint but unpleasant odour of panic will do little to help the cause. A mature and pragmatic attitude, however, will endear the security manager to those who more than anything look to this role for support and comfort, especially during times of crisis.

It is possible to prove that computer security can provide value for money. If information technology is already contributing to success, surely stable, efficient and effective information technology should make an even greater contribution. Increased trustworthiness of information technology must lead to increased growth and profitability and better use of computing resources. Yet this is still a most difficult concept for management to accept.

So, what might be the ways to show competitive advantage? How might a security manager earn an increased budget? It might not be enough merely to recite tales of gloom about the possible consequences of catastrophic security breaches, since human nature dictates that there will be no reaction until after the event, and in any case such major tragedies will not happen to the majority of us. Obviously, any reduction in direct losses through inefficiency or 'shrinkage'—that quaint old term for theft—should be held up for measurement against the security costs. Evidence that due care has been taken to look after computer systems and their data will help prevent allegations of negligence or breach of fiduciary duty (and of course the subsequent claims for compensation). More abstractly, computer security put in place at the start of any new project will allow management to press ahead more confidently with data processing innovations, which in themselves might produce competitive advantage.

Charles Cresson Wood lists four other benefits which might be cited as potential gains from a committed investment programme in computer security:

1 *Improved image* Competitive advantage can be gained by cultivating a public image of conscientiousness and prudence. This can help generate new customers, job seekers and business partners. It may also help to keep regulators and other government officials at bay.
2 *Enhanced customer confidence* Customer confidence in any enterprise is notoriously fickle. Any assurances which can be made about the care an enterprise takes to ensure service continuity, accuracy and privacy and to guard customers' assets will help bolster that confidence to the business's advantage. Indeed, increasing numbers of customers are now demanding that such security features are provided, and look to ensure that their business is in more secure hands than with any competitors who do not advertise the care they take.
3 *New products and services* Computer security products and services developed for internal use can often be marketed to other enterprises to offset their costs. Good security work may also be the source of an idea for new products and services.
4 *New security features for existing products and services* By adding security features to existing information technology products and services, enterprises can breathe new life into old lines, and tired sales figures can be given a boost. Indeed, market opportunities may be lost if such features are not included as standard in all new lines.

There are bound to be other unique ways, for each enterprise, in which security can be shown to be singing for its supper. What is certain in today's tightening economy and enhanced competitiveness, however, is that unless adequate proof can be given that security is contributing to profits, the likelihood of management support will be greatly reduced or might disappear altogether.

Gaining management support is not an easy task in any business function, but the odds are increased against success as soon as the word 'security' is mentioned. There are some ways, though, to improve the odds:

- *Be positive*   Do not present security as preventing something bad happening. Show that it will provide secure and stable computers for continued profitability and growth. Instead of 'half empty', stress 'half full'.
- *Talk management's language*   Business talk is less technical than computer-speak, and it does not help to label the IT security manager as a white-coated electrical magician from another planet.
- *Have a plan to present to your masters*   Make it manageable, and do not try to make it too grandiose or all-encompassing. Justify your plan, and provide detailed costings where possible. Anticipate the obvious objections and have your answers ready. Do not set deadlines, especially those you cannot hope to meet.
- *Deal with the biggest risks first*   Aim to introduce your plan progressively. Address the activities with the highest profile and which have the greatest chance of success—nothing breeds success and support like success in the early stages—and which provide the best value for money. The more difficult and expensive tasks can wait until you have the board convinced. Go for the lower fruits first.
- *Stress that security is a process, not an event*   It will require maintenance costs and continued effort. This will make your task easier later on, and saves you convincing management all over again once their initial enthusiasm has worn off.
- *Justify security on business impact*   It is the effect that counts, not the risk that caused it. It is, for example, important to have a business continuity and disaster recovery plan, full stop. It is not absolutely necessary to explain why the disaster might happen, just that it might happen.
- *Press for sufficient resources* for what you hope to achieve, both in terms of skills and funding. Never assume you will get all you need or were promised. Have fall-back plans in the event of the bosses changing their minds, so that you can continue with your work, albeit in a reduced way.

8
Allocation of computer security duties

While the routine administration of all aspects of security should be delegated to lower levels within the enterprise, top management needs to take the initiative, and must always retain overall responsibility, for security in all its guises. Without such support from the highest levels, security can never be effective, and will be relegated to a second-class role it does not deserve.

The organization of, and responsibility for, security, especially if no dedicated security manager or professional security force is established, will inevitably vary between enterprises. The effort applied to the security function will also vary, depending on the role of the company and the associated need for protection of company assets. This is true, too, for computer security.

8.1   Naming names

Having recognized the differences between computer and security staff, and that each group has its part to play towards the ultimate aim of good computer security, it is an important next step to allocate each of the specific computer security tasks within the enterprise. A fundamental principle of any security policy is that responsibilities must be clearly stated. It is important that persons are identified, either by name or appointment, and their specific tasks listed so that every person is aware of his or her individual part in the security policy and of others' roles. Unless the jobs are thus given, they will simply not get done. Just as important, though, is that everyone can then be held to account for their actions or omissions, not simply to serve blame in the event of a security or safety incident but also to protect those who have completed their part satisfactorily, only to be let down by another's carelessness or dishonesty.

8.2   Who's in charge?

Computer security in an enterprise should be one particular element of the overall security policy, dealing specifically with the safety and security of the company's electronically stored and processed information. As such, it should remain part of the security function, and the security manager should be nominated to take the lead in assuming responsibility for the implementation of computer security regulations alongside the other traditional aspects of corporate security. In this way, not only is computer security laid positively and publicly at somebody's door, but the special skills of the security officer, when applied in harmony with advice from computer staff, can be employed to ensure that an independent computer security policy is merged with existing security practices to produce the safest and most cost-effective solution.

8.3   Chain of command

The security function within any enterprise must have a clear reporting chain, to allow rapid communications about incidents or emergencies, and to make clear who is responsible to whom. That chain must include a direct link to the very highest level of the enterprise, to be invoked at the discretion of the security manager and to ensure that person's ultimate independence. Control of the security function will fall within normal company arrangements, but the security manager must be able to disregard these constraints when it is felt necessary in the interests of security. The security chief must be a trusted ally of top management, and be able to communicate freely with management, and vice versa. In turn, however, the security manager must use that privilege sensibly and sparingly.

8.4   The allocation of computer security duties

The following description of computer security duties and responsibilities applies, necessarily for the sake of completeness, to an enterprise of some size with significant computing assets. Clearly, though, companies will differ in size, will have greater or smaller dependence on information technology, with unique combinations of risks requiring differing emphasis on the various available defences, and will have differing available security resources.

8.4.1   The system manager

The computer system manager is the key person with any system and has responsibility for all aspects of that system's operations, including its security. He or she is the captain of the ship, who must ensure the safety and security of all parts of the system so that the data is protected from the risks directed against it. For the security function, the system manager, along with the managers of any other computer systems, works with and receives guidance from the departmental or site security officer. The system manager is charged with the task of formulating an appropriate security policy for the system, in line with the company's computer security policy, and then seeing that it is adhered to by all members of the staff. The specific tasks of the system manager include the following:

1   Preparing, maintaining and enforcing clear security operating procedures, so that all system staff know what to do in order to achieve their individual security tasks, how to do so, and most importantly why they are doing so. Security operating procedures are described in more detail in Chapter 6.

2   Arranging for independent inspection of the system's security, at regular intervals. Testing of security measures, at random intervals by an independent body, should also be arranged. Appropriate security documentation—system, security and maintenance logs, for example—should be included for review in these inspections. Observations or recommendations from any such inspection must be acted upon.

3   Reporting to the departmental security officer any breach of computer security, or any incident with security connotations. In addition, the system manager should report any changes to the computer hardware, software or procedures which could affect the security policy or security measures. In the event that the system manager is unable to comply with the security requirements and regulations—perhaps because of staff shortages or a breakdown of some of the security defences—the departmental security officer must be informed of the circumstances of non-compliance and the possible effects on data security.

4   Ensuring that a suitable business continuity and disaster recovery plan has been prepared, tested and maintained. (This aspect is discussed in Chapter 8.)

Information owners have been defined in Chapter 4 as 'those individual managers or representatives of management who have responsibility for making and communicating judgements and decisions on behalf of the enterprise with regard to the use, identification, classification and protection of a specific information asset'. Sometimes such owners will be the originators (authors) of that information, but more likely information ownership will have to move upwards to that level of management capable of providing an accurate assessment of the information's overall worth to the enterprise. Many system users originate information, but are not in a position to judge its greater worth properly. System managers will often therefore assume this role of information owner, at least temporarily, and will need to ensure that all information on the system is properly classified and access authorizations have been clearly and comprehensively designated.

8.4.2   *The system security officer*

The system manager should appoint a member of staff as the system security officer, and should delegate the daily administration of the computer security regulations. In this way the system manager can still monitor the security of the system but be relieved of the time-consuming and routine security workload; if this is not done, especially on a larger installation, then it is inevitable that the security measures will be neglected as tasks of seemingly greater priority bombard

Date	Time	Person reporting incident	Details of incident	Action taken/results of investigation	Date/time reported to ISyO	ISyO initials

Figure 8.1.   System security log.

the busy system manager. The system security officer has a number of important tasks:

1   The maintenance of a system security log (Fig. 8.1) which records, against time and dates and in sufficient detail, any incident that might have an effect on system security so that, in conjunction with the normal system log and a suitable engineering log, any event can be reconstructed at a later date during any subsequent investigation or counter-compromise action.

    Items for inclusion could include such things as the failure of a security feature of the computer, unauthorized attempts to gain access to the system, or unauthorized use of the system for private purposes.

2   With the assistance of the system's engineers and in liaison with contractors, monitor all instances when the system has received attention. In this way, breaches of security can be prevented during implementation of software and hardware modifications and enhancements. An engineering log should be maintained by the system security officer (Fig 8.2).

    Items for inclusion would include attendance by the engineer for routine maintenance of the system, replacement of faulty components, or modifications to the system in accordance with the manufacturer's specification. More detailed advice on maintenance procedures is included in Chapter 13.

3   Submit all logs for inspection at regular intervals by the departmental security officer, in order that any trends, not just at the particular system, but throughout the branch or depot, can be spotted. (In turn, the departmental security officer should pass the information upwards so that a company-wide picture can be formed.)

Date	Duration of visit (times)	Engineer's name	Signature	Firm	Reason for visit	Action taken	IM/ISyO initials

Figure 8.2.   System engineering log.

4   Ensure that only personnel with the appropriate security clearance have access to the system and its valuable data. A record should be maintained of all persons authorized to access any restricted part of the system or data, and the extent of their authorization. Other uncleared personnel must be denied access to the system and/or secure/restricted areas, or supervised and escorted at all times by a suitably cleared member of staff. Secure areas and areas of restricted access must be clearly defined and known by staff.

5   Provide security advice and proper security education to all system staff and users, especially newcomers, to include instruction on the security operating procedures and guidance on the security measures applicable to the system. Such a programme could include publicity about any praiseworthy (or not so praiseworthy!) achievements by system staff towards the system's security. Certainly there should be a minimum annual computer security training allowance for all staff of, say, two hours, during which security awareness can be reinforced. Records of such training should be kept. (Training and awareness is discussed in greater detail in Chapter 22.)

6   Control and issue user passwords or other access control devices. However, if a combination of such devices is in use (e.g. passwords and a personalized magnetic stripe card), the system security officer should be responsible for only one of these elements, and another member of staff entrusted with the other(s), thereby reducing even further the risk of corruption.

7   Ensure that all computer documents, including magnetic media, are properly registered and stored. Carry out random and irregular checks on these documents—their location, the accuracy of their markings and the suitability of the storage facilities.

8   Ensure that any surplus magnetic medium has been properly purged of any
    electronic data held before it is released from the system (see Chapter 11).
    Any eye-readable markings on the container or tape headers/footers should
    also be removed, as they may inadvertently reveal details of tape usage, if
    only by deduction. Any other form of computer document (waste printout,
    for example) should be destroyed in a manner appropriate to its sensitivity
    and worth.

9   Investigate security breaches and incidents, or report to more competent
    agencies if the matter is beyond system resources.

10 At least once every three months, inspect off-site data storage facilities; at
    least every six months inspect any stand-by computer facilities; at least
    annually test the stand-by facilities by exercising the business continuity and
    disaster recovery plan. The form and extent of such exercising should be
    decided in consultation with the system manager, departmental security
    officer and senior management, since there may be significant financial and
    performance costs incurred by the testing.

11 At least quarterly, or whenever a significant security incident or breach
    occurs, when a loophole or other vulnerability in the system's security comes
    to light, or when there is a warning of an increased or changed risk against
    the system's security or safety, submit a (written) report to the system
    manager. Such a report should contain full details of all incidents or those
    other factors giving rise to the report, and should describe any required
    improvement(s) to the security measures in force.

The system security officer is the system manager's key person for enforcing
and monitoring on a daily basis the security measures at the installation. He or
she reports to the system manager from whom direction is received. Nevertheless,
this is a vital position, and as soon as possible after appointment the incumbent
should become knowledgeable about the system and its security features, and try
to be well known, respected and trusted. Computer staff will be more likely to
seek advice if the security officer is approachable and helpful, and a bumptious
and aggressive approach will merely antagonize the system staff. In traditional
terms, the system security officer should be the 'village constable' of the system,
and a good one.

8.4.3   Computer users

Under the direction of the system security officer, all users have a responsibility
to their system's security, safety and integrity. Their role is perhaps the most
important, because of numbers alone—the security officer is but one person, but
with all users briefed and conscientious about their security duties there will then
be many pairs of eyes and ears looking out for dangers to the data and the
system. In particular, each user must:

1   Be fully familiar with the rules and regulations contained within the system's

security operating procedures. For security practices to be totally effective, every user must know what to do, how to do it and why.

2   Properly classify all inputs, programs, data files and outputs created, according to their sensitivity and/or value, and clearly mark such data appropriately as directed in the security operating procedures. Whenever in doubt about information classification, users should seek guidance from the system security officer and system manager. The user is both the biggest creator of data, and the greatest risk to any system regardless of its size and importance. Ironically, at the same time, the user can be the greatest asset to the computer's security.

3   Report at once to the system security officer any security breaches or incidents that come to light, or any other matter that might have a security significance, including suspicions about the activities or security reliability of other staff members. It is in this respect that the importance of good security awareness and education among staff members, and the good standing and trustworthiness of the security officer, become most evident.

4   Attend any computer security education presentations as required.

The users can be the greatest aid to security officers, and with them on their side much better security can be achieved. But to do this involves much hard work in educating the staff members, gaining their trust and convincing them about the necessity and importance of computer security measures for the well-being and safety of their own and the company's future.

8.4.4   Heads of departments

The heads of departments which have computers, even though they themselves may have little or nothing to do with the actual beasts, retain the normal supervisory role over their computer staff, including the security of those computers. Such supervisors cannot abdicate responsibility on grounds of age, status, ignorance or senility. They may be members of the last generation to grow up without computers, but nevertheless they must take a leading role in ensuring that the computer security policy and associated rules and regulations are enforced and adhered to.

8.4.5   The departmental security officer

In charge of the various system security officers at a site or within a department will be the departmental security officer, responsible along with his or her traditional security duties for the satisfactory security of all the computers at that site or within the department. This is the first point of contact on the site for all matters to do with computer security. (For sites with a particularly large or complex computer establishment it may prove necessary and expedient to appoint a departmental computer security officer, reporting to the departmental security officer on all matters concerning computer security.)

8.4.6   The corporate security officer

The corporate security officer will have responsibility for the security of all assets, including the computer systems within the enterprise. This role involves:

1   Supervision of the work of the departmental security officers.
2   Development of corporate computer security policy, ensuring that it is followed and that current regulations are promulgated and adhered to.
3   Monitoring the development of new computer systems as they pass through the various stages of design and procurement (purchase) so that security can be introduced early enough for it to be effective, and of course much cheaper.
4   Arrangement of, or even for the more essential company computer systems personally carrying out, appropriate risk analyses, though clearly such evaluations will contain a considerable degree of commonality between systems. Such evaluations should be updated at least annually or whenever the nature or value of the system or its data changes or whenever the risk(s) against such systems changes.
5   Adjudication when networks extend between departments and responsibilities can become blurred or duplicated.

8.4.7   Network security officer

Where a computer network exists, the responsibility for the overall security of that network, like all security responsibilities, must be assigned to a named individual, the network security officer. Independent elements of that network will have their own system security officers, who should be accountable to the network security officer for the security of their terminals and data links. Network security is considered in more depth in Chapter 17.

Figure 8.3 summarizes the typical hierarchy of security officers within an organization.

8.5   System security committees

It may be necessary, for a particularly large or sensitive/valuable system and especially where there is a large or widely dispersed staff, to set up a system security committee. Membership of the committee could include all the appointments so far described (especially representatives of the users), together with the person or persons responsible for the security of remote terminal areas, the data custodian and any specialist advisers (such as external software development agencies, or building maintenance staff).

The nature and size of the system and the risks against it will dictate the size and composition of the committee. It could involve formal and minuted meetings, while for a small system it may consist only of the system manager and the departmental security officer chatting informally. The requirements for most

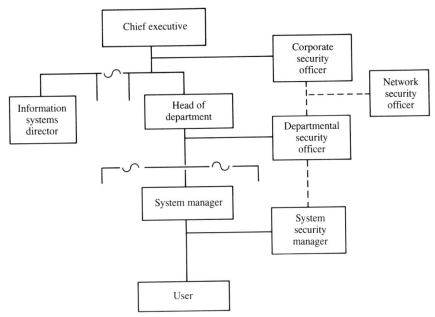

Figure 8.3.   Typical organizational structure.

systems will fall somewhere between the two extremes. Whatever the case, the composition must be reviewed regularly, for example on an annual basis.

Terms of reference for such committees will vary between systems. The committee should be responsible for obtaining appropriate threat assessments through local security staff, identifying particular vulnerabilities, assessing impacts and carrying out an objective and realistic analysis of the risks to the system. It is the system security committee that will be charged with specifying the classifications and types of data that may be processed on the system. Its members will be responsible for providing advice on security matters to the system manager and the system security officer, and for the approval and periodic review of the security operating procedures. The system security committee is the ultimate authority for the security of the computer system for which it has been formed; it should, therefore, address and then supervise all aspects of that system's security.

8.6   Security working groups

At a higher organizational level than system security committees, within a large company at least, it is often useful to create a security working group to draw together the various elements of company security, and the disparate individuals and departments possibly working along the same lines but ignorant of each other's contribution or even existence. The corporate security manager is usually concerned with guarding, physical security and investigations. The IT director will be steeped in the technical aspects of the systems and motivated by their potential contribution to the business. The data security staff will in their turn be handling almost exclusively the access control software, with perhaps some involvement in disaster recovery. System managers have to face the everyday implementation of and fallout from computer security matters. All these will benefit enormously from a common talking ground. At first this forum will serve simply to introduce the various parties to one another and help dispel the inevitable ignorance and suspicion about each other's roles. Slowly, though, and hopefully with increased enthusiasm from all sides, it will improve computer security standards throughout the enterprise and get everyone at least pulling in the same direction. At the very least it should help eliminate duplication of effort and remove unnecessary and unhelpful demarcation of duties. It is not uncommon, for example, for data security staff within the IT department to be unaware even of the existence or identity of the corporate security officer, let alone to have any contact, or for that corporate security officer to deny all knowledge about or responsibility for anything to do with computer security. These 'them and us' barriers must come down.

9
Registration of computers

Larger enterprises, especially those comprising a variety of independent departments and/or a number of dispersed sites, may lose track of exactly what computer resources they have.

With the cost of personal computers decreasing all the time, and as staff become increasingly confident in and knowledgeable about computers and their applications, the number in use in the office and on the factory floor will continue to grow, and at an accelerating pace. Previously prejudiced and suspicious anti-computer colleagues will become interested in the new additions to the workplace, especially as they notice the time-saving benefits and improved standards of work achievable on them, and so even more will spring up. Then, after computers are installed, they will be modified and improved as the manufacturers ply their additions and modifications to the equipment. The software will be patched, tinkered with, altered and added to. Finally, after only a short while, the use for which the computer was originally intended will inevitably be smothered by the numerous other tasks heaped upon its willing shoulders.

This dynamic change is not necessarily to be avoided; flexibility, capacity and adaptability are the very qualities sought with any move from manual towards automatic data processing methods. Staff should be encouraged to make the most and best use of their new information tools, and experiment with new applications. Nevertheless, there are sound practical, economic and security reasons for central control of all computer assets within an enterprise. The creation by central staff of a comprehensive and accurate company-wide register of such computer assets will not be just a bureaucratic exercise; if used properly it should pay for itself many times over in reduced costs and increased computer efficiency and security throughout the enterprise.

9.1   Why register computers?

There are three main reasons for registering all computer systems within an enterprise:

1   Unless the appropriate departments are aware of a particular computer's existence it will not be possible to ensure proper and efficient control over its security and operation. Registration will benefit the security manager and those responsible for company-wide computer operations and procurement.
2   A registration document, if suitably designed and then completed correctly, will provide a wealth of information about a system. When collated with similar facts about all other company computers, this can be used to improve computer operations in general throughout the enterprise.
3   Any insurance may usefully only be taken out after an inventory has been made of exactly what is to be covered. Such an inventory should include all software, hardware and data, and it must be up to date.

9.2   Responsibility for registration

The departmental security officer is responsible for maintaining an up-to-date register of all the computer assets at his or her site. This should include all computer systems such as word processors, automated offices, test equipment, large mainframes and the smallest personal computer. Privately owned computers used by staff either at their workplace or at home for official business must also be recorded; the risk of virus transfer by uncontrolled software exchange must not be ignored. The requirement for the registration of computers should be well advertised among staff so that they complete the registration forms willingly, promptly and accurately.

A copy of each registration document should be forwarded by the departmental security officer to the corporate security officer. At the highest organizational level the responsibility for compiling a company-wide register of all computer assets should be given to a named individual, who should be given sufficient resources to create a viable computer register. This task could lie within the security function, but as the use of the register will not be limited to security personnel, and as access by all personnel to the register for an on-line enquiry service is to be suggested, there is no reason why central management or computer personnel should not take on this task.

For each system the system manager, or in the case of a privately owned system its owner, should complete a computer registration document, purpose-designed for that particular enterprise. In this way, not only is the workload spread thinly throughout the enterprise but those with the best knowledge of each system are the ones describing them to the registration authority. Everyone has a responsibility for ensuring that computer systems and associated peripheral equipment are registered with the appropriate company authority.

Computer security regulations are obviously primarily intended for those computers processing sensitive or valuable data, or those where loss or reduction of service would impact significantly on the enterprise's performance. Nevertheless, many security measures are equally relevant to unclassified information needing protection for privacy, administrative or indeed commercial reasons. It is for the security authorities (with advice from management) to decide which regulations should be applied to a particular system. It is not for the users to dictate the security policy of the company. Therefore, all computers, regardless of their size, purpose or classification, should be registered. All parts of the computer should be registered.

9.3 Uses for the register of computers

For ease of handling, the computer registration documents should be designed for easy inputting into a simple computer of their own, which can manipulate all the gathered information about the enterprise's computing assets. The following functions will become possible:

1 The development of a rationalized maintenance policy for computer equipment, with likely savings in costs and an improvement in services to computer users. As an example, one particular site may have several exactly similar personal computers, each with its own hardware maintenance policy costing between 15 and 20 per cent of the initial hardware cost and rising by about 4 per cent each year, and all with the same company. This clearly does not make financial sense, but would be impossible to rationalize without a central register of all these PCs.

2 The procurement and development of standardized hardware and software. By buying items of computer equipment in larger numbers, and then utilizing common software between them, savings can be made at all stages and efficiency is quickly and cheaply improved. Applications can be swapped between systems. The many hours of work involved in writing and testing software can be usefully employed on systems away from the original development site. The cost of buying, maintaining and operating a diverse range of incompatible computer equipment is notoriously high, and the frustrations of using such a fragmented set-up are legend. Any possible method of reducing incompatibility and purchase/maintenance costs must be employed, and registering all computers is an excellent first step.

3 Monitoring Data Protection Act registration. Are all computer users within the organization aware of the need to register with the registrar under the Data Protection Act? Do all those users comply with the Act?

4 Improved automatic data processing (ADP) training, and identification of the type of training needed and by whom. Associated support services can also be arranged in the most efficient and economical way.

5 The provision of an on-line enquiry service. For example, the register will identify to an enquirer any other company computer assets of a similar nature and/or role to help the interchange of information. Before undertaking any development work, a user could discover if any existing facilities are available either to aid the development work or even remove its need—thus preventing the re-inventing of wheels! Business continuity and disaster recovery planning

is also simplified with a knowledge of who else uses the same type of equipment.

6 A major improvement in the monitoring of computer security. Before any security advice and assistance can be given to the users of a system, and before security regulations can be applied to that system, its existence must be known to the appropriate authorities.

7 The register will provide an inventory of computer assets for insurance purposes, and help reduce theft.

9.4   Updating the register

The computer registration documents are of little use unless they are kept up to date. At first, they should be created for new or existing systems, but then it is important that they are amended as those systems change and develop, and of course cancelled when systems are run down. To assist in this process, each system manager should annually be sent a copy of the most current registration document for his or her system, and should check it for its accuracy; any amendments should be returned so that the central records can be updated.

9.5   Serial numbering of computers

All computers registered should be awarded a unique serial number—the form of this number will depend on the organization, but for example could comprise a site prefix and serial number (LON/019). All parts of that system should then be marked clearly with this serial number, either by label or indelible pen. In this way, the process of keeping track of all the systems, as they are moved about the place, added to or split up as a result of 'swaps', should be made easier. It would also identify those systems not registered—no prefix number marked on the equipment, not registered.

9.6   Contents of computer registration documents

The computer registration document should elicit the following information:

1 Computer serial number (unique, allocated to each registered computer), site, location within the site (or home address for privately owned systems to be used at home).

2 System title—this should be clearly understood, and the use of abbreviations without explanation should be avoided.

3 Computer type and model number—for example Amstrad PCW8256 Personal Computer/Word Processor, or ICL 2930 Mainframe.

4 Date commissioned, and due replacement date.

5 Is the system registered under the Data Protection Act?

6 Brief description of data processed and a clear descriptive narrative of the authorized role of the computer (which often differs from its actual use!).

7 Mode of secure processing.

8 An estimate of the percentage of data processed at each security/privacy level.

9 The types of magnetic storage media used by the system, for example, floppy disks, or exchangeable hard disks.

10 On-site and off-site communications links—nature (copper wire/fibre optic etc.), connected to? Is encryption used?

11 Are remote diagnostics used? Such a facility, offered by many computer suppliers, can speed maintenance and therefore reduce costs and the time a system is off line. But security can be easily breached by this uncontrolled line straight into the heart of the system.

12 Operating system in use; applications languages in use; software packages/ utilities in use and licence arrangements for these (see Section 9.7); who is authorized to maintain software, and who supervises this?

13 Peripherals—specify printers, VDUs, graphic plotters etc.

14 Details of maintenance contracts for hardware and software. Give contract number and start/finish dates. Name the person to be contacted for each contract. If known, give costs, number of visits by maintenance engineers since the system was installed, number of visits per annum (estimated), assessments of service provided by contractors, average callout time compared with promised response time, and any other relevant details.

15 Details of any independent security checks, with dates and results.

16 System manager—by name, appointment and with contact telephone number.

17 System security officer—as above.

Finally, once the registration document has been completed, an appropriate classification for the document itself must be assessed; the information provided on the form may in itself be of value, such as the location of the equipment, or the use to which it is being put.

9.7 Illegal software copying (piracy)

It is illegal to make copies of proprietary software without the copyright owner's permission (see details of the Copyright, Designs and Patents Act, 1988, in Chapter 24). Unauthorized duplication of software can lead to penalties of unlimited fines and up to two years in prison. To reduce an enterprise's exposure and that of its employees to prosecution and adverse publicity, the following rules should apply:

1 Unless a special arrangement has been made with the software publisher, enterprises should follow the one package/one computer rule. With an equivalent number of software packages purchased for every piece of hardware in use, the incentive for users to make unauthorized copies is reduced. This does not rule out the making of a working copy of the software

disks, usually recommended anyway; the original is thus preserved as a primary back-up safe from corruption, but of course it may not be used in addition to the working copy.

2 Where appropriate, an IS department may, on behalf of other departments, negotiate site licensing purchase agreements with publishers. It is becoming increasingly common for publishers to automatically authorize a second copy for use on an 'associated portable machine' providing both machines are not in use at once, but this ruling is not universal, is somewhat woolly and difficult to enforce, and is ripe for abuse.

3 Software applications sold in local area network (LAN) versions must be used in accordance with the publishers' conditions and guidelines.

4 A full software census should be maintained, details for which can be gathered from the registration document.

In 1984 in the UK the Federation Against Software Theft (FAST) was launched to combat the major threat that software piracy posed to the entire computer industry in terms of investment, innovation and jobs, quality and viruses. Details about FAST and the procedures to be followed in reporting actual or suspect infringements of copyright can be obtained directly from:

Federation Against Software Theft
2 Lake End Court
Taplow Road
Taplow
Maidenhead
Berkshire SL6 0JQ
Telephone: (0)628 660377
Fax: (0)628 660348

Part 3
The countermeasures

10
Physical security

The means by which an enterprise provides and manages protection of its physical assets to prevent or limit their loss and damage, and maintains a secure and safe environment for its staff.

There is nothing new about physical security. Such measures are well tried and tested; for centuries men and women have been erecting physical barriers to protect their property and to keep them safe from enemies. The physical security of computers is achieved using these traditional techniques, with perhaps slight adaptation and updating, but the principles are the same as for those of a medieval castle.

10.1   Defence in depth—the fortress concept

The computing function within an enterprise has, in the past, been contained within a computer centre, with the assets clearly within a defined domain deep within the heart of the empire. This is not so much true today, with the mainframe dispersed in the form of the PC around all parts of the enterprise, networking having created vulnerable communications links, and remote terminals located often hundreds or thousands of miles away from the main site. The sharing of office buildings means that immediate neighbours or the hazards they create may be unknown. This complicated computer physical security problem calls now for measures to be extended to include the whole of the company's premises and its environment, not just that small part which was previously the computer room. However, the principle of defence in depth, where numerous layers of protection all need to be breached before access to any asset is gained, readily absorbs this enhanced requirement.

Concentric shells of physical security, as strong as necessary for the nature and role of the system, should be placed around the computer and its equipment wherever it is to be found, the buildings in which it is housed, around the site, and around any exposed components such as communication links or external essential supplies (electricity, water, telephone junction boxes etc.).

10.2   Aims of physical security

Physical security is intended to *deter* intruders by its overt presence, sending them to an apparently softer target. If deterrence fails, then barriers should *delay* the attacker. Then, *detection* of any attempted or successful intrusion is necessary. Finally, the capacity for *defence* from attack by reaction to protect the assets and fight off the attacker is required. Facilities for the admittance of authorized persons—control of entry—and all other physical security measures should be designed to channel, steer and control as you wish.

In addition to deliberate attack, physical security should protect against the threats of fire, flood and other natural disasters. Whatever physical security measures are to be incorporated, however, proper assessment of the nature of, and risks to, the system should be made. Physical security is readily understood by everyone and is relatively cheap to install; security and management staff can easily convince themselves that they have taken all necessary computer security precautions with the erection of a fence, the fitting of a smoke detector, and the introduction of security passes. The nature of the threats, the extent of any system vulnerabilities, and the risks to the enterprise of loss, compromise or unavailability of the computing function must be taken into account when developing the computer security policy, of which physical security is but one part.

The efficiency of that main component of physical security, the barrier, can be measured by the following criteria:

- the time or cost needed to breach it;
- the speed with which it identifies an attempted or actual intrusion;
- the accuracy with which an offender is identified;
- its non-interference with other security measures;
- its transparency to authorized persons, and its non-interference with the operations of the enterprise.

Any physical security must be applied throughout all parts of the system and its parent enterprise. The same standards should be applied to, say, a remote terminal as to the heart of the system. As with all other forms of security, physical security should be designed into any project from the earliest stages. The addition of physical security at any later stage is certain to be vastly more expensive, can never be properly efficient, and will inevitably impinge more significantly upon the operations of the system. Physical security must be consistent throughout; standards must not slip at the time they are most needed—for example, in the early hours of a Sunday morning.

10.3   The physical protection of computers

There are a number of physical security measures particular to computer security. It is not intended in this book to discuss the minutiae of physical security—there are endless textbooks on the subject—but to consider those aspects of special significance to the computing environment. The following sections assume a mainframe system of some importance, radiating a number of terminals to the immediate site. Any greater or lesser systems will require similar considerations for their physical security, but clearly to a differing degree of significance.

10.3.1 Location of the computer centre

Siting the computer correctly in the first place is an opportunity not always presented to the security manager. Sometimes the computer centre will be placed in a building specially built for the purpose, and such 'green field' sites are to be preferred. However, often computers are installed in existing buildings, either with or without existing physical security measures and which may or may not already house other computers. Buildings may have to be shared with other departments within the company, or even with other, unknown companies. They may be in enterprise zones, surrounded by other industries. Buildings, then, themselves present hazards to any computers introduced into them, and their security may not be all that is required. Nevertheless, security must live in the real world, and it is inevitable that constraints and imperfections will have to be accepted and measures adapted and strengthened accordingly. The following points should be borne in mind:

1　The site should be on solid ground free from the dangers of subsidence, and not over tunnels, main drainage sewers or any other underground hazards.
2　The level of the local water table is a vital consideration. The site must be free from the danger of flooding.
3　The environment of the site is important. Are there any other unavoidable hazards such as earthquakes (unlikely in the United Kingdom but possible), airfields and their flight paths (noise, vibrations, crashes), strong electromagnetic fields (from radar), or heavy air pollution? Is there a high crime rate in the area, or is there a history of public unrest, vandalism and violence? Are there any public rights of way through the area or site? What are the neighbours like, and what is their business? Do any of them present particular hazards? Being next to a fireworks factory is not such a good idea, but other occupations present less obvious dangers (chemical plants, or any site that stores and uses hazardous chemicals, to name but two). Remember, too, there are 24 hours in each day, and seven days in every week; what happens at weekends, or during the silent hours? Do not inspect a potential site just during the working day.
4　What are the local services like? Are there reliable electricity and water supplies? Are there good roads to the site? Are the local emergency services (fire, ambulance, police) located nearby, what is their strength, and do they have experience of dealing with an emergency in a high-tech computer centre?
5　The site should be large enough to allow the creation of a 10 metre sterile zone around the computer building, and so that car parking may be kept to a

distance from the building of at least 30 metres. It should be surrounded on all sides by company buildings, shielding it entirely from the outside world, but clearly this is not always possible. Locations are preferred which have open space around and where the dangers from physical attack and damage, overlooking, overhearing and technical eavesdropping will be reduced. (Rural locations, however, can bring their own problems, such as slower responses from emergency services.)

10.3.2 Design of the computer centre

With the site chosen, the construction and layout of the computer building should be carefully planned. All elements of the installation must be considered, not just the more obvious components, and protection should be afforded to utilities (water, electricity, air conditioning), heating, lighting, and specialized but closely associated equipment, areas and functions, as well as the computer room and its hardware and media.

Take care to guide and advise your advisers; architects and builders are highly qualified and experienced, but they will not be intimately aware of your enterprise's needs and you must ensure that their enthusiasm and love of the aesthetic do not detract from your efficiency or security. In particular, one should ensure the following are taken into consideration:

1 The building should be of solid construction, able to withstand forcible and/ or surreptitious entry, and provide a degree of blast resistance. The building and its fittings should be constructed of non-combustible materials. Flimsy, wooden, or glass-sided buildings should be avoided. Ideally the computer room should nestle within the computer centre as a windowless, environmentally controlled kernel, surrounded on all sides, above and below by its support functions; the room may comprise a number of separate rooms, each containing a portion of the enterprise's computer equipment.

2 The number of entrances and exits to the building should be minimized, in accordance with any safety regulations governing the evacuation of the building in the event of an emergency and which demand a statutory number of escape routes. Suitable access must be provided for larger items of equipment, but such entrances should not be used routinely. Control of entry to the computer centre should be effected at the main external entrance, with a 'buffer zone' or people-lock provided to assist in the physical control of personnel seeking ingress and egress. (There may then be separate and more selective access controls within the centre itself.) A suitably designed reception area should be at the main entrance to deal with and control visitors. The number of people in the computer room must be kept to a minimum—a crowd will cause mistakes and muddles, such as loading the wrong tape, and will hide strangers.

3 Keys, especially those protecting multiple access (master keys), should be

strictly controlled and treated with at least as much care and respect as the areas, material or information they protect. If their pedigree is suspect—for example, if key management has been lax and duplicate keys abound in all sorts of pockets—there should be drawn a 'red line' by replacing the locks and new keys closely managed from this time onwards. Full records of keys should be maintained; ideally they should be stored under secure conditions, and they should be regularly accounted for. (Keys that are removed from site are inherently less reliable than those retained on site under secure conditions when not in use. They are prone to getting lost or loaned, or even copied surreptitiously.) Keys must only be issued to and held by authorized persons under signature. Keys should not be issued to visitors or contractors, but to authorized staff on their behalf who should retain control over them even when this is inconvenient. Keys should be marked only with codes; master records of these codes may then be used to identify the keys, but these records must be protected.

4   External windows at ground and first floor levels should be avoided whenever possible because of their vulnerability to overlooking and forcible entry. If such windows already exist, they should be blocked up with glass bricks; if such bricking up is not possible, or windows that open are required for other reasons, the glass should be strengthened and opaque, and the frames strong and secure. The requirement for emergency exiting, access by firemen and proper venting of accommodation must, however, be considered.

5   Raised floors and suspended ceilings can allow access between rooms, unless partition walls extend from solid floor to structural ceiling; such full height separation is especially important in sensitive areas such as the computer room itself, where secure conditions are to be imposed. Fire safety regulations may also require such barriers.

6   Computer rooms should not be in basements, because of the danger of flooding. Ground floor sites are usually the most convenient and suitable of all the other options, provided of course the building is strong enough. If accommodation of less than a robust nature is to be used, then a first floor site will allow more effective access control and increase the difficulty of gaining unauthorized entry, but appropriate measures must then be made for the supply of equipment and usables (paper etc.).

7   Within the centre, compartmentalization of the various elements should be enforced. At the core, the computer room itself should be protected from entry by all except the minimum necessary number of operations staff. Other areas, such as media libraries, plant rooms, data preparation areas, printing rooms, paper stores, administration offices, programmers' accommodation, and areas for all the other functions should be segregated and access allowed to staff as appropriate and necessary. There are a number of electronic access control systems working on magnetic stripe and other tokens unique to each member of staff, which can allow strict control over access to a number of separate zones. Alternatively, 'Simplex'-type push-button

combination door locks are less sophisticated but cheap and convenient, but overlooking by unauthorized staff can reveal their combinations. Most importantly though, when access control is provided, use it! Doors held open by fire extinguishers are a common sight but are of little use. The shutting and locking of doors to such as the computer room can provide massive improvements to the physical security of an installation at no extra cost. Furthermore, a door is only a barrier when it is closed and locked, so reduce the number of times it has to be opened; hatches to allow items to be passed through should be used whenever possible, though they must not be large enough for a person to pass through. Doors to, say, fire-safes left ajar because they are used many times a day are no use to anyone. No matter the inconvenience, shut and lock each time; in this example, in the event of a fire and evacuation, the fire-safe will inevitably be left open in the confusion, and the data inside will be damaged or destroyed. Finally, the more people around a door, then the more people will go through it; keep staff away from a particularly sensitive door (such as into the computer room itself) by placing a not-so-important door to the room outside the computer room.

8   The building should be alarmed against fire and unauthorized incursion. Alarms should terminate in a central, permanently manned security control, probably most conveniently placed at the main entrance so that access control may also be supervised. Surveillance of the exterior, and parts of the interior, of the building can be achieved using closed circuit television, the monitors of which should be placed in the security control office. Any guard force should operate from this control. There should be planned procedures for responding to a security incident. Such procedures should be comprehensively documented, tested and regularly practised by all staff, not just any guards established. Such procedures should include reporting actions, search techniques, cordoning, first aid and firefighting. There should be a clear establishment of an incident command and control structure and care should be taken that procedures are included for maintaining the physical security of the data centre during the emergency—an obvious ploy is to set off a false fire alarm, wait until everyone has fled the building and then gain access through one of the fire exits which will have been left open during the panic.

9   Controls should provide assurance that resources in transit—magnetic media, reports, pro-formas, documentation—are physically protected especially where courier runs are outside the site over long distances, or where a large volume of data or especially sensitive data is being transferred. Courier runs should be authorized by specified managers. Resources should be properly and securely packaged and sealed, accounted for at both dispatch and receipt, and handled only by authorized staff or recognized and authorized couriers. Identification of dispatches should be forwarded separately to the recipient. There should be formal control over the routes used by couriers. Such routes and timings of journeys should be varied. Couriers

should be properly identified before resources are released into their custody; they should sign for the consignment at both ends of the journey and not release resources except to authorized nominated recipients—not just dumped at reception! Couriers should not leave the resources unattended *en route*.

10 Controls should be in place to prevent the unauthorized transportation of materials into or out of the computer data centre, and which control and record the authorized transportation of materials into or out of the data centre. Staff should be made aware of these controls and signs should be clearly posted at entrances and exits prohibiting the entry of unauthorized material or the removal of proprietary material. Regular but random searching of staff/visitor/contractor belongings on entry and egress should be performed with a high profile.

11 Incoming services such as water, electricity, gas and communications lines should come into the building underground. Service tunnels and manhole covers should be locked to prevent unauthorized entry to them. Internal water or sewage pipes should not pass over any computer equipment, but should be routed around such areas. If this is not possible, emergency shut-off valves should be provided for immediate use by staff in the event of leakages, buckets should be to hand to collect drips, and polythene sheeting should be provided to cover the equipment and protect it from the most serious ravages of this danger. Water tanks should not be installed over the computer room. Water detectors should be fitted in floor spaces, the first places where water will gather.

12 Accommodation for back-up media stores should be located in a separate building at least 100 metres from the main computer site, preferably further, and ideally at another site entirely. Such accommodation must be fire resistant, physically secure to at least the same standard as for the main centre, and of limited size and replicated so that no inordinately large amounts of back-up media are stored within a single back-up library.

13 Any externally sited support facilities, such as air conditioning heat exchangers, telephone junction boxes, and transformers and other electricity supply components, must be physically protected against attack and damage.

14 Paper stores should be located away from the computer room, and daily supplies of stationery brought forward as required. Proper physical control over blank pro-formas will reduce the risk of their theft and subsequent improper use. Waste paper, which until destroyed remains as sensitive as any data on it, must be protected appropriately until destroyed under secure conditions; it may be necessary, depending on the volume of waste paper generated, to allocate a separate and physically secure waste storage and disposal area.

15 Good housekeeping procedures should be rigorously enforced throughout the computer centre. Waste materials, especially paper, should be removed before they begin to accumulate. Smoking, eating and drinking should not

be allowed within the computer room and associated areas. Staff canteens should be separate from the computer centre, and staff property boxes for prohibited items (matches, cigarettes, etc.) should be placed at the entrance to the building. Rubbish must not be allowed to gather in any underfloor recesses, and a generally high standard of cleanliness and orderliness must prevail. Running and horseplay should be forbidden. Strict handover/take-over procedures should be devised and enforced.

16 Dust control is particularly important; computer rooms must have vinyl flooring, painted walls and ceilings, contain only metal and plastic furniture, and there must be no carpets, curtains or other soft furnishings present. Air must be filtered, and supplied under positive pressure so that any draught from the computer room is outwards. Dirty processes such as printing, shredding, or card or paper punching, should be performed away from the more sensitive equipment and processes.

10.4   The physical protection of computer installation services and utilities

Services and utilities are often the weakest part of the computer installation; power failures or fluctuations, cuts in the water supply which affect the air conditioning plants, or the breaking of communications links, for example, are each capable on their own of bringing to its knees the most modern and reliable computer equipment.

Services and utilities, including those serving other parts of a multi-occupancy building, should be routed clear of the computer room and any other critical parts of the installation, so that maintenance work will not interfere with the functioning of the system. In addition, the following specific points should be observed:

1 *Lighting* Continuity of computer operations and safety of staff will require a certain amount of lighting. The main lighting switch needs protecting from unauthorized interference, and adequate emergency lighting good for some hours should automatically cut in in the event of a power failure.

2 *Heating* The temperature of the computer room should be maintained within the limits set by the manufacturers of the computer equipment, usually around 70°F; fluctuations in the temperature should also be avoided. The heating of staff accommodation should be maintained at an appropriate level; a walk-out by frozen workers is not to be recommended!

3 *Air conditioning system* Even the most modern computer hardware requires adequate cooling and appropriate humidity. A breakdown of the air conditioning system will normally cause a rapid automatic computer shut-down; its protection is therefore essential. Apart from being of a suitable specification and capacity, it should be separate from the systems which serve the rest of the building, and should comprise at least two separate units, each supplied

from independent power sources and water supplies. It should be protected from unauthorized access and interference. Any external heat exchangers should be physically protected, and all air intake and extract vents should be out of sight, protected by wire mesh and out of range of hand-thrown objects. Any supply of cooling water should be adequately protected, if possible duplicated, or at least emergency water supplies provided. Any cooling pipes should be lagged to prevent condensation and subsequent water damage to the computer equipment, and should have emergency valves to shut off the supply if faults occur.

4 *Electricity supplies* Electrical power is usually obtained from a reliable source. Even so industrial action, storms, accidents or sabotage can disrupt supplies, so:

(a) At least two separate feeders should be installed, drawing from different local transformers. These transformers should be adequately protected from physical attack or damage.

(b) Emergency power from a stand-by generator should be provided for the computer, the lighting circuits, heating, the air conditioning system, security systems and any other critical services. Such alternative sources of supply should carry the load of the computer system and support services until normal power sources recover. Even if back-up supplies cannot support long periods of operation, they should provide sufficient power to allow the computer system to close down 'gracefully', that is in a controlled manner that protects the equipment and data from immediate loss or corruption. Stand-by generators should be regularly serviced and tested at least weekly to ensure they cut in and run as required.

(c) Any power supply should be free of fluctuations in voltage and 'spikes', and filters must be incorporated to clean the supply; these filters must also be provided with adequate physical protection. Change-over from main to emergency power should be uninterrupted.

(d) Authorized staff should be capable of easily and safely switching off the computer's power supply in an emergency, either by quickly powering down in the normal way or by operating emergency switches clearly marked, not capable of inadvertent use and located by the exits to the computer room so that staff may actuate them as they leave.

(e) Lightning conductors should be fitted to the building.

Electrical wiring and installation should be carried out by a qualified electrician and conform to all the relevant standards. No unauthorized or untested electrical appliances should be introduced into the computer building.

10.5   Fire protection

Physical security measures often satisfy the necessary fire protection features within a computer centre. We have already mentioned the use of non-combustible products in buildings and fittings, and floor to ceiling barriers, which not only prevent unauthorized access to other areas via underfloor or over-ceiling gaps but which stop the spread of fire and fumes through these passages. Owing to the large quantities of combustible materials stored within, and the electrical complexity of, an installation, the dangers of fire are nevertheless very real, and the effects from both the heat and the smoke devastating. To protect against fire, the following steps should be taken:

- No smoking in the computer area, or paper/combustible store.
- Regular inspections and clean-ups of the computer centre.
- Maintain stocks of computer paper products outside the centre, keeping only supplies necessary for the day's work in the computer area.

These procedural measures must be supported by a comprehensive fire safety programme, employing all the standards and products of the modern firefighting and fire prevention industry. The help of experts in this field must be sought, and one's local fire department officers will always be delighted to advise on the incorporation into new or existing buildings of the most appropriate combination of alarm, prevention, detection and suppression systems. Some points and features that will probably be of issue are listed below, but it is emphasized once again that expert advice must be sought:

1 Doors and walls should be fire resistant. All internal and external computer building doors should be able to withstand fire for up to one hour, should automatically close on the activation of the alarm system, and should be both sufficient in number and proportion and clearly marked with illuminated signs powered by batteries to facilitate safe exiting by employees in the event of an emergency. Partition walls should also be fire resistant for one hour. Any breaks in the fire separations, such as by air intakes for the air conditioning, should be baffled in the appropriate way to close these potential supplies of fresh air and breaches in the barriers. Air conditioning should shut down in the event of a fire alarm, to avoid any conflagration being fed fresh air, but should be brought on-line again as soon as the danger is over in order to get rid of smoke.

2 There should be an effective emergency fire plan, which must be tested to ensure that it works. It should include evacuation, firefighting, the maintenance of physical security during the emergency and the protection of classified material. Most importantly, all staff should be aware of the emergency procedures and their part in them, and be well practised:

   (a) The first priority of any fire drill must be to save life. Everything else must take second place to this.
   (b) There should be nominated wardens and searchers, alternate exit routes and rally points at places of safety well away from the building. All staff must be aware of the need to call the fire brigade at the first sign of trouble, and not to wait until they have attempted and failed to put out the fire themselves—such actions are meritable, but should begin only if there is time after help has been summoned.

(c) Unannounced fire drills are a most important element of any workplace's routine, but in a computer centre this is especially important. Remember, too, the other reasons for evacuation, such as a bomb threat, and practise these scenarios too.

3 Proper stocks of emergency equipment such as hoses, axes etc., should be immediately available. In particular, hand-held fire extinguishers for both electrical and non-electrical fires should be placed around the centre appropriately, and maintained properly. Personnel should be trained in their use. Although carbon dioxide extinguishers are normally recommended for electrical fires, the gas is expelled at such low temperatures that the computer equipment may be damaged as much as by water extinguishers.

4 Smoke and heat detectors should be installed to detect the outbreak of fire anywhere in the building; do not forget floor spaces, where the greatest combination of wiring is to be found. Such alarms should activate an area fire suppression system after a short period unless cancelled, during which time the presence of fire can be confirmed and first-aid firefighting employed by staff. If a fire is large or out of control the suppression system should then activate:

(a) *Halon*   The traditional medium for extinguishing fires in computer rooms is halon gas. This smothers flame by interfering with the chemical reaction of combustion, and does not damage any computer equipment in the area. After a warning period, during which the presence of a fire can be verified or the triggering overridden, the area will be flooded with the gas, and although it is not lethal it is important that evacuation of staff is completed promptly. This solution is not entirely without fault, though, and while ideal in many circumstances there may be occasions when its drawbacks must be weighed against its advantages:

   (i) The installation of a halon system is expensive, and is thus best suited to small or inaccessible areas. If large areas are to be protected then the costs may become prohibitive.

   (ii) Stored in liquid form under pressure it can leak over a period so that the cannister is empty just when it is needed most.

   (iii) Once discharged, it needs replacing, which is in itself expensive, especially when the activation was caused by a false alarm. Unless the system is duplicated, the area is unprotected until the gas has been replenished—during the very period when a fire may suddenly spring up again.

   (iv) To be effective, the area needs to be sealed, and then kept sealed for a period while the suppression works and the fire scene cools to below the temperature for re-ignition. This may be quite some time in some circumstances, denying access to the entire computer area when one may wish to enter to limit further damage or to recover media left in there during the evacuation.

(b) *Water sprinklers* Clearly one should avoid contact between water and sensitive and valuable electronic equipment. False alarms will be especially frustrating if the hardware is ruined, and so any sprinkler system must incorporate a delay to allow manual override if the presence of fire is not confirmed. Sprinklers are cheap, very effective on all types of fire, virtually inexhaustible, immediately available for reuse and actually facilitate entry to the danger area while operating. It is only the damage they inflict on any electrical equipment which is their real drawback, and it has been the traditional view that they should not be used in computer centres. However, since hardware costs are only a small part of the investment, with buildings and plant far more valuable and more difficult to replace in most instances, perhaps it is most important to put out the flames and worry about consequential damage later? Any fire officer will tell you that after saving life, the first priority will be to extinguish the flames as quickly as possible, since while the fire burns it harms; this rationale presumably should apply to the computer centre. The importance of proper backing up of data and storing it away from the computer centre is paramount.

(c) *Mist* There is a new development in suppression systems—mist—which is a fine fog of water droplets. It seems to have the qualities of halon without the disadvantages. Mist does not wreak the damage that standard water sprinklers cause.

5 Do not concentrate fire precautions around the computer itself, which is probably one of the least flammable components of the installation. All the other functions within the installation—data preparation, media library, programmer accommodation etc.—are in their way just as essential to the efficient operations of the installation and probably constitute a greater fire hazard. Even the loss of the staff canteen and the associated effect on the morale and performance of the staff could be critical at certain times within the commercial cycle.

11
Document security

A computer document is any input, output or storage medium or associated material upon which information is recorded or displayed.

Computer documents, like many other aspects of computing, appear strange and special at first sight. Apart from some particular qualities and weaknesses which need to be taken into account, though, they can in truth be looked after in exactly the same way as traditional paper. They can be secured in appropriate containers, recorded and traced from creation to destruction, destroyed in such a way as to ensure any information upon them cannot be surreptitiously re-created, and marked at all times with an indication as to their worth or sensitivity.

Existing corporate procedures for document security should be transferred to the ADP environment. By using tried and tested methods with which the staff should be familiar, this aspect of computer security can thus be kept as simple and reliable as possible. There is little merit in making a security measure more difficult than necessary.

11.1   What is a computer document?

Computer documents take many forms, and the information on them can be magnetic or otherwise, recorded in either visible or invisible form, either permanent or volatile:

1   *Paper and card*   Such obvious things as printer output, punched card or paper tape, graphs, charts, flow charts, logs and plans, but also any other document relating to the computer and its operations—for example manufacturers' manuals which explain how to use the system, or which describe its security features and thus give clues about how to circumvent them.
2   *Film*   Computer output to microform—microfilms and microfiche.
3   *Magnetic media*   Electronic information is stored on a variety of magnetic media. Magnetic tapes are now being superseded by cassette tapes, data cartridges, removable or fixed magnetic disks, magnetic drums, and floppy disks.

4 *Hardware* This includes the electronic circuitry, and associated core and hard disk memory.

5 *Firmware* Software code or data can be contained within non-volatile hardware chips. There are two main types:

   (a) Programmable Read Only Memory (PROM) Once implanted, the software or data can only be read, and cannot be altered or deleted.
   (b) Erasable Programmable Read Only Memory (EPROM) The software or data can be altered, erased or replaced.

6 *Visual displays* The information being displayed on a computer VDU is a computer document.

7 *Ancillary materials* Those items used in computer operations and which are often forgotten—carbon papers and backing sheets, for example, or printer ribbons (especially those which strike only once and thus create a perfect record of what has been typed)—can hold information as sensitive as anything held on the system. They must be treated accordingly.

8 *Optical devices* The new generation of storage media—optical storage devices—at first could only be written on once and then read many times ('worms'). Now they can be altered or overwritten, and provide massive amounts of storage capacity on very compact disks which are almost invulnerable to damage.

11.2   Handling computer documents

Assuming that the basic rules of secrecy such as the 'need to know' principle are being applied, and that all information has been valued and assigned an appropriate classification, there are some special rules for handling computer documents:

1 *Aggregation* Computers can produce documents which are more sensitive than the composite parts of the information held on them. A host of detail can reveal more than that detail itself when gathered together—aggregated—especially if the computer can then manipulate such data. Computer documents may need to be looked after more carefully than the apparent worth of data held on them would suggest. The originator of any computer document should seek the advice of the system manager if there is any possibility of such aggregation occurring, and the classification increased if necessary.

2 *Retention of information* Rather like pencil on paper leaves readable indentations after it has been rubbed out, electronic information leaves traces on magnetic media which can, with a little effort, be read even after the data has been deleted. More significantly, many computers do not actually erase data on magnetic media but merely remove the label to the 'erased' file and then allow overwriting when that space is needed; until then the original data is available to someone with the necessary and easily available software tools and a modicum of skill. Thus, a magnetic computer document should retain

the highest classification of data ever held on it, until it is either purged in an approved manner or destroyed.

3 *Treat as plain text* If data is in machine coded form, invisible on a magnetic drum, or is a series of holes in a long punch tape, do not assume that it is unreadable; treat it as if it were in plain text. To some it is. Columns of data, if missing the headings of those columns, must be treated as if all the information is present, since it does not require a great deal of ability to work out what the data means. Software programs, apparently a jumble of numbers and lines of instructions, should be protected as if they were readable to the man in the street, especially if, as is likely, they are valuable in their own right or contain classified data.

4 *Clear desk policy* All documents, computer or otherwise, should be locked away in appropriately secure containers whenever the workplace is left unattended, even for lunchtimes, coffee breaks or visits to the lavatory. In addition, at the end of the working day all working surfaces should be cleared of all items so that any documents left lying about will be immediately obvious. Such tidy routines will also aid good housekeeping and administrative routines. As an aside, recent bomb attacks in London have highlighted the need for the clear desk policy; loose papers were blown in the blast like confetti at a wedding, and lost forever.

11.3   Marking computer documents

Marking paper documents is straightforward. Company policies will differ, but a usual method is to indicate the classification of the document in the centre at the top and bottom of each page, including the blank side of single sheet print, and these markings should be overstamped in red. It should be easy to tell the worth of a document from a glance, no matter from what angle or which way up it is. This is not possible with many computer documents. How do you stamp a disk pack? But as ever, application of a measure of common sense will reveal a sensible solution.

It must be possible to mark:

- *On the VDU* When processing sensitive data, the classification of the information displayed on the screen must be visible in eye-readable form at all times, no matter what is happening on the screen.
- *In the machine* Even when packets of data are within the computer, or moving around a network, they must be marked with their sensitivity so that appropriate security can be applied. Machine code must be headed by certain labels within the file identifier to show the nature of the data to follow, and how it and any files created/hard-copy produced from it are to be handled, stored and distributed.
- *On the physical documents* All documents should be marked in eye-readable form, in letters larger than the text, with the highest classification held, or

previously held (on magnetic media) since the last purge. Colour codes for each level of classification or privacy will help. Any markings must not affect the document, and must not be removable by accident or wear. It may be appropriate to make them indelible; it may be necessary to be able to remove or alter them from time to time.

There are various methods of marking the differing types of computer documents:

1   *Paper*   Graphs, charts, flow charts, plans, maps and drawings should be marked in plain language; such markings should be visible on rolled or folded documents. Each page of printout should be marked either automatically or manually. Paper with the classification marking pre-printed could be used. Especially sensitive printout should have each page consecutively numbered, with the total number of pages and the last page indicated (. . . 16 of 26, etc.); it may be necessary to mark each copy produced (. . . copy no. 16 of 26, etc.). Large runs of printout should devote the first page to a large pattern print showing the overall classification of the run. If possible, multi-page documents should be bound securely, in which case each page need not be marked providing the external covers show the document's worth clearly and unambiguously.

2   *Punched cards*   A deck of punched cards should be treated as a single document, and its overall classification should be marked in plain language on the front of the first and back of the last card; the total number of cards should be shown on the last. Colour-coded card can be used. Individual cards need not be marked unless they are removed from the deck. It is often easy and effective to stamp the edge of the deck of cards with the classification.

3   *Punched paper tapes*   Punched paper tapes should carry a plain statement of their classification at the beginning and end of the length of paper used, and for more sensitive tapes at regular intervals throughout the tape. The edge of the roll can be written upon. Colour-coded paper can be used.

4   *Magnetic tapes and cassettes*   The magnetic tape held on a spool should have headers and footers marked with the classification, but the tape itself should not be tampered with in order to mark the classification. The spool itself should carry classification markings. It is important when using magnetic tapes to ensure the correct tape returns to the correct spool. Cassettes should be marked on the front and back, and the cassette box should also be marked appropriately.

5   *Removable magnetic disks*   Removable magnetic disks and disk packs should be marked on the top of the disk or pack, and on the dust covers normally surrounding the disks. Take special care not to damage or unbalance disk packs with any markings. Make sure disks are returned to the correct dust cover.

6   *Fixed magnetic disks and drums*   These vary in size and type, and are often contained within the hardware in inaccessible places. It is often adequate to

mark the hardware itself, though if the disks or drums are removed from the computer equipment then it will be necessary to mark their classification.

7 *Floppy disks and diskettes* Floppy disks are robust if treated properly, but fragile if mishandled. Do not mark directly on to the disk. Only write on the dust jacket and then where the manufacturer indicates. Do not press heavily and do not use a fountain or ballpoint pen. Use a felt tip pen, or write on to a self-adhesive label and then stick it to the cover.

8 *Computer output to microform* Microfilm and microfiche must be marked appropriately, both on each frame in microform itself and in eye-readable form on the transparency itself. Containers of microform should be marked appropriately.

9 *Firmware* As soon as the item is programmed, it should be marked with a coloured dot denoting the correct classification of the data held on it. It must then be handled throughout its life in the appropriately secure manner. EPROMs should retain the highest classification ever placed on them, no matter what subsequent erasures and reprogrammings occur.

11.4   Accounting for magnetic media

Since electronic data is easily copied on to small areas, to be subsequently stolen in great amounts, by tightly controlling magnetic media within the area of computer operations it should be possible to reduce this risk. Additionally, magnetic media are attractive and valuable in their own right; the stockroom has always been rich hunting ground for the pilferer. All magnetic media should, for security and crime prevention reasons, be accounted for from the moment of receipt into the enterprise until the moment of final disposal or destruction. They should be booked in and stored under secure conditions from the moment they are received. Each item should be allocated a unique, eye-readable identification number, assigned in order to enable that item's use, movement and destruction to be recorded throughout its life, to aid checks and musters, and to help during investigations into loss, corruption or compromise of data. This number must be easily seen and it should not be possible easily or accidentally to remove or alter.

Marking magnetic media with easily understandable titles can in itself breach security, and place that particular disk or drum at greater risk. But magnetic media cannot be 'read' in the normal manner, and it is important that some secure but efficient cataloguing system is employed to keep track of what is where. The identification number can be used for this, the contents of each item of media entered into a central library document—itself protected according to its own aggregated classification. The contents of each tape, for example, are then easily determinable from this library document, but the registration number will in itself reveal nothing. The maintenance of these records must, as with every other security task, be allocated to a named individual. If this central register is held on the computer itself, regular back-up copies must be made, since the loss of this data would be especially painful.

Firmware should be registered like any other computer document. In order to attribute a readable identification mark, it may be necessary to mark the circuit board upon which the chip is mounted, and treat the whole board as the classified document.

Take care with shared printers. When a printer is shared by more than one user, it is often difficult to judge when a wanted document will be printed. The owner may not go to collect the printout as soon as it has been produced, and anyone can read and/or copy it during the intervening period.

11.5   Accounting for associated documents

There are many documents, apparently unimportant or not directly associated with the operations of a computer, which do need protection since their abuse could lead to circumvention of the security measures of the installation or place its safety in jeopardy:

1 *Blank pro-formas*   There will invariably be a host of blank pro-formas which can subsequently be turned into extremely valuable items. Blank cheques, once processed through the computer printer, become negotiable. The speed with which the modern computer can process and print such output often means that whole boxes of these things are left lying around the computer centre, while those same staff happy with this would never dream of leaving their own chequebooks unattended. Bills, receipts, invoices, licences, accounts, statements and endless other process-specific blanks can all be used to defraud, and should be properly protected and accounted for as if they were already processed and printed.

2 *'Handle as if . . .' documents*   There will always be computer documents which, although in themselves unimportant and unclassified, contain information that in various ways could allow access to more valuable information. Such items as the manufacturer's technical publications and instruction manuals for the computer equipment, the master copies of the controlling system software, programs used to test the security features of the controlling system software, directories of user files and details of their contents, programs used to overwrite data storage media, and other such documents need to be handled as if they were in themselves classified. Often they are the equivalent of keys to doors opening on to a treasure garden of secrets. Often, too, they are essential to the continued operation of the installation, and their loss would have a serious impact on efficiency and survival.

11.6   Purging magnetic media

Magnetic media can be re-used. As a video tape can be used many times over to record different television programmes, so too can magnetic tapes, disks and drums record, store and process different sets of information. There is a danger, though, that data is inadvertently left on the magnetic media to be passed on to unauthorized parties during such re-use. The media must be wiped clean, or purged, of the recorded images on them:

1 *Re-use within the department*   If a tape, say, is to be re-used within the same department, where it matters not if the data is retained on it and seen later by the same staff who probably put it there in the first place, then there is no real need to purge the medium. The tape must, though, be protected throughout its life in a manner appropriate to the highest classification of data ever stored on it, regardless of whatever is overwritten on it.

2 *Re-use within the enterprise*   If the medium is to pass out of the immediate control of those responsible for its initial use, but it is not to pass outside the control of the enterprise, it will be necessary to purge the medium to a level where it is unlikely that any data is retained. Since it would not be too serious if some other member of the company's staff caught sight of the original data, there will be no need to expend a great deal of effort on this process. Data should simply be overwritten at least once. Again, though, regardless of its subsequent use, the medium must always retain the classification of the most valuable or sensitive data ever written on it.

3 *Release from the enterprise*   If the medium is to be released from the control and custody of the enterprise, then more stringent purging must take place to ensure that no data remains. The ultimate destination of such media can never be known. Hard disks returned to the manufacturers, for example, can be refurbished and sent anywhere in the world. The embarrassment and damage caused if sensitive or valuable data turns up elsewhere could be immense. It is sensible, then, to take more care during the purging process:

   (a) All markings on the medium must be removed or defaced so that they cannot be read. This prevents any information being passed on inadvertently about the previous use or value of the medium.

   (b) Either the medium should be overwritten many times, or it should be treated with a degaussing device (to swamp the medium with a much stronger magnetic force to distort any patterns of data). The following points are important:

      (i) Are you sure the surface has in fact been overwritten? Is there any record of mechanical problems, either with that piece of medium or with the machine being used to overwrite, which could lead to parts or the whole of the surface being missed?

      (ii) Check afterwards by attempting to read the medium that nothing has been left on.

      (iii) It may be that the medium is faulty and cannot therefore either be overwritten or the overwriting cannot be checked. One of the most obvious reasons for releasing an item of media from company custody is because it needs to be returned to the manufacturer for repair—a head crash, for example, or a hardware failure on a board containing classified firmware. Degaussing must be used in these circumstances.

(iv) Floppy disks are so cheap that it can never be worth while releasing them outside the enterprise; they should be destroyed.

(v) PROMs cannot be cleared, and should therefore never be released. EPROMs should be cleared prior to release by programming all data locations with 1s and 0s several times over.

(vi) The potential damage from the inadvertent release of sensitive or valuable information contained on, say, a damaged disk, drum or board, may likely be far higher than the worth of the item itself. If in doubt do not take the gamble, and destroy rather than release.

(vii) There will be information of such importance to the enterprise that release of any media which have ever contained it should never be permitted. The apparent costs of this policy are far outweighed by the potential cost of this data's unauthorized release. Details of exactly which categories of classification come under this rule must be laid down by senior management in advance, and affected items must be clearly marked with a warning that they are never to be removed from company premises.

11.7   Backing up magnetic media

Copies of magnetic media must be made accurately, regularly and religiously. The magnetic medium itself can become faulty and its data not easily retrieved, or it can be destroyed or lost in some way (physical damage, theft, fire). With the amount of data possibly held on, for example, a floppy disk the loss could be enormous. Magnetic media must be duplicated at least once and stored away from the computer. Since data, and to a lesser extent software, files will change as time goes by, such copies need to be updated, each new version replacing the previous.

The established method of backing up is the so-called 'son, father and grand-father' system (Fig. 11.1):

• The in-use (live) copy—the son—is backed up to become the father copy; the new copy is now the son.
• The father may be stored alongside the son, for immediate access if it is needed.
• The grandfather copy, produced from the father during the next repetition of the backing-up process, must be stored at a remote location, certainly in a different building at least 100 metres from the computer but ideally at another site altogether.
• Old grandfathers can be returned for re-use.
• Great-grandfathers, and so on, can be created if necessary or appropriate.

The frequency of updates will be determined by the nature of the operations.

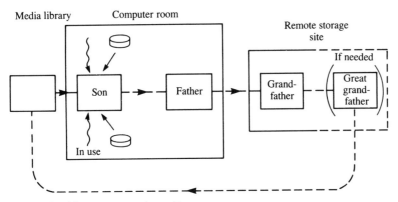

Figure 11.1.   Backing up magnetic media.

Software media will need updating less often than data files, and the remote copies (the grandfathers) may miss a father or so to reduce the administrative burden if this is acceptable, since they are the last resort.

The loss of the son will inevitably lead to the loss of the data since the last back-up. Either this loss must be predicted and planned for, or the intermediate transactions must have been manually recorded between updates. For example, it may be wise to keep all source documents—sales invoices, bills and so on—until backing up has placed their data on to at least one remote copy of the media.

It is best to update at regular, recognized times to reduce the effects on operations and to minimize inconvenience. Keep track of which version is in use, and advertise this well so that staff all know.

Test the back-up copies to ensure the copying process has been working. This is very important.

Access to back-up copies should be strictly controlled. Loss of the son may have been due to operator error. That same operator may reach for the father and promptly wipe it out in the same way. Keep the grandfather out of reach! Spreading responsibility for updating, and for drawing on back-up copies, will help prevent this nightmare. The older the version then the higher (older?) the authority should be to order its breaking out for use.

Finally, remember to keep copies of associated documentation, including operations' manuals and disaster plans, with the grandfathers. Such paperwork, if destroyed, can become the bottleneck which strangles the company, no matter how up to date is the magnetic storage media.

11.8   Destruction of computer documents

The useful life of every computer document should end with its destruction in a safe and secure way, preferably on site:

- Computer documents should not be hoarded, but destroyed as soon as they are no longer required.

- Whenever possible, classified data recorded on magnetic media should be overwritten before the media are destroyed, as an added safeguard.
- Larger systems will probably produce large volumes of sensitive or valuable waste documents of all kinds including magnetic media, paper printout, ancillary materials and firmware. There should be bulk secure storage facilities for this until it has been disposed of in the appropriate manner.
- All waste should be considered as classified to its highest level. It is safer and more economical than trying to sift out the more sensitive and then dealing with it separately.
- Those documents attributed a unique identification number will be being traced through their life, and so the record must be annotated accordingly when each of these items is finally destroyed.
- Paper and card waste and ancillary items such as carbon papers and unwanted blank pro-formas should be shredded, or burned in an incinerator. The latter should have a filter on its chimney to prevent large pieces of paper being wafted into the air in the smoke and heat, and the ashes should be probed before final dumping in case all the paper has not been burned.
- Magnetic tapes and printer ribbons should be cut into short lengths before being mixed in with large volumes of paper waste and burned—some types give off toxic fumes, so ventilate well. A radial cut from the centre of the spool will suffice: there is no need to chop chunks off one by one! Cassettes and cartridges should be broken open, and the tape dealt with accordingly.
- Floppy disks should be removed from their cardboard jacket and shredded, or cut into small pieces and burned with paper.
- Those magnetic disks and drums and optical disks, which have held very sensitive or valuable data, should be melted into ingots using an oxyacetylene torch. Less important ones should be broken into small pieces with a large hammer, and mixed with large volumes of other solid waste.
- Microfilm and microfiche do not burn satisfactorily and cannot be shredded. They should be cut into small pieces and torched along with the very valuable disks and drums.
- Firmware should be destroyed by incineration after being hammered.

11.9   Checks and musters of computer documents

To reduce the risk of loss or compromise, all computer documents, but especially those containing sensitive or valuable data, should be subject to the same security checks as conventional documents, in line with the enterprise's overall security policy. These checks should include routine and surprise (regular but random) musters and physical inspections. Selected media should be physically produced or conclusive evidence of their location obtained. It should be determined:

- whether correct classifications have been assigned;
- whether correct and effective handling, recording, copying and transmission

methods have been enforced from receipt of the document into the establishment until final disposal;
- that appropriate destruction methods have been employed;
- that all documents can be traced and accounted for.

Personnel carrying out these checks must be independent of the department
under review. Records of all such checks must be maintained.

12
Personnel security

While a computer system's greatest asset is its staff, ironically the greatest danger to that system, and thus to its data's security, lies with those very same people. They will be entrusted with its programming, maintenance, operation, use and security, but they may be dishonest, disaffected, incompetent or careless. No matter what other measures and regulations are introduced to protect the data held within the computer, at the end of the day the staff involved will have to be entrusted to carry out their duties securely, responsibly and safely. And no matter what care is taken in other ways, unless personnel security is sound then all the other measures will be of little worth.

12.1   The elements of personnel security

As systems become smaller, more powerful and more widely dispersed, a greater number of staff gain an increasingly comprehensive access to the growing database, and often at more and more isolated and unsupervised remote sites. Add to this the fact that the computer's abilities to store, process and produce vast amounts of valuable and sensitive data make them very attractive targets, it is therefore vitally important that:

1   Only trusted staff are allowed access to a computer system, and then only:

   (a) to those parts they require access to in order to carry out their duties ef-
       ficiently;
   (b) to a level of sensitivity for which they have been cleared.

2   Untrusted staff and strangers are denied access to the system, and thus the opportunity to do damage.
3   The trusted staff remain trustworthy, and that any who become risks to security are identified and removed at once from the 'danger areas'. This requires constant and close supervision by supervisors and other staff.

User malpractice and error, caused by a lack of knowledge, skill and understanding, can be as devastating to a system as any well-planned, deliberate attack. Many instances of data loss/corruption or computer service unavailability can be avoided if personnel are properly trained in their normal duties, and additionally are aware of the risks to a system and the correct countermeasures that should be employed. A comprehensive training and computer security awareness programme is therefore a vital element of any personnel security policy for computer staff—this is addressed in Chapter 22.

These, then, are the elements of personnel security:

- Screening
- Security clearances
- Supervision
- Training and security awareness.

Computer staff—especially those entrusted with the most sensitive and responsible appointments, but ultimately all those who have any contact with system assets (including security guards, contract (external) staff, and cleaning/ancillary staff)—must be of the highest integrity. Management should pay constant attention to their conduct, reliability and personal behaviour.

12.2   Fundamental principles of personnel security

There are fundamental principles that should govern the personnel security measures at any computer installation:

1 *The need-to-know principle*   Possession or knowledge of information, what-ever its classification, must be limited strictly to those who have both the authority for access (clearance) and a clear need to know that information for the efficient performance of their duties. Status or appointment does not on its own imply entitlement to knowledge or possession of that information. The more sensitive or valuable that information, the more important becomes this principle. Sales managers should not automatically be allowed, by virtue of their position within the company and despite the fact that they carry a high level of clearance, to have access to, say, research data held by other perhaps more junior staff. Human nature dictates that the 'brass', with their confidence and authority, will attempt to brow-beat more lowly staff in order simply to know what is going on. Management and security staff must make it clear, and show it to be true, that when those receiving such brow-beatings refuse to disclose information, they are supported and that there are no adverse, only positive, consequences of their compliance with this principle.
2 *The need-to-go principle*   Staff, again of whatever rank and appointment, should be allowed physical access within the computer data centre and any associated areas only as far as is necessary for them to perform their jobs. They should also be denied unnecessary access to data areas and functions within the computer itself, even though they may be legitimate users of the system for other reasons.
3 *The two-person principle*   In order to reduce the opportunities for any person to breach system security, those responsibilities and duties which would

afford particularly useful access to the system or its security features should not be carried out by one person alone. This individual should be accompanied at all times during the performance of such duties by an authorized person, where 'authorized' infers an equal knowledge and the ability to detect any unauthorized or dangerous practices; it is of no use for a security guard to accompany the system manager during very technical operations, since the security guard will not understand what is going on and will not, therefore, recognize an illegal or incorrect action.

(a) This principle is particularly relevant to security-related tasks such as:

   (i) Control of access-control procedures (issue of passwords, etc.).
   (ii) System start-up and shut-down.
   (iii) Periods of classified processing.
   (iv) Modification or maintenance of software/hardware.

(This list is not exhaustive.)

(b) However, when a certain procedure or operation is subject to the two-person rule, this then raises the possibility of collusion between the two staff members. To avoid this, as much as possible and practical should be done to vary shift rosters and working practices so that the same people are not always working together, and vital functions should be well dispersed among staff members.

(c) There are certain computer functions that should not be carried out by the same person:

   (i) A programmer should never be allowed to operate the computer system, and operators should not act as programmers. Certainly this rule should apply for particularly sensitive computer operations, though the constraints of live operations and on-line computing may make this difficult.
   (ii) The introduction of any system security features must be carried out by staff entirely independent of programming or operational staff (security staff, perhaps).
   (iii) The data preparation and data processing functions should be entirely divorced from each other, not only organizationally but physically too.
   (iv) Data custodians/librarians should not be directly responsible to, or connected with, any operations or programming staffs.
   (v) The custodian of any classified/sensitive material should not be allowed to authorize its reproduction, issue or destruction, and independent checks of this person's work must be carried out at regular but random times.

4 *The rotation of duties* No one person should be kept in one particular post for too long, especially if that appointment carries with it any specific security

responsibilities or opportunities for dishonesty. This will help to avoid the errors that emerge from boredom or over-familiarity with duties, and it will prevent an individual from continuing any crooked activities indefinitely. This replacement process often reveals dishonesty or inefficiency that would otherwise have remained concealed. Predictable working routines should be interrupted without notice. Enforced holiday periods should be introduced (during which the absence of the perpetrator may cause the offence to emerge). 'Old Harry', who has been in charge of the data preparation room for years, who has never given cause for concern, who works every weekend and who never takes a holiday, may not be the faithful retainer everyone supposes; he may be milking the computer system dry. As a rule, always avoid predictable routine as much as possible, though remember at the same time that we are all creatures of habit and your staff will always prefer their routine to be preserved.

12.3   The threats from staff members

An individual's role and status within an enterprise will dictate the nature and amount of damage—inadvertent or deliberate—that he or she can cause to the computing service and data.

12.3.1   Users

The majority of staff who have access to a computer system will comprise low-level users—those with terminals on their desks and with limited access to, and use of, that system. Yet the effects of their actions can be considerable, since there is often little control or supervision over them. Their level of training and often the mundane nature of their duties result in high error rates:

1 *Failure to apply checks* In the interests of expediency, or as a result of ignorance or laziness, users will often ignore or deliberately bypass the in-built security and validation checks designed to protect the system and its data.
2 *Operator error* 'Finger trouble' is inevitable and costly.
3 *Dishonesty* False entries; deliberate omissions and transcription errors; misuse of resources; unauthorized disclosure of company trade secrets; the clogging up of the system with unauthorized processes (football pool permutations, stamp club membership lists etc.): these are all potentially extremely damaging to the company.

12.3.2   System support and development staff

The small number of system support and development staff have immense responsibilities towards the system's well-being, efficiency and security. They will have a deep understanding of the system software and security features, and almost endless opportunity to commit dishonest or damaging acts either by manipulation of the software code or as a result of the inefficient performance of their duties. Apart from programming errors, deliberate acts such as the insertion of software bugs or the avoidance of in-built software security features are easily committed.

12.3.3 Computer operations staff

At the heart of the system are the well-trained, confident and influential computer operations staff. These personnel can fall prey to human temptation like all others, but their actions can have profound effects on the system. Simple errors can have catastrophic results. Manipulation of data and the subsequent suppression of audit and security features (in order to hide such unauthorized or dishonest acts), unauthorized disclosure of data, and theft of computer resources are all easily achieved. Furthermore, these staff will tend to be blind to their computer's faults and weaknesses. They will have great faith in the infallibility of their system and its own security and safety features. They will be a closely knit group and be blind, too, to any suspicious activity of a close colleague. They may indeed cover for any incompetence of a colleague. There is, therefore, an even greater need for personnel security measures and supervision over these staff members, and it is more important than ever that they are trustworthy and conscientious.

12.3.4 Security staff

Who checks the checker? Security staff are only human too, and the dishonest guard or subverted security manager will have ample unsupervised opportunity to commit illegal acts. The security manager will, of course, have an intimate knowledge of the system, but for the guards their activities would be limited in the main to the less technical attacks—theft of computer resources, vandalism, sabotage. Coercion with dishonest computer staff members could, however, lead to other dishonest acts which require both knowledge and opportunity. Security staffs must be cleared for access to the highest level of information held, processed or produced within the computer centre they are protecting. (Do not forget cleaners, who also have unescorted access to the heart of the installation, building/equipment maintenance staff, computer maintenance engineers and other contractors.)

12.3.5 Outsiders

An enterprise will have no control over outsiders who, deliberately or inadvertently, damage or attack the system. Although the greatest dangers to any system come from those who work within it, criminals may attempt fraud or theft, 'hackers' may attack the system for fun, and terrorists or vandals may attack and damage vital equipment, especially those remote and therefore easily accessible components such as communications links or power supplies.

12.4 The motivation for crime

Why do not only strangers, but also those within an enterprise's computer department who should hold allegiance to, and have an interest in, that enterprise's well-being, efficiency and profitability, commit dishonest acts against the security and safety of the computer? If we can recognize these motivating factors, then we can adapt and improve still further the personnel security features.

People will be tempted into committing a crime if:

1 They are unhappy or disgruntled. Good morale is an important aspect of not only an enterprise's performance but also its safety and security.
2 The crime is easy to commit and there is a reasonable chance of getting away with it.
3 There is the opportunity and the reward is sufficient—'every person has a price'.

People will commit a computer crime for a number of fundamentally different reasons:

1 *Because it is there . . .*   Hackers seem to lack any real malice towards the owners of the computer systems they love to try to break into. Time and again they admit merely to wanting to crack any security measures simply as an intellectual challenge or to satisfy their curiosity, with no real thoughts of personal gain.
2 *To gain personal advantage*   The step from the challenge to the crime is a small one. Personnel, especially those with access, will, given the opportunity and often whatever the prize, no matter how small, use any security weak-nesses within the computer system to their own advantage—personal, financial or competitive. Extra motivation occurs when an individual encounters a pressing need for extra cash—blackmail, during sticky divorce proceedings, gambling, over-extension of borrowing etc.
3 *Retaliation*   Individuals may retaliate against the computer to deliberately damage it or the parent enterprise—relieving a real or imagined grudge, displacing their animosity of management and/or work practices, or simply as a result of fear of the computer and its effect on future job security. Indeed, computers are often thought of as fair game, and public support will tend to be against the computer. Tales of old-age pensioners receiving bills for £50 million are often related. Computers have also been attacked as part of a wider campaign against an enterprise, such as during industrial disputes.
4 *The modern criminal*   Computers can be used simply as tools to carry out a crime. The present generation is the last to grow up without computers; my son could punch his name into my PC before he could write it for himself.

12.5   Personnel security measures

Computer staff should display high personal and professional standards and qualities:

- *Intelligence* Judgement, commonsense, imagination, perception, problem-solving abilities.
- *Compatibility* Cooperation, tact, teamwork, relationship with superiors, peers and subordinates.
- *Strength of character*   Maturity, stability, integrity, moral courage, determination, honesty.
- *Loyalty* Sense of duty, reliability, dedication to the enterprise, enthusiasm for its aims.
- *Professional knowledge and abilities*   Ability to perform current duties, efforts made to keep abreast of new developments in the individual's field of employment.
- *General characteristics* Breadth of interests, social attributes, powers of written/spoken expression, energy, appetite for work, staying power, drive, health.

Sadly, companies have been known to recruit data processing staff with less diligence than for personnel of other departments. Indeed any strict company procedures for recruit selection can be deliberately waived or ignored in respect of the computer department. Qualifications often outweigh all other qualities and considerations within the current market place where there is a serious shortage of good computer staff. Post-employment supervision is then rarely carried out by management on those staff now absorbed into the insular and mysterious computer world.

There are several stages involved in the achievement of sound and comprehensive personnel security measures.

12.5.1   Stage 1: Identify sensitive jobs and key personnel

In order to apply most cost effectively the available personnel security resources, those persons who hold the most sensitive appointments, those who have access to the more sensitive and valuable information and assets, and those on whom computer operations most depend, should be identified and concentrated upon.

12.5.2   Stage 2: Screen personnel

The screening process is best achieved before employment, during the recruitment of new staff, but it can be applied retrospectively. The simple methods of screening are often the most effective.

If designed well, application forms completed by prospective employees will contain a wealth of personal and background information. More can then be learned about the individual from character/professional referees. These should include at least the previous employer, and at least one character referee whose credentials are provable, such as a senior public or government servant, a member of one of the professions (lawyer, doctor, teacher) or a commissioned officer of the armed services or civil police—we need one to attest to our worth for a passport, why not a job? Private background investigations may be considered appropriate in the case of applicants for very sensitive appointments. Finally, whatever is learned about an individual in other ways, a properly structured interview should be conducted in order to gain a 'feel' for that person.

The personal qualities that should be considered in an applicant are:

1   Previous employment and positions held, and career pattern/development. In particular, any mysterious gaps in this history should be thoroughly accounted for—do they represent a prison sentence, or a period in hospital?
2   Check references and qualifications thoroughly. There are numerous examples of fictitious 'previous employers' and legendary 'university of life'-type diplomas and degrees. Nothing should be taken at face value. Find out about:

   (a) *Competence*   The most highly qualified individual can be useless in practice, and a polished performance during interview can be little more than a façade for incompetence. Devise some simple test of an individual's abilities in the work for which he or she is to be employed. Incompetent individuals are more prone to cause operator errors, and will be more vulnerable to the pressures of blackmail or subversion.
   (b) *Time-keeping and absenteeism*   How reliable is the individual?
   (c) *Disciplinary record*   Are there any continuing involvements with legal proceedings, either criminal or civil?
   (d) *Medical history*   Is there any evidence of mental instability, or protracted/chronic illness which could place financial or social pressures on the individual? One effective method of obtaining these facts is to offer a company-paid life insurance policy which requires a medical examination of the person to be insured; medical-in-confidence details may not be forthcoming, but if the candidate is fit to insure then there is probably no serious affliction.
   (e) What were the reasons for termination of previous employments?
   (f) Would any previous employer re-employ, or would any referee?
   (g) Are there any continuing obligations upon the individual from any previous employment?
   (h) Was the individual ever employed in the past by one's own company, and if so when and under what circumstances and for what reasons did the individual leave?
   (i) What were the individual's relationships with colleagues—was the person able to work as the member of a team? Was he or she liked and respected? Were there any problems that arose concerning ability to work

with others and vice versa? There is one recorded case where a programmer with the most atrocious body odour disrupted an entire data centre.

3   Consider the individual's origins, domestic and family circumstances, and contacts or family connections with competitors. Ask for proof of identity and nationality such as a passport or birth certificate.
4   Is there any evidence or history of alcohol or drug abuse?
5   Is the individual a member of any professional or business associations? Are any strong political views held, and if so what? Does the candidate hold any public or other responsible office (councillor, trades union official etc.) which may occupy an inordinate amount of time and thus detract from performance at work, or which may bring the candidate or the company into unwanted conflict or limelight?
6   What is the individual's lifestyle? What are his or her social and sporting activities? Are there any signs of excessive or unexplained wealth or extravagance, and is there any indication that he or she may be over-extended?
7   Consider the individual's driving record, which will reveal much about character, emotional stability and maturity.
8   If possible, elicit information about the individual's creditworthiness within the banking, mortgage, credit card and private finance circles. There are specialist services available in this field.
9   If the individual has previously served in the armed forces, discharge papers will be available for scrutiny.

Background or field enquiries beyond the scope of company resources can be contracted out to firms specializing in such work. The voluntary use of lie detectors may be considered worth while at times, but these can create unwanted animosity and mistrust from the very start of one's relationship with a prospective employee.

Personality—or psychometric—testing is used by many large companies when recruiting for jobs where an employee's personality is an important factor in his or her future job; these tests can also reveal inherent security weaknesses in an individual. They should be used to complement the job interview not replace it, and will indicate such diverse qualities as leadership, teamwork, sociability and reaction to stress. There is resistance to such tests, mainly due to ignorance, fear and suspicion, and cost is often cited as a major objection. But modern techniques are vastly improved over the original tests of 15 or so years ago, and an accurate personality profile can be gained from a test lasting only 45 minutes. They are designed so that they cannot be 'best-guessed', and are resistant to deception by the person under review. They must, of course, be professionally administered and analysed properly, or they are of little worth. Like any tool they will only work satisfactorily in the right hands, and the subject needs to be honest and accurate. Finally, the tests are of greater worth if the results are explained to the candidates, giving them an insight into their strengths and weaknesses.

Some final words of caution about references and testimonials:

1   Referees are usually nominated by the candidates, and so are biased.
2   The motives of the referee, especially present employer, cannot always be determined. A good reference may indeed reflect the individual's worth or it may be that the present employer is trying to get rid of a poor worker; a poor reference may be about a good worker whose boss is reluctant to release.
3   References are written in a language all of their own, and often a translator is required to reveal the true meaning of faint praise. 'Bloggs has tried hard . . .' (failed); 'Bloggs' satisfactory performance . . .' (pathetic); '. . . has shown average intelligence . . .' (has more teeth than brain cells); '. . . a person of sound qualities . . .' (I would hesitate to breed from this individual); how often have we used such phrases ourselves because we are weak and wish to avoid the unpleasantness of confrontation with our staff, or simply because we are naturally considerate and do not wish to offend?

12.5.3   Stage 3: Award security clearances

Classification of data provides adjustable levels of worth; security clearances provide adjustable levels of trust. We must be able to indicate who is and who is not to be allowed access to the various classifications of data, and this is achieved by granting security clearance levels to individuals depending on their trustworthiness. The higher the level of clearance, the greater the trust we place in the individual, and the more sensitive the material we allow such a person to see. This process is linked to, and follows on from, the screening process.

There are essentially three types of employee:

1   *Unchecked*   Uncleared personnel will not have been checked in depth or at all for their honesty, reliability, integrity or loyalty to the enterprise, and their contact with sensitive data must be limited accordingly. There is no suggestion that such people are dishonest or untrustworthy, it is simply that we do not know. In this group, though, will be those, who because they have failed checks or have proved to be of doubtful character, must be kept away from sensitive data.
2   *No reason to doubt*   Those employees about whom limited checks have been made, and which they passed, will be awarded a level of clearance to allow some access to classified data of a certain value.
3   *Highly trusted*   More exhaustive and positive checks into an individual's history, background, family, personal life, moral views and previous employment will indicate those who may be trusted with the most sensitive data. This positive screening is only good as to the day of completion and cannot guarantee reliability and honesty, but in the risk-taking business of security it must reduce the chances of loss or compromise of data by dishonest activity.

Each level of clearance will allow a greater level of access and a greater award of responsibility. An unchecked employee may be allowed to work in the receipt and dispatch section, a no-reason-to-doubt employee may be allowed to program or operate the computer, while the highly trusted person would fill such sensitive and responsible appointments as system manager. It may, indeed, be prudent to screen such as the system manager to a level higher than apparently necessary, since the aggregation of data and the importance of the role may make this person vital to the survival of the company.

The work of a newly-arrived or obviously unstable employee must always be treated with more suspicion than that of a senior and long-standing employee. But take care with the latter, too.

12.5.4   Stage 4: Arrival procedures

An employee's contract of employment should state clearly and unambiguously:

1   His or her personal responsibilities and duties towards the security of computer assets, including information, so as to:

   (a) Remove doubt as to exactly who does what.
   (b) Bring this vital topic to the employee's attention from the time of his or her earliest associations with the enterprise.
   (c) Allow the medium for any necessary subsequent disciplinary action.

2   The formal disciplinary procedures adopted by the enterprise as well as the type of behaviour/offence which will cause it to be invoked.
3   The constraints to be placed on the employee in the event that he or she leaves the company's employ, in particular the non-disclosure of sensitive or proprietary information to a competitor (the so-called confidentiality clause).
4   That any professional books, papers and presentations written or given are to be approved in advance by senior management.

The employee should sign as having read and understood the contract of employment and all general security regulations in force. The employee should also agree in writing to the random search of his person and belongings at work, or on entering or leaving work.

There should then follow an agreed and clearly understood period of probationary employment of, say, six months. During this time special note should be taken by supervisors of the employee's behaviour, performance and apparent security awareness. At the end of this period, a deliberate review and decision should be made about suitability and retention. The probationary period should not be allowed simply to fizzle out.

12.5.5   Stage 5: Training and awareness

There should be established an effective computer security training and awareness programme to ensure the continuing reliability of employees. (This is discussed in greater depth in Chapter 22.) Such a campaign can be formal or informal, but it should be kept simple, enjoyable, understandable, innovative, cover the salient points of computer security over a recurring period of, say, two years, and draw upon company experiences and those of other organizations. Posters, beer-mats, and notices in routine company orders/newsletters can all be used to disperse the message, and a number of firms produce specialist video films that have been found to be a particularly effective medium.

Properly conducted and controlled visits around the computer centre, and a comprehensive and detailed briefing about computer operations within the enterprise and the employee's part, should be given to new arrivals. This will emphasize but also take away any fear or misconceptions about the nature and importance of the computing function within the enterprise. Mystery creates fear in many, and in others the 'jar of sweets' effect where they become intent on the forbidden and unknown.

Teach staff above all else to challenge strangers, and not to accept identity or story at face value. Always encourage them to check back, no matter what the embarrassment or inconvenience.

12.5.6 Stage 6: Supervision

Most larger enterprises already use a formal system of annual appraisal of individual performances in order to guide careers and to select those more able candidates for further promotion. Such a system is ideal for monitoring those personal qualities which indicate an individual's security reliability and honesty, and any rotten apple will be identified before any significant or lasting damage can be done to the computer operations.

More informal, everyday monitoring and supervision of personnel is in any case a vital element of any supervisor's role, and the disloyal, disaffected or dishonest worker should be recognized. Low morale, which is a common precursor to incompetence or disaffection, should also be identified and its causes dealt with, as much a matter of good practice as a security measure.

Remember to reappraise an individual's security clearance and reliability if jobs are changed within the company, including promotion, or if performance or personal circumstances change, especially for the worse.

The security education programme should encourage all staff to be vigilant and to report any security matters, especially the suspicious activities of a colleague, boss or junior. Such things as illegal orders to contravene security regulations, irrational or unusual behaviour, unusual spending and apparent wealth, or unexplained absenteeism or lateness for work should all ring alarm bells in people's minds. The Big Brother image of such a requirement should be countered by a clear understanding on everyone's part of the greater need of the enterprise over the individual. More importantly, though, such prompt reporting may save an individual from falling into even deeper trouble.

12.5.7 Stage 7: Termination of employment procedures

Formal termination of employment procedures should be introduced for persons leaving the company. It may be necessary to ban some employees from the system as soon as they make known their intention to leave. Post-employment agreements should be re-stated, with individuals being reminded in particular of their agreement not to tell competitors any company secrets they may know. A suitable signed statement to this effect should be obtained. Any access keys or tokens for the site and the computer should be recovered and computer access authorizations (passwords) revoked. Finally, the rest of the enterprise should be informed of the individual's departure, so that combination settings, etc., can be changed.

It may be appropriate to include in these procedures any employees moving posts within the enterprise.

12.5.8 Stage 8: Miscellaneous considerations

1 *Contract employees* Do not treat contract employees as if they were employed by the company—they are not, and their loyalties will be to their own firms. Personnel security measures must be bolstered for such individuals. Do not forget the maintenance engineers, even though they may be regular visitors. Contract cleaning, increasingly common in many enterprises, results in a variety of possibly unsavoury individuals being admitted without supervision to the data centre. Consultants, for all their qualifications and assumed importance, are also outsiders; usually they can be trusted since they would soon be out of business if they broke confidences, but there may be things you do not wish them to know.

2 *Remote sites/terminals* Do not forget that remote sites/terminals' staff, who are often out of mind, are a greater risk to security since they often work unsupervised, can remain anonymous, and often have direct access into the very heart of the system. Included in this group should be any maintenance firms with whom remote diagnostic contracts have been arranged.

3 *Visitors* Visitors to the computer installation, either regular or unknown, should be included within the personnel security procedures as appropriate, including background checks and authentication of those to be allowed access. If necessary, and in any case as good practice, all visitors to the installation should be escorted at all times during their stay by a member of the computer or security staff.

4 *'Remote control' over employees* A member of the system staff, who apparently has insufficient skill or knowledge to subvert the system security features, may be being guided by someone from outside with such knowledge.

5 *Act positively* If an individual's security reliability has been brought into

doubt for any reason, then until any such suspicions have been entirely resolved access to the system should be denied *at once*. Often, the individual's access authority (password etc.) can be revoked by system management without the person's knowledge or help, but it may be necessary to remove an individual physically and with surprise. For a software bomb, placed in advance by a dishonest employee in case of detection, the touching of a key sequence on the keyboard could be sufficient to demolish the whole database; if the stakes are high enough and a crook realizes the game is up, then this is just what might happen. Do the same for an employee who resigns; give him or her pay in lieu of notice and get the individual off the premises straight away, or at least away from the computer.

6 *Loyalty extends upwards and downwards* Employers must treat, and be seen to treat, their staff fairly and honestly if they are to expect fair and honest treatment in return. This is especially true for one's ADP staff who are by nature intelligent and perceptive.

7 *Walk the shop* Managers must get away from their desks on a regular basis, to walk the shop and talk to the employees. The perspective from below is entirely different to that from above, but often equally valid. An eagle is invisible from above, but from below can be seen silhouetted against the sky; such 'eagles' are stalking every enterprise, ready to pounce on any weakness in the system and invisible to the bosses on the top floor.

8 *'If you pay peanuts, you get monkeys'* If you require high quality and trustworthy ADP and security staff, especially in today's competitive market where there is an overall shortage of computer skills, then you must be prepared to pay at least the going rate. This alone will not guarantee security reliability, but cheap wages will attract the less able and more unsavoury members of the security and ADP communities.

9 *Set a good example* A company that operates efficiently and honestly, treats its staff and clients fairly, and is thus respected by its competitors will tend to enjoy higher standards of personnel security. The expected standards of corporate conduct will always be perceived by the staff as the minimum. The higher such standards in the first place, the better will be individual honesty and efficiency. At the same time, make security rules applicable throughout the enterprise; it is demoralizing for lower ranks to see different standards, usually less stringent, for the bosses.

10 *Do not be fooled* Throughout the history of crime and espionage, the most convincing and successful crooks have been the most unlikely. Remain vigilant at all times, and never assume anyone's honesty.

11 *Escape route* Employees must always be able to escape the consequences of their actions in the interests of security; they must not be so afraid of the punishment that they fail to admit to the 'crime' when it highlights some security weakness. There must be some sort of confessor figure, available to all staff and able to listen to, and react to, anonymous reports of security incidents and breaches. At the same time, employees must be able to report

their superiors without fear of retribution, if those superiors are putting security at risk by careless or deliberate breaches of the rules. Anonymous reporting can, however, result in maliciousness, but attributable reporting will cause shyness and reluctance. A balance must be developed for all these elements of the security reporting procedures.

12 *Never assume* Never assume, check. This is especially true when dealing with people. An assumption is usually the first step towards a foul-up.

13 *'If it looks like a duck ...'* Trust your judgment and instincts. If a bird looks like a duck, flies like a duck, sounds like a duck and mixes with other ducks, it is almost certainly a duck!

13
Hardware security

The protective security features provided by and applied to the physical components of a computer system.

The items of equipment that make up a computer system need to be protected:

- An effective way of compromising the security of a computer is physically to modify its hardware in such a way as to divert the routines and procedures that have been carefully set up. Modifying the circuitry, adding the infamous 'bugs', tapping into the communications links, circumventing the circuits and chips which provide software security measures, surreptitiously reading the memory which stores the passwords for the system, and altering the use for which a terminal or other peripheral is configured so that it can carry out unauthorized tasks are all possible ways of breaching the security of what would otherwise be a secure system.

- Computer hardware, despite the claims of the manufacturers, is prone to failure and bad workmanship. It can be faulty on supply. More insidiously it can fail in an endless number of ways during operation, thus at best making the system and its data unavailable, or worse actually corrupting, compromising or destroying vital information or software.

- There is no guarantee as to the pedigree of computer hardware and the myriad of its component parts. It need not have been manufactured by a reliable and known firm, and is likely to have originated in the Far East, or from other European countries or the United States. We can neither be sure what exactly it is we have bought nor necessarily have recourse in dispute or emergency to anyone but the supplier, who is in the same vulnerable position.

- In case of fault, or merely for routine maintenance, we must accept into our secure computer centre an engineer of whom we may have no knowledge. This person will be allowed to tamper with the very heart of our computer system. A bug could be inserted, or firmware removed containing vital and sensitive data or software. It is unlikely that we will understand what is being done—how many of us understand what the TV engineer is doing to the relatively simple television set in our lounge? Furthermore, it is impossible except for an engineer to identify easily which individual elements of hardware

119

perform which specific functions, since a cabinet may house a confusing number of differing modules of equipment. We are entirely in the hands of the computer maintenance engineer.

Defence against these problems is vital. But at the same time, those same items of equipment, vulnerable in these ways, can include features which themselves improve the security of the system.

13.1   Securing hardware from tampering

All hardware should be protected, if only from theft or criminal damage. But there will be those items which, for a number of reasons, will be more important to the efficiency, security and continued operation of the system. Defence should be concentrated here. For example, user terminals with no ability or licence to access the heart of the computer do not need to be guarded as much as a console in the computer room itself which is configured to allow the system manager to go right into the operating system.

Terminals must be protected from tampering:

- Cabinets containing hardware should be locked, or sealed with a paper or lead seal. These seals must be regularly inspected to detect signs of unauthorized access. There are available now holographic seals which contain unique images impossible to re-create. The backing of these breaks up if an attempt is made to remove them so that it is obvious when they have been tampered with and they cannot be stuck back on. Whatever seals are used must be properly controlled so that they cannot be stolen to replace a broken seal after an attack.
- Hardware items should be segregated whenever possible, thereby limiting the number of personnel with access to the most highly classified work.
- Hardware items of special sensitivity, for example circuit boards with firmware holding very sensitive or valuable data, could be photographed at regular intervals so that the photographs can be compared with previous ones to detect any unauthorized changes, such as the removal or insertion of chips.

13.2   Hardware identification devices

It is possible for each item of peripheral hardware to be issued with a unique identification device, to be read by the computer during the logging-on process and confirmed throughout the period of connection. Each printer, or terminal, or link to a remote site can be set up to handle or store information of a certain classification, or to carry out predetermined functions on the system. The unique identification devices confirm and allow these privileges. For example, terminals throughout the enterprise used to input data by uncleared members of staff should not be used to access the operating system of the computer, or even perhaps to retrieve the data of others, or manipulate it. Similarly, a printer in the general office should not be used to print classified data, which should only be produced on a printer in a physically controlled and supervised area. The times a particular peripheral or user may operate can also be set up, so that, for example, terminals or printers in a general office cannot be operated during the silent hours, or uncleared clerical staff cannot use the computer out of hours.

Strict measures must be enforced to protect these control mechanisms from unauthorized or accidental tampering and modification. They should only be set up and changed under controlled circumstances by trusted staff.

13.3   Hardware integrity checks

13.3.1 Self-diagnostics

Computers can check themselves to ensure all is well, or discover exactly what is wrong when the system breaks down. These self-diagnostic processes will help ensure the correct and reliable operation of the system. They can include all aspects of the machine's workings, including monitoring of the hardware security features and access control facilities. Self-diagnosis is specially useful for:

- accurately confirming the identity of the devices, media and users forming the individual elements of the system;
- checking that access controls are restricting users to those items of hardware, software and data to which they ought to have access, and that unauthorized access or use is being positively denied;
- ensuring that unauthorized attempts to access or use hardware, software or data are blocked and system supervisors alerted.

The provision of these facilities alone will not, of course, provide complete system security, and should be used as only an element in an overall defence in depth.

13.3.2 Remote diagnostics

A number of computer manufacturers provide remote diagnostic facilities that can check the computer from a distance—usually the service centre—to ensure it is working correctly and diagnose faults that may not even yet be apparent. Such a service is attractive since it reduces maintenance costs and is often quicker than calling out the engineer, thus reducing the time the system is unavailable or operating at reduced capacity. It can be as simple as a remote terminal provided for the manufacturer at the service centre, or as sophisticated as the linking in of a full diagnostic computer to the machine under test. The thoroughness with which such testing can be carried out is quite remarkable.

But remote diagnostics are a danger to computer security. From a distance a complete stranger is being allowed into the heart of the computer system, quite often in an uncontrolled and unsupervised manner right down to the very lowest levels within the software. What this person does to the system, its software and its data is entirely unknown and unaccountable, and for sensitive or valuable systems this is unacceptable. Even assuming the engineer is entirely honest and legitimate, there is during this period of testing an open line into the system which could be used by others for dishonest purposes, or which could accidentally allow software or data to escape or to be altered or erased.

At the very least, all sensitive data must be purged from the system before testing commences. All classified media must be removed from the machine, and any main memory wiped clean. If possible, the 'remote' diagnostics, as a compromise, could be carried out on site so that the engineer is able at least to employ the tools developed for checking the system but within the secure confines of the computer centre and under the supervision and checking of system staff.

Do not be tempted to jump for the apparent savings offered by remote diagnostics; the final costs could be more than you could ever afford to pay.

13.4   Maintenance procedures

The maintenance and repair arrangements at any site can prove to be a major weakness to the safety, security and availability of data within the computer system. It is important to control access to the system hardware and software, and to supervise closely any maintenance engineers and the work they carry out:

- The maintenance log, recording details of all maintenance carried out on the system, is the first line of defence in this respect. It should provide details of the date and time of any visit, the engineer's identity, the reason for the visit, and the actions and repairs carried out, including the specific details of any equipment installed, repaired, replaced or renewed. This record should be countersigned by the system security officer at the time of each entry. The log should be independently inspected at regular intervals by the departmental security officer to detect any trend or pattern that might suggest suspicious circumstances. A suggested layout for this log is shown in Fig. 8.2.
- As for remote diagnosis and as a general rule, maintenance should only be carried out once any data or software of any value has been removed from the system. Magnetic media should be taken off all tape and disk drives, all memory, buffers and spoolers should be purged of all data, and the system powered down and reloaded with a version of the operating system kept specially for the purpose. Maintenance engineers must be denied access to any sensitive or valuable data—especially passwords.
- A more than likely reason for maintenance is that the computer is faulty. If the system and its magnetic media cannot therefore be purged of data, or for some reason it is not necessary or desirable to go to the lengths of download-

ing the system, then the maintenance engineer must be supervised continuously, and by someone who knows what the engineer is doing. It is of no use putting a security guard on duty to watch, if that guard's total knowledge of electronics is limited to the ability to change a fuse. A reputable manufacturer will be willing to give instruction which, while not qualifying users to maintain their computer, will at least give an insight into the system, what the various bits are, and the maintenance and repair procedures and methods they can expect any visiting engineer to use.

- There should be a planned maintenance programme incorporated into the scheduled operations, aimed at preventing faults by regular and timely service rather than by reaction to problems. The manufacturer's warranty conditions will almost certainly require such proper and regular maintenance. The maintenance programme should be designed to ensure minimum down-time while different elements of the system are being worked on.

- The system manager must authorize in advance all maintenance and repair visits, and approve any proposed repair, replacement or renewal of equipment before it is carried out. Engineers should not be allowed just to pitch up and wade in with whatever checks and repairs they say are needed, treating the installation as their own. They should, it goes without saying, be positively identified before they are allowed access. If in any doubt check back to the service agents or manufacturers the engineer claims to be from, to make sure the right person has appeared and was in fact sent.

- Keep stocks of spare parts, including replacement printers, terminals and VDUs. Ensure adequate re-ordering procedures to ensure availability of consumables such as standard stationery, special stationery, printer ribbons and so on.

- All work must be carefully inspected in the presence of the engineer and before the latter's departure. Quiz the engineer if you are not sure what has been done and why. Make accurate notes in the maintenance log of the engineer's comments.

- Thorough testing of the routines and security features affected by any changes should be carried out prior to live operations, or certainly any classified processing.

- The engineer should be contactable at all times; the telephone number should be posted on the wall near the computer. Do the same for support facilities, such as the air conditioning engineer or the person from the Electricity Board.

- If the engineer requires to remove any items of equipment or any documentation from your site, ensure they do not contain company data of a sensitive or valuable nature. Better still, they should hold no information at all relating to the company or its operations. The special conditions governing the release of magnetic media are discussed in Chapter 11 on computer document security. In cases of doubt, the equipment or documents should not be released, but stored on site until either the information is no longer of any worth or you decide to destroy the offending items rather than release them. This may mean an increase in the maintenance costs but could prove to be a cheaper alternative in the long term.

- Software patching should be treated with extreme caution. When the software instructions contain a fault or omission it is possible to insert coding to overcome such a problem—the software can be patched. Most times such a process, whosoever carries it out, is legitimate and useful, and is often the only way to overcome a shortfall in the system's software. But the dishonest person can use such a ploy to insert unauthorized coding designed for some dishonest purpose—a 'bug', for example, or something to divert/bypass any password routines in the access control software. Even stricter supervision, testing and recording of such maintenance procedures must be taken than for any other work carried out on the system. Ensure all software patches are recorded in the maintenance log, to be reviewed regularly by the system manager.

- When the time arrives that your expensive computer equipment is no longer anything but as much scrap metal, take care during its final destruction and disposal. Information can be retained in the circuitry, and no check will ever guarantee that all traces of magnetic data have been purged. Reduce equipment that has been used for classified storage or processing to small bits, torching any particularly valuable items. For large items of hardware it may be necessary to employ contractors; make sure they are established and trustworthy and that they agree in writing to break up the scrap before its final disposal.

13.5   Fault tolerance

Aircraft are designed so that, if some vital component should fail, there are reserve systems at once brought into play. Some equipment, such as flight controls or hydraulics, can have several duplications, so that a major catastrophe will have to occur before these eventually fail. The aircraft can tolerate a fault without crashing; for all computer systems this is an important quality, but may be absolutely vital for critical systems. Fault tolerance can help prevent the loss or corruption of data, and every single keystroke should ideally be recorded somewhere, and retrievable in some way. Fault tolerance should also be able to allow secure, controlled and supervised on-line repair, ensuring continued service from a computer with a fault, even a major one, while that fault is being worked on.

There is no such thing as an unstoppable computer. There will always be single points of failure, which cannot be duplicated practically or economically or which are simply overlooked until they break. But if such critical components can be reduced in number and importance to a minimum, then the safety and security of the computer must have been improved.

There is a range of computers that run two central processing units in tandem, each fully up to date with the processing and holding the same complete sets of data and software. In this way, with the loss of one the other is able to continue until the first is brought back on-line and updated. The equipment is housed in the same or adjacent cabinets, and shares many features such as air conditioning, communication lines, disk drives and associated magnetic storage media, power supply and other utilities. Since many system failures are caused by the processing microchips and the software contained within the operating system and application programs, however, such tandem computers are a sound and well-tried method of providing a high level of fault tolerance.

Other computer systems are built to contain duplicated functions. Such methods as mirror disking, where two disks at once are written to, prevent loss of the data in the event of the all-too-familiar head crashes. Equipment destined for rugged use, such as mobile computers for military use, can be built into very strong containers, and even made resistant to water by coating components in resin or other damp-proof substances. Cabling can be sheathed in metal to protect it from damage. Back-up supply can be provided, at least for a graceful shut-down, by internal batteries. The extent to which fault tolerance is employed, and the particular parts of the system to which it is to be applied, must be determined from the nature of the system and the risks ranged against it, and the importance of its role.

13.6   Contracts

One of the most frustrating 'disasters' to happen at a computer installation is for a lengthy wrangle to develop with the suppliers of the system and software if the system breaks down or simply fails to come up to its expectations. Bugs and other common system breakdowns are an accepted aspect of the computer world. Manufacturers are anxious to keep their good reputations, and so tolerance and good grace prevail on both sides.

However, claims about what your new system will be able to do are usually exaggerated. Sales persons are sometimes liars or totally over-confident in their product, and the end result is largely the same. Sometimes deliberately under-sized systems are recommended to allow the suppliers to submit a much lower tender than their more honest and realistic competitors; the intention to come along afterwards to provide the necessary enhancements at inflated prices is rarely far away. On the other hand, customers often underestimate what they want in the first place, or fail to carry out proper research into the intended use of the system. They often go for the cheapest option even though this is unlikely to be the best or most suitable. They simply cut corners to save a few pennies. They change their minds about the use of the system once it has been installed. Companies will invest vast sums installing a computer before they have even determined whether they want one, just because it seemed a good idea, or in order to spend taxable income, or to look good in the eyes of their competitors and the public. Companies can buy systems not secure enough for the intended use.

Blame usually lies on both sides when the whole project turns into a lemon. It is vital that contracts are properly drawn up from the earliest stages of project development in order to protect all parties.

In order to ensure the correct system is procured in the first place, and then to have recourse to the supplier in the event of contractual disputes, the customer should from the first dealings with the supplier always:

1 Provide a clear definition of the system's use:

   (a) Describe the required functions and facilities of the system in order of priority. If you want a word processor, say so. If you want an automated office, make this clear, but do not expect a word processor to do anything else.
   (b) Describe future intended developments of the system. If you want only a word processor now, but might need an automated office or wish to connect to a network at some time in the future, make this clear.
   (c) Detail the intended workload of the system, the intended number of users, the type of work it will be performing, network requirements, the importance of the system and hence the need for reliability or rapid repair/maintenance and any other details which at first sight seem obvious. These points do need to be explained to the supplier, and they are quicksands for any claim you may need to make in the future.

2 State the system's security policy in understandable terms so that the supplier has a complete and coherent statement of all the measures that are to be taken by the customer to protect the information processed and stored.
3 Retain all documentation relating to any dealings with the supplier. Minutes of meetings, notes of actions taken and phone conversations with dates, times and with whom, promotional literature, presentations given by the supplier, all are important evidence.
4 Quantify where possible the (consequential) effects of both the computer system's total failure or its failure to perform as intended. Inform the suppliers in writing of these sums.
5 Place an official order in writing, in which relevant aspects of the above precautions should be included. The supplier should acknowledge in writing receipt of this confirmation of intention to purchase.
6 Ensure that service contracts guarantee restoration within an agreed time, assume liability for the behaviour of engineers, define responsibilities of contractors, and fix liability, responsibility and accountability.

Finally, as with all security-related tasks, the duties of steering the purchase through safely and the preparation of suitable contracts should be given to a named individual who should be given clear instructions in writing.

14
Software security and logical access control

The protective security features provided by and applied to the system's programs.

The software within a computer comprises (among other things) the instructions which that computer will operate to. Those instructions—the programs—will tell the computer what it should and should not do with the data, how that data is to be stored and handled, what end result is required during any manipulation of that data, and in what form and state it should be in. The computer will perform its work to the programs—no more, no less, and slavishly. A computer cannot think for itself. It is an obvious step, therefore, to include in the programs some which dictate the security of the software itself and the data contained within it. The software can be made to tell itself how to take care of itself and its data; software security refers to those protective security features provided by, and applied to, the system's programs.

14.1 The aims of software security

There are three main functions that software should try to provide, to an extent dictated of course by the nature and classification of the data being stored and processed. These functions concern in the main the confidentiality of the data, rather than its integrity or availability:

1 *Access* The software should be able to discriminate between authorized users and strangers, and deny access to the system to the latter.
2 *Separation* The software should separate the work of the various users, giving privacy to an individual's data and allowing that data to be read and manipulated by others only with its owner's permission, and in the ways that the owner allows. The database should, in effect, be compartmentalized, with crossings between discrete areas governed by predetermined rules.
3 *Audit* There should be a selective record of what has been happening on the system—such things as who has been using it, when, for how long, and what did this person do with the data. There must be a way of analysing this record.

It is these three tasks, intermingled and interdependent, that the software of a computer system should aim to perform. The computer's operating system should automatically block any unauthorized person from using the computer, prevent authorized users sharing the system from gaining access to other users' data without permission, and record system activity in order to account for the actions of those users and detect errors, abuses and security breaches.

14.2   The limitations of software security

Historically, most people working within the field of computer security have been computer professionals, and it is only recently that security staff have become involved. The security to be provided by software has always, therefore, seemed an attractive option. The computer person can understand it and relate to it. Its improvement and refinement is a challenge, regardless of cost or effort. It resides neatly within the computer system and should be entirely effective and extremely cost effective once set up. And it is potentially capable of providing everything any manager could ever hope for in looking after the confidentiality of the electronic data. Of course, there are as ever some problems to ensure that we cannot relax with software security alone in place. Indeed, the very name 'software' suggests impermanence and fragility:

- Software is very expensive to produce. Even simple programs can occupy many thousands of lines of coding, each one produced by hand. Software security programs are similarly intricate and expensive, and the more strict those measures then the more, and more expensive, coding is required. Software security can quickly become uneconomic and unworkable, and only a limited level of reliability in that software—assurance—is normally affordable by most users.
- With programs come errors. It is impossible to produce any software that does not, at least at first, contain errors. These must be removed if the software security programs are to be trusted, again an expensive process and one that can never be completely achieved.
- In any case, no software can be tested to ensure it is entirely free from error and anomaly; the larger the system and the greater the required level of assurance, then the more likely it is that the software security programs will contain errors despite rigorous checks.
- Software security occupies space within the system, reducing its available processing power. Whatever the size of the system this must be an overhead, but for a smaller system will be more significant.
- Most enterprises import hardware and software from the manufacturers and there can be no guarantees about the pedigree of any standard software, especially that which provides system security. The operating system lies at the very heart of the computer and will control its every function. Trust it to

do its job, of course, but to place total reliance on such a beast would be foolhardy.

- System staff will not normally have very detailed knowledge of their system's inner workings, having the ability only to monitor it and make minor adjustments. Deliberate or accidental flaws in the system software which could lead to a breach in security will remain undetected. Such imperfections in the software could have been introduced at those very manufacturers over which the purchaser has had no control.

- Any system evolves. The errors in the software will be repaired, improvements will be introduced and new facilities and functions incorporated. After a short while the original software will be significantly altered, and any one of those changes could have weakened, bypassed, altered or suppressed the software security features. Indeed, these software changes present in themselves an ideal opportunity for skilled programmers—perhaps the maintenance engineer about whom little is known—to deliberately bypass the security controls.

- The operating system compromises separate packets of instructions merged and knitted into a whole. Several utility programs, which perform set routines, such as add or sort into alphabetical order, will be present, and these autonomous sets of instructions can hide a multitude of sins and be used dishonestly to circumvent software security measures within their common operating system.

- Mischievous coding within the software can lie hidden, and can carry out subversive activities unseen and undetected. These 'sleepers', 'Trojan horses', 'viruses' or 'trapdoors' to name but a few can, in time, do untold damage to the software itself, get it to perform the most outrageous acts, and leak the most sensitive and valuable information to unauthorized personnel.

- The greatest threat to any computer lies with the personnel charged with its use and operation. It will be these who will be the only ones to understand to any degree the software security features of the system, and management and security staff set to monitor the computer staff will be at a great disadvantage in this respect. Any abuse of the software security features could go undetected.

- Finally, with the advent of more open systems, and networking connecting between enterprises and even countries to produce massive databases used by thousands of workers, the software security measures necessary to protect these vast computer systems are extremely difficult to achieve.

Because of its considerable limitations—the expense, the difficulty in ensuring total reliability, and the frailty—and the effectiveness and cheapness of other defensive measures that can be used to improve a computer's security, software security is not the panacea many in the computer security world would claim. It has its very great merits, and it is a vital component of any rounded computer security policy, but it should not be embraced to the exclusion of more efficient and cost-effective security solutions. A manufacturer will always push the virtues of software security to a potential customer—there is rarely any profit to be made by suggesting locks on doors, or better screening of staff, for example.

Market forces have accepted the limitations of software security. Even the most secure commercially available computer operating systems provide a far from complete degree of assurance, and the work in producing more sophisticated security features is confined almost exclusively to the government/military sector. Since computer users will therefore be provided only with a degree of assurance, certainly not to a level where total reliance can be placed on it, there will still be a need for a wide range of other security measures of the more traditional variety.

Software security is only one more of the weapons in our armoury, one more of the imperfect rings of defence in depth. With a sense of perspective, then, and with the word of caution that all manufacturers will express understandably proud but almost certainly overstated capabilities of their software security features, let us now consider in more detail exactly what it is that we must do to protect the computer software. What can it do to protect itself and the electronic information within the system? This discussion will not be technical. There is no need for a deep understanding of computer science to understand software security, as there is no need for a police officer to be a pathologist in order to investigate a murder.

14.3   Software security—general measures

There are a number of important general measures that should be taken to protect the operating system itself and other programs from damage or subversion:

- All programming activities (repairing, writing, using, etc.) must be performed under the strictest codes of discipline and procedure set down in writing and followed rigidly. The requirement to follow these rules should be included in the terms of employment in the contract signed by the employee. Any divergence from them should be dealt with severely and publicly. A company with poor programming controls will pay dearly, to everyone's disadvantage.
- Essential programs and associated documentation must be physically protected and secured to a degree appropriate to the value and importance of the computer system they serve.
- Copies of these programs and all the electronic data (and do not forget the documentation) must be stored at a back-up site, and protected to the same degree as the primary copies at the main site. This procedure is fundamental to computer operations; lack of back-up for a computer is like tightrope walking over the Niagara Falls without a safety net—it can be done, but one slip and you are dead. This aspect of computer security is discussed in more detail in Chapter 11.
- Program development must be performed in an orderly fashion, closely

monitored and supervised, checked and tested at all stages for completeness and correctness.

- Program development must be accompanied by full documentation; in a sloppy outfit this is the first area to be neglected.
- Program development must be carried out separately from the live running of the computer. Either a spare computer must be used, or the computer must be taken off-line and purged before program development or testing is carried out. The system should be once again purged before it is returned to main running.
- Programs should carry with them some form of signature to identify those members of staff who wrote them or subsequently worked on them.
- Tapes and disks containing the system's software should be identifiable at a glance and from data storage media. Access to them must be restricted to the minimum number of staff, on a strict need-to-know basis. An access list, authorized by the system manager, should be strictly adhered to and kept up to date at all times.
- A master copy of the operating system must be kept under secure conditions by the system manager and system security officer, the in-use operating system being a copy of this master. The in-use copy should be checked against the master to detect any changes to it during its exposure. Disreputable staff or accidental errors could lead to alterations to the operating system, which could harm or divert security features within it, and by comparing the two versions any such changes will show up. 'Compare' programs are available, and the system security officer should insist they are used periodically, and after system malfunction and scheduled or unscheduled hardware or software modifications.
- Other test and security routines to check the integrity of the operating system should be similarly used. Protect all such software from itself being modified or interfered with.
- Other programs within the operating system should be prevented from modifying the software security features, or from interrogating or bypassing them.
- It should not be possible to access or obtain copies of the operating system software or parts of it from any except the most trusted control terminals. Remote terminals in particular must be stopped from doing this. The operating system should have built-in protection to prevent the bypassing of security controls, for example by system staff who have gained an intimate knowledge of the computer and its software.
- All known loopholes in the operating system should have been identified by the system designers, the hardware manufacturers and the users, and the degree of exposure or risk attributable to each of these loopholes within that specific environment must be documented and brought to the attention of senior management. Forewarned is forearmed, and appreciation of one's Achilles' heel allows preparation elsewhere in the defence in depth.

- Procedures should exist which ensure that more than one person prepares, implements and tests operating system patches or new versions, to reduce the opportunities for system subversion by a single individual.
- There must be strict procedures governing the loading up and the down-loading of the operating system software. Any re-starts in the event of system failure should be especially well controlled and logged.
- The system log should include details of all system faults, either fatal (leading to system crashes and/or loss of, or corruption of, data) or non-fatal (temporary loss of facility, minor inaccuracy or abnormally long response times), and these must be reviewed regularly to detect patterns or trends of unreliability. These may reveal some inherent fault in the system or its software, or lead to the detection of some subversive change which is causing the problem and possibly some other unforeseen ones.
- All problems must be diagnosed thoroughly until the person, software component or hardware device causing the malfunction has been identified. Action must be taken to rectify the fault—do not run with 'acceptable defects'.

14.4   Software security—logical access control

The first barriers erected by the software of the computer are those designed to check on the identity of all those asking permission to use the system. Only those users authorized by the system manager should be let on to the system, and then only to those areas and/or classifications necessary and appropriate. In this context, a user can be an individual or a group of workers on, say, a project or who all carry the same level of security clearance, or indeed a computer program or routine operating on behalf of some other authorized program or person.

There are three ways of identifying a user trying to access the system:

1 *Something he or she has* Possession of such items as keys, magnetic cards, smart cards, personal identification devices and tokens is regarded by the computer as authority to access the system, but clearly loss of the token can lead to its use by some unauthorized party. Lending of tokens is another danger.

2 *Something he or she is* Biometric identification is an alternative which involves 'reading' a person's fingertips, or signature, or voice print, or hand geometry, or retina image, or pattern of veins on the back of the hand, or size, or weight . . . the list can continue. These techniques are not reliable, are expensive, and often inconvenient and unpleasant to use. There is little mileage in this area at present, since there is much work still to be done before such techniques are technically and economically viable. In any case, there is little merit in making matters more complicated than necessary when there are perfectly acceptable alternatives that are cheap and simple.

3 *Something he or she knows* A password. The only problems with password

access control involve the people who use them. If managed properly, password identification provides security of a standard quite sufficient for all including the most sensitive and valuable computer systems, especially so if combined with something the user has. It is your staff who will let you down before the password system does, and no fancy means of identification will change this.

Ideally, an access control policy should bring together at least two of these: most often a password is combined with a token. An everyday example is the bank chequebook with a password—the signature, something the owner knows— having to be presented with a cheque card—the token, something the owner has—before the presenter is permitted 'access' to the money.

14.4.1 Password security

Passwords are used to afford access to a computer, and are associated with individual users, groups of users, or system staff. After identifying themselves to the system, and possibly presenting a key or token, users offer the password to the system either by entering it via a terminal or by including it with documents used in the processing. The computer compares the password with a list of approved passwords held in the software. If matched, the user is 'authenticated', awarded access, and granted predetermined privileges that specify those actions the user is able to perform on the data he or she has been allowed to get to:

- *Execute* A user can execute (run) a program, but will not be allowed to read the coding or alter it.
- *Read* The user can read a file, but no data can be written back into it.
- *Write* The user can place data into a file, but not be able to read any of the data in that file.
- *Read–Write* The user can read a file and write into it; in effect the file becomes part of the user's space on the computer.
- *Append* The user can add to the data within a file, but is not allowed to read the file or change any data already within it.
- *Delete* The user can delete the data in a file.

Depending on the nature of the privileges granted in advance by the system manager, the user may access certain (or indeed all) areas of the database and perform work on the files again as determined in advance. The detail with which this is achieved, and the control the system can exert over each user, each privilege and each file is called the granularity of the software security, in the same spirit as the granularity of a photograph.

The comparison between a user's password and the agreed password held by the system against this name does not in itself provide any security protection and cannot be made to do so. The security of the password system depends entirely on the protection afforded to the password, both in the possession of the user and in the computer's master list. Password security is paramount. No matter how strong a door, or how clever a lock, all is worth nothing if the key is not cared for and falls into the hands of another.

The use of passwords has fallen into disrepute, since users are notoriously difficult to educate about the weaknesses they themselves introduce by choosing very short passwords, or by choosing items like the names of their children or their spouse. The practised and determined attacker, if this is allowed to happen, can carry out a little research and with only a few guesses find the right password. Even if users are given passwords, they immediately become convinced they will forget them and resort to writing them down on the backs of their desk calendars or on scraps of paper fixed to the undersides of their telephones! Strict procedures will make the password an adequate form of access control for all but the very sensitive or valuable systems, but poor control over their generation, issue and use will make them less than useless.

14.4.2 Issue of passwords

A password should only be issued to a user holding the appropriate security clearance and authority for access which that password will permit. Knowledge of passwords should not be granted solely on account of position or status. Passwords for classified systems should be allocated by the system security officer. Passwords intended for such issue should be protected by this person as if they were able to gain access to the most highly classified data on the system. They must only ever be issued once, and not used again after being withdrawn.

Passwords may be created by the users for less sensitive or valuable systems, but the dangers associated with this option include:

1   Users not changing their passwords at the proper intervals, or changing them only slightly.
2   Users not recording their passwords anywhere, nor updating the record after any change.
3   For ease of memory, users choosing some obvious or associated word, such as spouse's name, or car registration number. Such passwords, with only a little knowledge of the individual, can be easily guessed. Indeed, it is the disaffected worker who represents the greatest threat to the system, and just this sort of person will have the necessary personal knowledge to figure out the office companion's password. Incidentally, a recent review discovered that the most common passwords in use were the words PASSWORD and SECRET . . . need any more be said?

14.4.3 Protection of passwords

A password is a key, and it must be looked after in a manner appropriate to what it is protecting. Indeed, as a computer password will often give access to great volumes of data its worth is even more enhanced.

The rules governing the control of passwords are as follows:

1   Passwords must be changed at least every six months, though this period should be much less for access to valuable or sensitive data and can be as short as you like.

2   Shared passwords should be changed as soon as a person with knowledge of that password is replaced, or leaves the job (even on promotion and/or within the company), or no longer requires access.

3   A password should be changed immediately if it is in any way suspected that it may have become compromised, or if access to it has been necessary for emergency purposes. Any actual or suspected compromises of passwords must be investigated. Any misuse of passwords must be reported to the system security officer.

4   Passwords should be committed to users' memories and not recorded anywhere, especially in the user's desk diary and so on, except in the following circumstances:

   (a) They are to be written down for emergency use only.
   (b) Each written record is to be sealed in a separate envelope marked on the outside with brief details of the computer to which it allows access, and the names of those users authorized to have access to the password.
   (c) The envelope is to be graded to the same level as the highest classification of data within the computer to which the password refers. The user of the password is to sign across the flap, and add the date, after the flap is sealed.
   (d) The envelopes are to be held by the system security officer or the departmental security officer. Knowledge of the password is to be limited to those persons nominated on the envelope.

5   If duplicate passwords are to be stored electronically instead, within the computer itself, such files must be carefully protected from unauthorized access, and backed up in case the in-use software is lost or damaged. Authorized access to the list must be strictly limited to the minimum number of highly trusted members of staff, and then under the two-person rule. Password listings should whenever possible be stored in encrypted form to make them unreadable should any unauthorized access be effected.

6   Passwords should never appear on any output, especially hard copy. They should not appear on the VDU screen during log-on, to prevent overlooking. Overlooking of terminal keyboards should also be prevented during the log-on process, and staff should be alert for, and report at once, others attempting to look over shoulders.

7   Passwords should normally have a minimum of eight characters. These should be of alphanumeric construction—letters (upper and lower case), numbers and spaces—in a random order. There are ways of trying the few thousand common words of eight letters or less in the English language in

only a few minutes, given access to the computer. It is inevitable, though, that words will be chosen, in which case they must at the very least not be connected in any way with the user.

8   Computers should allow only a limited number of attempts to enter a password, normally a maximum of three. If this limit is exceeded by a user, this fact should be reported at once to the system manager or security officer, with an attention-getter alarm if necessary, and investigated. At the same time, the user should be locked out of the system and denied access until the matter has been satisfactorily resolved and the system manager has re-authorized the user. For classified systems, it may be prudent to lock out the user without letting him or her know; while the user continues the attempt to access the system, he or she can be apprehended in the act and asked to explain these actions.

9   Once into the system, users must not be able to change their identity after initial log-on in order to confuse the system or nullify the security features to allow access to data to which they are not entitled, or to perform actions for which they have not been granted privilege. Users must not be able to leave their assigned space, nor to violate the space of other users.

10 If a terminal is used for a long period, the authentication process should be repeated at intervals to make sure the authorized user has not been replaced at the terminal by some usurper. If a terminal remains inactive, it should log off automatically after a given period (say 10 minutes), in case the authorized user has wandered off.

11 At log-on, the computer should let the user know the last time his or her password was used, as a check to the user that it has not been used by someone else.

14.4.4   Dual passwords

For very sensitive areas of the computer's database, such as the operating system itself or the files containing the password listings, there should be a dual password control, like the dual keys on a bank vault where both the manager and the chief cashier need to be present before it can be opened. The advantages are clear—the two-person principle is enforced without exception, no one person is allowed unsupervised access to these most valuable and sensitive areas of the software and database, and any actions taken during the period when access is granted can be checked at all stages by the second person. However:

•   The two people should not always be the same, to inhibit collusion between individuals.
•   The procedure must be properly followed; there is little point in Freda and Harry accessing the operating system together if Harry then wanders off to do his own thing, leaving Freda a free agent.
•   Both people need to know what is going on. Harry, the guard, will not know

if Freda, the programmer, is doing something dishonest or dangerous, even if he watches her every move.

14.4.5 Tokens

The principal difficulty with access control security is that it is a nuisance to the authorized users. This nuisance factor cannot be easily removed, but it is possible to design systems which enforce better discipline on the part of the user, and which make the user more accountable for the secure access rights that have been granted. One of the main ways to do this is to provide the user with a token over which physical control must be maintained. It can be emphasized that the user is responsible for the use of the token, and any breach of the security by its misuse will be regarded as a personal failure. Such can be included in the contract of employment.

The tokens themselves are various, starting with the simple console key. The magnetic stripe card is now common too, though card readers are needed at every terminal, which is a definite cost disadvantage. Smart cards—magnetic stripe cards with implanted microprocessors—have the ability to decide how, when and where they are to be used and will become more popular as their costs reduce.

There are now available products that make use of a hand-held calculator-style device. The calculator is a special encryption unit which produces random personal authentication values (passwords) which are keyed into the terminal in the normal way and matched with a similar device within the computer. No special card readers are required, the process being controlled from the heart of the system. These, then, are an attractive enhancement of the simple password principle.

14.5   Software security—separation

Allied with the techniques for identifying users and awarding them access to the computer system are the software security measures that build separations between items of data held on the database. Whatever their form, the purpose of these barriers is common: to prevent unauthorized access by one user to the data or programs of another, especially if either differing levels of security classification or need to know are involved.

In the good old days before computers, information resided on paper, on files contained within filing cabinets within registries large and small. Sometimes the files within a registry were all the same classification, or files of differing classifications were held together. Sometimes there were no controls at all over access to files, or what people could do with them; you just walked in and helped yourself. Sometimes registry clerks did their best to control the files, and usually you only got to those you were allowed to see; occasionally mistakes were made and you ended up with those belonging to someone else, or one classified higher

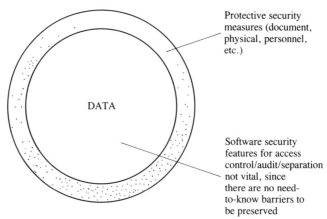

Figure 14.1.   Dedicated mode of secure processing.

than you were supposed to see, and you returned it at once with little more said since everyone trusted each other to be honest. If you were unlucky, the clerk was difficult and you saw nothing and did nothing unless you had his or her permission, often a real nuisance but always most secure and you could leave your files safe in this person's hands. The ways in which the registries were run depended on the nature and importance of the information, but also to a great extent on the effort management was willing or able to give to document security.

With the modern marvel of computers, all these files are held within the computer system, stored on magnetic media, called forward when needed and processed in a variety of ways. The computer is its own registry; the ways in which it controls access by the users to its files—the modes of secure processing—bear a remarkable resemblance to the traditional registry.

14.5.1   Dedicated mode of secure processing

The computer processes data of a single classification at any one time. There are no access or need-to-know constraints within the system, so that once a user has been allowed through the security screen surrounding the database he or she is entirely free to wander among all the information (Fig. 14.1).

Since total freedom is granted to users, each must be cleared for access to the most valuable or sensitive data held within the system.

14.5.2   System high mode of secure processing

Here, the computer processes data of more than one classification at any one time, but not all users will be allowed to see all the data. Privacy barriers are erected to prevent free range within the database, limiting access to files to certain approved groups of users (Fig. 14.2).

Since there is no guarantee about the strength of the internal privacy barriers,

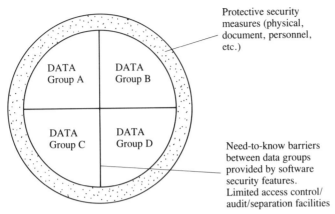

Protective security measures (physical, document, personnel, etc.)

Need-to-know barriers between data groups provided by software security features. Limited access control/ audit/separation facilities

Figure 14.2.   System high mode of processing.

all users must still be cleared for access to the most valuable or sensitive data in the system, just in case a mistake is made and they are allowed to see data normally beyond their remit.

14.5.3   *Controlled mode of secure processing*

The computer processes data of more than one classification at any one time. With a combination of extensive software security measures and supportive non-computer controls (such as strict procedures, tight supervision of staff, and physical, document, personnel and other measures), high assurance can be given to the barriers within the operating system. The fences between files are sufficiently strong and reliable to mean that, under normal conditions, no user can stray from his or her area or exceed the awarded privileges to gain access or interfere with the data belonging to another. Since one user is not able to gain access outside his or her bounds, there is no requirement to clear staff beyond their levels of access (Fig. 14.3).

14.5.6   *Multi-level mode of secure processing*

The computer processes data of more than one classification at any one time. The software security features within the system's operating system themselves ensure beyond any doubt that users are not allowed to access any data they are not authorized to, and there is therefore no need to clear personnel beyond the level to which they are authorized (Fig. 14.4).

Of these four modes of secure processing, the dedicated is the simplest and therefore the cheapest; indeed, there may be no software security features at all included within the operating system, control being restricted to non-computer features such as physical security. Multi-level standards have rarely been achieved, and then at such expense and with such constraints on system use and software maintenance as to make them all but irrelevant to the great majority of

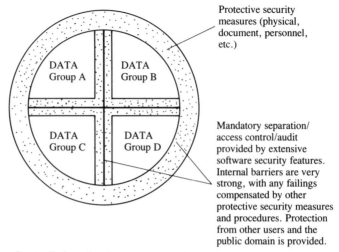

Protective security measures (physical, document, personnel, etc.)

Mandatory separation/ access control/audit provided by extensive software security features. Internal barriers are very strong, with any failings compensated by other protective security measures and procedures. Protection from other users and the public domain is provided.

Figure 14.3.   Controlled mode of secure processing.

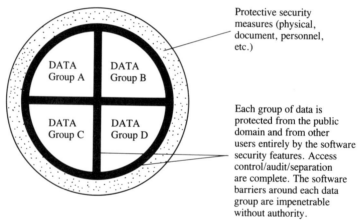

Protective security measures (physical, document, personnel, etc.)

Each group of data is protected from the public domain and from other users entirely by the software security features. Access control/audit/separation are complete. The software barriers around each data group are impenetrable without authority.

Figure 14.4.   Multi-level mode of secure processing.

enterprises. Controlled systems are feasible, but the security overheads are extremely demanding, and there is little need for this level of software sophistication except at the most sensitive or valuable installations.

The system high mode is the most common and the most convenient to use. It is achievable if only because it does not try for impossible standards of assurance; it is affordable since of the range of software security features it employs only the simple and practical elements, boosted by other non-technical security measures; and it allows the computer to work in that most common of work environments—the general office with a variety of users working with data of differing nature and classification. All users must be cleared for access to the highest classification held on the database in case the barriers fail, of course, but this is easier and cheaper than complicated software security.

The choice for most people therefore is between a system high or a dedicated arrangement. Both these provide software security which is incomplete but which can easily be boosted by other defensive measures. A good system high computer provides very adequate levels of data separation for the needs of most companies. There is no real need to understand how the software provides the security, simply what can be done.

14.6   Software security—audit

Software can be set up to monitor and record the use of the computer. An unbroken chronological journal—an audit trail—can be maintained of all programs, files and data records to which access, or attempted access, has been made for any job or transaction. Access to this log should be restricted to staff authorized by the system manager and system security officer. In most systems the following details should be recorded:

- date and time of access
- terminal used
- job identification
- program identification
- file identification
- activity (read, write, delete etc.)
- number of pages of printout produced, and the classification of this output

Tools should be available to allow the sifting and analysis of this record. It must be possible, for example, to find out such things as any user regularly using the system out of normal working hours, or taking an inordinate amount of printout. Without such tools, and for a busy system, an unmanageable and therefore useless amount of audit trail will soon build up. In effect, most operating system audit trails will selectively audit the system use, discarding records that fall within the acceptable norms and making note only of unusual actions or activity, such as an abnormally high number of incorrect log-on attempts by a user, or the unauthorized use of a peripheral (a printer, say) by a user.

In particular, the audit trail should be able to create and print out a system error log at regular intervals for inspection by the system security officer. This log should record:

1 Any failure of hardware or software mechanisms.
2 The abnormal termination of a job, and system crashes.
3 Abnormally short times between re-starts, indicating perhaps that a user is deliberately crashing the system either to cover up his or her crimes or while trying to find new back doors into the system.
4 Unsuccessful attempts to log-on to the system. A user might be trying to break a password, or might be browsing through the system. If a user appears to be logging on at very frequent intervals it may be that the password has become known to an unauthorized user and is being used for less than honest purposes.

5   Attempts to gain unauthorized access to files, especially sensitive or valuable
     ones, and an unexplained increase in the use of any valuable or sensitive files.
6   Attempts to use privileges not awarded.

It should be used to detect possible trends and thus track down individuals
who are misusing, or attempting to misuse, the system. Manual logs should be
used in conjunction with the audit trail, and a good security officer should view
all system activity with a jaundiced eye.

A system of automatic internal checks should be provided where a detected
failure of any protective security mechanism within the operating system, the
software or the hardware should cause the system to enter into a unique
operating mode whereby access is restricted solely to the system manager and the
system security officer until the fault has been tracked down and rectified. In
short, if something goes wrong with the system's defences the software security
features should lock everyone out and freeze the system until the matter has been
investigated by the authorities.

All these various logs and records should be retained for an appropriate
period. The information held within the records may in itself become classified,
and must be marked and handled accordingly. The custody of the records must
be vigorously protected, and strict measures taken to prevent abstraction and/or
substitution. The new technology of optical disks is ideally suited to the retention
of electronic audit trails; great amounts of data can be held on very small disks,
and since the information committed to the optical disks is not to be deleted and
the space rewritten, this medium is entirely satisfactory.

Audit trails should include all activities, even those of the system manager and
system security officer. The activities of any staff used to test the system's
security features, and any other specially privileged users particularly those who
are not from within the company's staff, must be audited. Do not forget the
maintenance engineer.

14.7   Software security—programming

Procedures should be established to provide control of software design and
development, to ensure that unauthorized changes to the software in general, and
the security features in particular, are not made. Such changes, either accidental
or deliberate, could simply harm the computer and its operations, or they could
subvert software security measures, or defraud and deceive. To prevent this:

1   There must be separate design, production and testing facilities so that
     software can be produced away from the live system until it has been fully
     checked, tested and approved.
2   Software that is not developed systematically in a controlled, supervised and
     fully documented manner may not meet the system's needs or standards and
     can cause poor service and generate system faults. Such software is likely to

contain more faults, making it easier for unauthorized personnel to penetrate the system. It is also easier for a member of the programming staff to misuse the system either for personal gain or as a result of subversion.

3   Programming activity should be assigned and initiated by the system manager, and individuals should wherever possible work in teams. The system security officer should be aware of all programming activities. Under no circumstances should programmers be allowed to generate system software without the approval in advance of the system manager and the knowledge of the system security officer. All programmers and their work should be uniquely identified to the system.

4   All system software must be thoroughly documented. This documentation must be up to date, and reflect all versions and the current status. It must be protected appropriately, bearing in mind that it will almost certainly contain information that could aid unauthorized penetration of the operating system. The system security committee should ensure that this proper documentation is maintained, and that the software does indeed contain the necessary security features.

5   All new software should be verified and validated prior to its introduction into active service. If possible it should be tested on a computer system separate from that used for live operations. If this is not possible, the new software must be loaded and tested on the live system in a way which has minimum effect on users and operations, and which leaves the system exposed as little as possible. The system manager should monitor the testing and maintain records as appropriate.

6   If possible, penetration tests should be carried out by knowledgeable programmers other than the software developers, to identify any obvious faults or omissions.

7   All changes to system software should be initiated and approved by the system manager. They must go through the same rigorous control processes as any newly written software (verification, documentation and testing), and again the system security officer should be kept informed of all changes.

8   There should be strictly defined procedures for initial start-up, re-start, scheduled and unscheduled shut-down, and system failure/crash, and the system manager must ensure these are enforced at all times.

9   The software security can be made to check the format of the data entered by users—input validation—to ensure it is in the proper form. A variety of checks can be carried out on data while it is being processed—processing controls—to check for and correct errors. A number of features such as item counts and control totals can be produced at the end of a job—output controls—to determine if an error has occurred.

10 While all programs should be protected as described, those which are particularly critical and require special protection and controls should be identified and security resources concentrated upon them.

14.8   Covert channels

Despite all the care one might take to secure the data within a computer system, all can be compromised by some hidden leak in the defences. Such covert communication channels can be exploited to transfer data out of the system by an unauthorized person. Covert channels come in two sorts:

- *Storage channels* These allow the direct or indirect writing of a storage location by one process, or the direct or indirect reading of it by another.
- *Timing channels* These allow one process to signal information to another process by virtue of its timing.

Such covert channels—an everyday example would be the number of boots ordered by a general revealing the size of his army—can never be totally excluded, since the very design of most systems creates them in many ways. However, for all except the most sensitive of systems, and provided the designers of the system have reduced them to a minimum number and then to a minimum bandwidth (size), covert channels are not a real danger and can be dismissed from the security considerations for all but the most valuable or sensitive of systems.

14.9   Some final thoughts . . .

Software security is a highly complex subject, and the measures for protecting information are numerous, varied and extremely useful. The security officer will need to rely heavily on the experience and honesty of the system staff, and the special relationship which should be developed between them is particularly important, if for this aspect alone.

System integrity will depend on the incorporation of a variety of software security measures both during the development of new software and during its maintenance. Testing of software security should be an on-going process, and adequate resources should be made available to ensure that the system's integrity is maintained.

Do not be frightened of software security. If you don't understand something, find someone you trust who does and ask. But also, do not be bamboozled by software security experts who try to convince you it is perfect. Remain sceptical, but at the same time recognize that it does have very fine qualities and uses.

Totally reliable software security is still a long way off, making the support of it with defence in depth using other, traditional, security measures that much more important.

15
Evaluation, certification and accreditation

When I was a lad, eggs used to come with little lions stamped on them. When I buy electrical equipment I always make sure it carries the British Standards Institution kite mark. My car carries the 'E' mark which confirms it has been manufactured to the Government's required standards. These are examples of certifications—formal statements that something has been evaluated (examined) against certain predetermined standards of safety, reliability or quality and has passed.

Now that it has as many wrinkles and dents and is as well passed its first flush of youth as its owner, my faithful old Volvo has to go through the annual Ministry of Transport test, which examines its roadworthiness. My many friends who fly commercial aeroplanes for a living passed the necessary examinations a decade or more ago, but they have to undergo regular stringent check-rides to confirm they are still able to fly the aeroplane under both normal conditions and during simulated emergencies; fortunately for us mere passengers they are not allowed to continue flying unless they pass these reviews. These examples of accreditation confirm that, regardless of certificates, the product or service is maintaining the required standards *within the real world.*

Evaluation leading to certification and confirmed by accreditation provide a degree of confidence in something or some service, for ourselves or of ourselves. I knew the eggs were British—of course that made them taste better but I still hated eggs—and I know my electrical equipment will be safe if I use it properly. I know my car complies to basic safety and quality standards of manufacture, and I and other road users know that at least once a year someone who understands these things checks the car over to make sure the brakes still brake, the steering still steers and the tyres aren't too tired! We can be confident that our pilots have not only passed their flying examinations but that they are regularly re-examined in the cockpit environment so that when they set off down the runway they still know what to do and how to get themselves out of trouble if something goes wrong.

In exactly the same way, owners, managers and users of computers need confidence in the security of their system, and yardsticks against which to measure the security capabilities of IT products they are thinking of buying. Of course, they could rely upon word of mouth from manufacturers or vendors of the systems and products in question, or they could test them themselves. But it must be better and more efficient to have some form of impartial assessment by an independent body against objective and well-defined security evaluation criteria of a system's security in its operational environment. In this context, then:

- *Evaluation* is the assessment of an IT system or product against defined security evaluation criteria, at present usually technical. It leads to certification.
- *Certification* is the issue of a formal statement (the certificate) confirming the results of the security evaluation. It is part of the more comprehensive process of system accreditation.
- *Accreditation* is the procedure for accepting an IT system for use within a particular environment. In addition to the certification it requires a number of other factors to be taken into account before a system can be viewed as fit for its intended purpose, such as:
  –compliance with relevant technical and legal/regulatory requirements;
  –confirmation of management responsibilities for security;
  –confidence in the adequacy of other non-technical security measures provided in the system environment.

The earliest work in the development of security evaluation criteria was performed during the early 1980s in the USA. In 1983 the US Department of Defense (DoD) produced the Trusted Computer System Evaluation Criteria (TCSEC) for product evaluation, in its document affectionately known as the Orange Book (simply because of the colour of its cover). Accompanying publications were later issued to offer guidelines for implementation and support in areas such as configuration management, password management, networks and databases. The whole series has come to be known as the Rainbow Series.

Portability of criteria, though, was a problem, and the Orange Book was a good start, but far from adequate. Military and Government demands are entirely different from those of the commercial sector, and the standards laid down in the USA were not always acceptable elsewhere. Political, technical and economic pressures lead to other countries, mostly European, and who themselves had gained significant experience in IT security evaluation, developing their own IT security criteria, with inevitable confusion, duplication of effort, unnecessary artificial barriers to international trade, and unnecessary development and implementation costs. In the UK, for example, the Department of Trade and Industry (DTI) published evaluation criteria for commercial IT security products in its Green Book (DTIEC). The German Information Security Agency (GISA) published a first version of its own criteria (ZSIEC), and at the same time criteria were developed by the Service Central de la Sécurité des Systèmes d'Information in France, the so-called Blue–White–Red Book (SCSSI).

Harmonized criteria became essential and have now been produced, building upon these various national initiatives and merging the best features of what had already been done and extending them where appropriate. In its first draft in 1990 the *Information Technology Security Evaluation Criteria (ITSEC)— Harmonised Criteria of France, Germany, the Netherlands and the United Kingdom* became known at once as the White Book!

15.1   The 'Orange Book'—the US Department of Defense trusted computer system evaluation criteria (TCSEC)

The US Department of Defense (DoD) has adopted a policy of describing the efficacy of the software security features on a system's operating system by allocating it to one of a range of divisions. In this way, it is hoped to identify easily those computer systems that come supplied with hardware and software security features of given standards, rather like the various models within the range of a particular car can be described according to the extras provided and the size of engine—'2.0 GLS', or '2.3 Ghia Fuel Injection', for example. The DoD divisions and their criteria have been developed to serve a number of intended purposes:

1   As a guide to manufacturers as to what software security features should be built into their computer systems;
2   As a benchmark against which the software security features of computers can be judged;
3   As a basis for specifying what software security features are required in any new or planned computer system.

These trusted computer system evaluation criteria concentrate on confidentiality and envisage that the security features of the operating system are contained within one area of it. This so-called trusted computing base (TCB) is considered as separate from the rest of the operating system, isolated and protected from abuse and subversion and providing, as the name suggests, a base from which the rest of the system's programs can operate safely and securely. The TCB should be as simple as possible consistent with the degree of security it has to supply, to help this isolation and to make it as reliable as possible. The TCB should be seen as a trusted base from which computing may safely proceed.

15.1.1   The divisions

There are four divisions of criteria, from D to A, with the latter proving the most comprehensive security. Each division represents a major improvement in the overall confidence that can be placed on the ability of the system and its software security features to protect sensitive or valuable data. The criteria are based on four factors, each of which must be proved acceptable before the TCB can be said to be in the designated division.

Security countermeasures

The actual software security features which aim to prevent deliberate or inadvertent access to data by unauthorized persons, and stop unauthorized use of the computer system, fall into three specific types:

> *Mandatory security controls* Access control measures to ensure that only authorized personnel have access to the system, and then of those any who do not have the appropriate security clearance or need to know do not gain access to information to which they are not entitled. Users must not be able to change the location of classified data within the system (in order that such information is not made available to unauthorized users). Equally, it must not be possible to transfer data to a storage area designated for a lower classification unless that data has been correctly downgraded, and the downgrading and transfer properly authorized. These are the strict security controls intended for multi-level or controlled modes of secure processing. They are mandatory, the user has no part to play in them.

> *Discretionary security controls*   A less strict regime of controls, where an individual user is allowed to specify access by other users to his data. Access-control is implemented on a need-to-know basis. Discretionary security controls are not a replacement for mandatory controls, but provide additional restrictions within the security safeguards of the operating system software. On their own, however, they are best suited for system high or dedicated modes of secure processing.

> *Labelling controls* To enable security controls to work, especially the mandatory ones, the computer must label each item of information with its appropriate security and/or privacy classification. The labels must be at least at file level, and must be inseparable from the information. In traditional terms, this equates to marking paper files in indelible ink with the appropriate classification for the papers inside. Once data is thus unalterably and accurately labelled, control over it can be properly and consistently enforced. The label must be generated automatically whenever the data is printed or displayed.

Accountability

The computer must identify each user, and authenticate this identification and the user's access rights to the information that is demanded. In addition, an audit trail must record all access to, and manipulation and production of, information so that the actions of an individual user can be monitored and traced by management and security.

Assurance

The computer must ensure that its software security measures have not been corrupted or bypassed. The TCB must be carefully evaluated and tested during the design and development of the computer system, and re-evaluated at regular intervals and whenever changes are made which could affect the integrity of the TCB and its security measures. There must be assurance that the system's software security is working as designed and intended.

Documentation

There are certain items of documentation which relate to the system's software security features, and which must be prepared and maintained correctly:

• security features specification
• trusted system manual
• test documentation
• design documentation

Such documentation will differ in depth and nature according to the extent of software security measures within the TCB, but will always try to detail the security features of the TCB to provide a record of the design of the security features, and to describe the manufacturer's tests on them and the results.

15.1.2   Summary of evaluation criteria divisions and classes

The divisions of systems recognized under the TCB evaluation criteria are as follows. The divisions can be further split into classes.

Division D: Minimal protection

This division of one class only is reserved for those systems that have been evaluated but that fail to meet the requirements for a higher evaluation class.

Division C: Discretionary protection

Classes within this division provide discretionary (need to know) protection to the data, and through the inclusion of audit a degree of accountability of users and the actions they perform or attempt to perform.

> *Class C1: Discretionary security protection*   A TCB awarded C1 provides limited separation of users and data. Its access control facilities allow users to protect project or private information and stop other users from accidentally reading or destroying this data. This low level of software security is designed for cooperating users processing data at the same level of sensitivity or worth.

Class C2: Controlled access protection   TCBs in this class enforce a more finely grained discretionary access control than C1 TCBs, making users individually accountable for their actions through log-on procedures, auditing of security relevant events, and resource isolation.

Division B: Mandatory protection

TCBs seeking this award must be able to preserve the integrity of sensitivity labels on the data, and use them to enforce a set of mandatory access control rules.

Class B1: Labelled security protection   In addition to all the features of Division C TCBs, Class B1 TCBs must provide data labelling and mandatory access control over named users and items of data. The capability must exist for accurately labelling information exported out of the system (on printout, for example, or into a network). Any flaws identified during the testing of the TCB must have been removed.

Class B2: Structured protection   In this class, the TCB requires the discretionary and mandatory access controls present in Class B1 to be extended to all users and items of data, and there must be more extensive testing and documentation. Authentication mechanisms are stronger, and the system is relatively resistant to penetration.

Class B3: Security domains   Class B3 TCBs should mediate all access of users to data, be tamperproof, and be small enough to allow thorough analysis and testing. To this end, the TCB will be structured to exclude non-essential code, and will have been designed and constructed deliberately to minimize its complexity. Audit mechanisms are extended, and system recovery procedures are required. The system will be highly resistant to penetration.

Division A: Verified protection

This division is characterized by the use of formal security verification methods to ensure that the mandatory and discretionary security controls employed in the system can effectively protect classified information stored or processed by the system. Extensive documentation will be required to show that the TCB meets the security requirements in all aspects of design, development and implementation.

Class A1: Verified design Systems in this class are functionally equivalent to those in Class B3 in that no additional security features are added. The distinguishing feature of systems in this class is the analysis derived from formal design specification and verification techniques

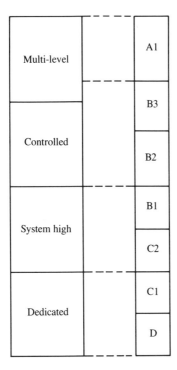

Figure 15.1.   Modes of secure processing and the 'Orange Book'.

(usually mathematical and very complicated) and the resulting high assurance that can be placed in the TCB. Procedures will be established for securely distributing the system to sites.

Beyond Class A1?   At this stage, systems beyond Class A1 are of academic interest only because most of the security enhancements envisaged for such systems, which will provide features and assurance in addition to those already provided by A1 systems, are beyond current technology. As more and better analysis techniques are developed, the requirements for these systems will become more explicit.

15.1.3 *Relating the orange book to the modes of secure processing*

The DoD criteria and the modes of secure processing are not unrelated—they each describe the capabilities of the operating system software security features, though from different perspectives (Fig. 15.1). It is reasonable to compare the two concepts:

- The dedicated mode of secure processing relates most obviously with the D Division and Class C1.
- The C2/B1 classes equate to the system high mode of secure processing.
- The B2/B3 classes equate to the controlled mode of secure processing.

- It would seem likely that a system would have to achieve a Class A1 rating before it could be considered as operating within the multi-level mode of secure processing. Some upper-B systems however are being regarded, possibly justifiably, as multi-level.

Most users need a dedicated or system high computer system; most computer systems provide from D Division to at best Class B1 software security standards. For those rare organizations that need to operate at controlled level, there are a few B2/B3 systems on the market, but they are expensive. Multi-level standards of software security are not generally affordable to the commercial sector. The standards, the requirements of users, the capabilities of the manufacturers, and market forces have all combined to create the inevitable compromise.

Software security can never be made totally reliable. As long as non-computer security measures are required, since software security measures are expensive, and since traditional security is invariably cheaper, users should (and do) settle for a compromise of a reasonable degree of assurance from the system's software boosted by traditional security measures. Most users need a system high system at the most; this is confirmed by the fact that of systems available commercially, two-thirds are of C2/B1 standard, and only a fraction achieve a higher level than this. Even within the military sector, only 10 per cent are B2 or higher.

15.1.4   The commercial product evaluation process

The commercial computer security evaluation process is aimed at 'off the shelf' commercially produced products, and is focused on general purpose operating systems that meet the needs of government departments and agencies. The evaluation does not consider overall system performance, potential applications, or particular processing environments. It is only the first part in the overall system security evaluation, which would take into account all the other security factors and features. The evaluation falls into three distinct elements.

Preliminary product evaluation

An informal dialogue between a vendor and the examining authority, to create an understanding of the product, the criteria and the rating that the product may expect to gain. Since it is generally very difficult to add effective security measures late in the project development and design, system vendors, who typically initiate the evaluation, should approach the examining authority as early as possible. After non-disclosure agreements have been signed, which require the examining authority to maintain the confidentiality of any proprietary information supplied to it, the vendor then provides details about the system, especially its internal designs and goals, in return for expert advice about its development and interpretation of the criteria as they apply. During the preliminary evaluation the vendor is under no obligation actually to complete or market the potential product, nor is the examining authority obliged to continue further into the evaluation process. Either side can stop the evaluation at any time. At the end, a private report for the vendor is produced.

Formal product evaluation

Once the product is ready, and the necessary documentation has been prepared, it can move forward to formal evaluation. A team is formed to test a working version of the product against each requirement, and the vendor is informed of faults or weaknesses as they are discovered so that as many as possible can be put right before the evaluation is complete. A final report is then produced which is publicly available (though any proprietary or sensitive information will have been removed); it will contain details of the team's findings and the overall rating awarded.

Evaluated products list

A list of products that have been subjected to formal evaluation and their assigned ratings.

15.1.5 The limitations of the Orange Book and the evaluation process

There is no doubt that the Orange Book has become an important reference document in the computer security world. Indeed, there are those for whom it has become a bible, and the evaluation process their all-consuming goal. However, there are some important aspects of the book and the associated evaluation process which limit their worth:

1 The book is some years old now, and relates primarily to mainframe technology. But since then networking has blossomed, resources have been distributed down to the user's desk, and the PC has come into being.
2 The book is not easy to read even for a computer expert. There are supplements to it, relating to such as passwords and networking, and these add to the confusion.
3 The book is designed with government needs in mind, with high standards of software security which are to the commercial sector perhaps irrelevant and unnecessary.
4 The examining authorities are overworked, and will concentrate understandably on the systems intended for government use. Purely commercial systems are unlikely to be so tested, and despite the fact that a system might provide perfectly sound software security, it will not be awarded a grading simply because it has not been tested.
5 On the other hand, and some say unfairly, those fortunate to have been evaluated have a great advantage.

6   Frustrated vendors, or indeed less than honest ones, attribute their own gradings—'B3 Equivalent' and the like. Such claims are misleading and meaningless, and are often exaggerated. They undermine the whole process.

7   Systems need to be shoe-horned into gradings. Unnecessary features are supplied simply in order to meet the requirements of the necessary grading, and some perfectly sound systems may not reach a higher grading because of a weakness in some feature which may not even be needed.

Nevertheless, the DoD criteria exist, they have won a place in the hearts of most computer security people, and they do have a useful role to play.

15.2   ITSEC—Europe's IT security evaluation scheme

ITSEC represents the European Community's commitment to a viable set of IT security evaluation criteria specifically designed for the commercial environment where integrity and continuity are often the major issues ahead of the all-important military consideration of confidentiality. They do not aim to challenge the Orange Book, but to complement it. Indeed, alongside the development of ITSEC have been equally conscientious efforts to ensure their applicability and compatibility with existing criteria, in particular the Orange Book. They were written to be applicable to all sectors (commercial, governmental and defence), to cover both products and systems, to cover all classes of security policy, to be equally applicable to technical security measures implemented in hardware, software or firmware, and to encompass confidentiality, integrity and continuity.

15.2.1   Terminology

The criteria use the following definitions, which it is important for us to understand before the scheme itself is described;

Target of Evaluation (TOE)   The product or system under evaluation.

Sponsor   The person or enterprise that requests an evaluation.

IT System   A specific IT System with a particular purpose and known operational environment.

IT Product   A hardware and/or software package that can be bought off the shelf and incorporated into a variety of systems.

Security Target   A specification in which the sponsor defines the security enforcing functions against which the TOE will be evaluated. It will comprise:

(a) either a system security policy or a product rationale;
(b) a specification of the required security enforcing functions;
(c) a definition of required security mechanisms (optional);

(d) the claimed rating of the minimum strength of mechanisms;

(e) the target evaluation level.

System Security Target   The technical security objectives of the system, fully stated in natural language.

Product Security Target   A developer's specific security claims for a product, made as a clear statement and in formal language.

Product Rationale   Description of the security capabilities of a product.

Functionality   The security functions (those active features which contribute to security) of the IT product or system under evaluation, taken as a whole but considered at three levels:

(a) *Security Objectives*   Why the functionality is wanted. The contribution to security which a TOE is intended to achieve.

(b) *Security Enforcing Functions*   What functionality is actually provided. The features of the TOE that contribute to security.

(c) *Security Mechanisms*   How the functionality is provided. The means, such as logic or algorithm, by which a security function is implemented.

Security Enforcing Components   Components of a TOE which contribute to satisfying security objectives.

Security Relevant Components   Components of a TOE which are not security enforcing, but which must nonetheless operate correctly for the TOE to enforce security.

Functionality Class   A predefined set of complementary security enforcing functions capable of being implemented in a TOE.

Assurance   Confidence in security functions, expressed as:

(a) *Correctness*   The correctness of the functions in development and operational terms.

(b) *Effectiveness*   of the functions.

15.2.2 *Functionality and assurance, classes and levels*

The criteria differentiate between functionality and assurance, and a product certified under ITSEC will receive a rating comprising these two components:

- an evaluation of functionality (why, what and how) (F1 to F10);
- an evaluation of assurance (correctness and effectiveness) (E1 to E6).

Functionality

In order for a TOE to meet its security objectives, it must incorporate appropriate security enforcing functions covering, for example, areas such as access control, auditing and separation. These functions must be defined either individually or by reference to a predetermined functionality class, in a way that is clear and understandable to both the sponsor of evaluation and the independent evaluator.

Generic headings   The security enforcing functions fall into the following natural groupings:

1   *Identification and authentication*   Any functions intended to establish and verify a claimed identity.
2   *Access-control*   Any functions intended to control the flow of information between, and the use of resources by, users, processes and objects.
3   *Accountability*   Any functions intended to record the exercising of rights which are relevant to security.
4   *Audit*   Any functions intended to detect and investigate events that might represent a threat to security.
5   *Object reuse*   Any functions intended to control the reuse of data objects.
6   *Accuracy*   Any functions intended to ensure that data has not been modified in an unauthorized manner.
7   *Reliability of service*   Any functions intended to ensure that resources are accessible and usable on demand by an authorized user or process, and to prevent or limit interference with time-critical operations.
8   *Data exchange*   Any functions intended to ensure the security of data during transmission over communications channels, under the subheadings:

   * authentication
   * access-control
   * data confidentiality
   * data integrity
   * non-repudiation

Predefined classes   ITSEC has been defined to permit reference within security targets to predefined classes of security—enforcing functions, grouped in their generic headings. The criteria give ten examples of such functionality classes, derived from the Orange Book and the German ZSIEC. The use of these classes is not obligatory, and security-enforcing functions may be specified individually. The classes are simply convenient benchmarks for all to use as they wish, and it is likely that more will be defined in due course:

1   Classes F-C1, F-C2, F-B1, F-B2 and F-B3 are hierarchically ordered confidentiality classes which correspond closely to the DoD Orange Book Classes C1 to A1.

2   F-IN is a class for TOEs with high integrity requirements for data and programs.

3   Class F-AV sets high requirements for the continuity of a complete TOE or special functions of a TOE.

4   Class F-DI sets high requirements for integrity during data communication.

5   Class F-DC is intended for TOEs requiring confidentiality of data during communication.

6   Class F-DX relates to networks needing high standards of data confidentiality and integrity.

Assurance

It is equally important to be assured that the security enforcing functions and mechanisms are actually achieving the security objectives. Such assurance is considered in the criteria in terms of both correctness and effectiveness.

Effectiveness   Evaluation of effectiveness assesses whether the security-enforcing functions and mechanisms in the TOE will actually satisfy the stated security objectives, i.e. whether things will work in terms of:

- the suitability of the TOE's security enforcing functions to counter the threats;
- the ability of the TOE's security enforcing functions and mechanisms to bind together in a way that is mutually supportive and provides an integrated and effective whole;
- the consequences of known and discovered vulnerabilities, and whether they might compromise the security of the TOE;
- the ability of the security mechanisms of the TOE to withstand direct attack.

Correctness   Correctness is addressed from the point of view of construction of the TOE—including both the development process and the development environment—and from the point of view of operation of the TOE. Seven evaluation levels in the criteria show ascending levels of confidence in the correctness of security enforcing functions and mechanisms within the TOE:

1   Level EO represents inadequate assurance.

2   At Level E1 a security target is defined and an informal description of the architectural design of the TOE is provided. Functional testing shall indicate that the TOE satisfies its security target.

3   In addition, at Level E2 there shall be an informal description of the

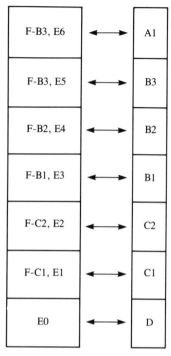

Figure 15.2.   ITSEC and the 'Orange Book'.

detailed design of the TOE. Evidence of functional testing shall be
evaluated, and there shall be a configuration control system and an
approved distribution procedure.

4   At Level E3, the source code and/or hardware drawings correspond-
ing to the security mechanisms shall be evaluated. Evidence of testing
of those mechanisms shall be evaluated.

5   At Level E4 there shall also be an underlying formal model of
security policy.

6   At Level E5 there shall be a close correspondence between the
detailed design and the source code and/or hardware drawings.

7   At Level E6, the highest level of assurance, the security enforcing
functions and the architectural design shall be specified in a formal style,
consistent with the specified underlying formal model of security policy.

Assurance   ITSEC considers first the correctness of security functions
and then their effectiveness (including strength of mechanisms), although
in practice there will be a concurrent assessment of the two elements.

   The relationship between ITSEC and the Orange Book is shown in
Fig 15.2.

15.2.3 Using the ITSEC

The sponsor of an evaluation should determine the security objectives of the TOE and then choose security functions to satisfy them. ITSEC thus gives a flexibility not present in the Orange Book, since it is possible to 'pick and mix' from the list of security functions and the levels of assurance required from each of these. A system with a high level of integrity might be needed, for example, where strict standards of confidentiality are not necessary. A product performing a specific and highly effective access control role might not need to achieve any other function.

ITSEC allows such discriminations to be made before evaluation, and confirmed specifically in subsequent certification. Unlike the Orange Book's 'all or nothing' classes, it is now possible to have increased tailoring of functionality and assurance, choosing from the much greater possible selection of combinations, to the advantage of both those procuring IT security systems and products and those selling them.

ITSEC is at the early stages of its evolution, and procedures for its practical implementation are still in their draft form. They relate to systems and products, and certification after ITSEC evaluation will not award any measure of accreditation to the system in its operational environment. They do represent, though, the intended and desirable route for the European Community, and the USA if ITSEC can be harmonized with the Orange Book, to take over the coming years. ITSEC may not be the final version of how commercial evaluation and certification of IT security systems and products will take place, but they are flexible and certainly the best guide we have so far on how such evaluation and certification should be addressed and evolved.

15.3 Accreditation

Accreditation as a process is not widely understood, since it has so far been restricted mainly to military environments. However, the European Commission has sponsored a study into the security accreditation of commercial IT systems, the results of which were published in 1993. During accreditation, system security is checked for completeness, effectiveness and conformance with the overall security requirements and objectives set by management. Accreditation:

- checks the corporate security policy;
- agrees that the system security policy was properly derived from the corporate security policy;
- ensures that the security countermeasures are sufficient to enforce this policy;
- ensures that enough confidence can be placed in the effectiveness of those countermeasures.

Accreditation can be performed internally on systems restricted within an enterprise. Its greatest benefits will be realized, however, when systems connected externally to other enterprises' systems are accredited. Then, if measured against known criteria by an external and independent accreditation agency, User A can have confidence to varying degrees in User B's system.

16
Compromising emanations (TEMPEST)

Transient ElectroMagnetic Pulse Emanation STandardizing: the Phenomenon of compromising emanations.

All electrically powered equipment, even washing machines and electric drills, produces electrical energy released as unintended electromagnetic signals travelling through the air as radio waves, or along wire and metal-work as electric currents. It is in the laws of nature that this should happen and there is nothing that can be done to prevent it. Such emanations from computers or communications cables might carry information which could be extracted after analysis by an unauthorized outsider. It is important to take steps to reduce the strength of these compromising emanations or to contain them within the confines of the establishment.

16.1   The nature of the problem

The strength and complexity of the compromising emanations depend on the device in question and its environment:

- Peripheral equipment, especially printers and VDUs, often emits strong, uncluttered signals that can be 'read' some distance away.
- Those signals produced by a mainframe CPU will be complex and difficult to decipher. Similarly, crowded areas with numerous VDUs and printers, such as to be found in the average automated office, will produce a similarly cluttered radio environment, and it will be difficult, though not impossible, to isolate a single signal for 'reading'.
- The way in which an item of equipment radiates depends greatly on the extent of the protective measures incorporated during its design, development, manufacture, installation and use. Care at these stages can reduce the problem significantly.
- Emanations from typical office equipment may be detected at distances of up to 100 metres.

16.2   The dangers from TEMPEST

- There is misplaced concern within the commercial sector about TEMPEST. Some years ago a popular TV programme showed how it was possible with a van-load of electronic equipment to read the display on a VDU within an office block in central London, and much has been made of this within the computer security fraternity.
- Among the most vociferous in this lobby are some of those selling TEMPEST-proofed equipment designed to reduce compromising emanations, and which is much more expensive than the standard equipment.
- Any signals intercepted are only those being transmitted at that time. In order to detect any particularly sensitive data such as passwords, all emanations need to be monitored and sifted, a time- and resource-consuming process.
- In order to gain a clear and useful signal, it is necessary for any miscreant to be virtually within shouting distance of the equipment under attack. Vans hanging around for any considerable length of time should begin to be noticed by even the most unalert enterprises. Less overt equipment will be correspondingly less effective. Any small enough to be portable will be of very limited use, and will only work at distances when the perpetrator would in any case be able to read the screen personally!
- The phenomenon of unintended radiation is not easy to attack compared with the less sophisticated but more effective methods described elsewhere in this book. It requires technical knowledge, expensive equipment, time and opportunity, and places the perpetrator at risk. An attacker is bound to use easier methods before resorting to TEMPEST.

It would be foolish, however, to discount the dangers. Sensitive systems must be considered to be at risk from it, especially those handling data very attractive to a competitor who may be prepared to use any method no matter how inconvenient to gather it. Computers housed in built-up areas, where a covert surveillance post could be set up close by, are also more at risk.

Certainly within the military environment, where highly classified data is stored and processed, TEMPEST is a very real consideration during the design, procurement and operation of such systems. Even under these extreme conditions, however, it is not always necessary to install TEMPEST-proofed equipment—equally effective low or no cost countermeasures are often employed instead. Within the commercial environment it would be rare indeed for TEMPEST-proofed equipment to be necessary, despite the protestations of some vendors, since these same traditional and commonsense precautions can be employed. And then TEMPEST-proofed equipment, if it is necessary, may be limited only to those most vulnerable components of the computer system.

16.3   Simple precautions against TEMPEST

There are a number of simple, obvious, and cheap or free precautions that can be taken to reduce the threat from data being inadvertently released via compromising emanations:

1 *Sterile area*   Create a sterile area around any hardware device, especially VDUs and printers, which keeps all metal items away. Do not use metal desks, for example, even those with only metal legs, or metal waste paper baskets.

2 *Telephones*   VDUs are information machines, and it is the most natural thing to place telephones next to them at the place of work. But while the screen is displaying the latest trading figures, or last year's profit and loss figures, the phone on the desk, even when it is at rest, can be transmitting that data anywhere, literally, in the world. Whenever possible, telephone instruments and their associated cabling should be kept away from sensitive computer equipment and its associated cabling. If a telephone is needed:

   (a) It should be fitted at the periphery of the sensitive area with a suitable filter to prevent compromising emanations (which will be at a differing frequency from the speech) from passing inadvertently along the line.

   (b) 'Secure at rest' phones should be used which physically disconnect the apparatus from the line when the handset is replaced in the hook. This prevents the phone remaining live even when not in use.

   Both these are available from the telephone company. Another simple ruse is to fit phones and computer equipment located in the same room with cables too short to allow them to approach each other. Don't forget the curly flex on the telephone: it can stretch across the English Channel in the hands of a desperate user.

3 *Filtered mains*   A bonus of a filtered mains power supply is the prevention of compromising emanations down the cabling.

4 *Access*   Unauthorized access to buildings, or unauthorized vehicular access in close proximity to the installation, should be prevented. When siting the computer installation, and as described in Chapter 10 on physical security, green-field sites are to be preferred, and the computer building should be located at the centre of the site. Shared accommodation, say within a multi-storey block occupied by other, perhaps unknown, companies, is especially undesirable for sensitive or valuable computer installations.

5 *Office arrangements*   Avoid placing computer equipment near to windows. Obviously, turning the VDU screen away from the window will prevent direct overlooking, but unfortunately any compromising emanations will be emitted from an entire peripheral, not just from the obvious parts and displays. It will be advantageous to place the computer equipment towards the centre of the building to make best use of the natural shielding effect of the concrete and

other building materials. If possible, place particularly sensitive items away from public view—say at the rear overlooking the courtyard and factory, rather than in the more prestigious offices at the front overlooking the gardens and main road. Internal office walls often provide no shielding at all, so care must be taken to prevent leakage to non-sensitive items including telephones in the next, lower or upper offices.

6 *Modern equipment* Modern kit tends to radiate less than older models—some of the latter need broadcasting licences! But some of the latest 'cheapies' are also particularly good transmitters. However, the latest generation of quality VDUs has been designed to radiate very low amounts of signal for the comfort of the operator—it is said to reduce tendencies for headaches and eye-strain among staff—and for sensitive or valuable systems it is prudent to invest in such modern technology.

7 *Clear the screens* Leakage can only occur while the screen is displaying the data, or the printer is printing, and so on. Encourage staff to clear screens of data as soon as it is finished with, and not leave displays on the screen when they are not needed. They should not produce printout, especially of sensitive or valuable data, unless necessary—the endless drafts after each spelling correction should be discouraged (which will also improve control over computer documents).

8 *'Swamping'* Hiding the sensitive leakage within a barrage of non-sensitive leakage is an effective way of preventing it being easily picked up and deciphered. To this end, sensitive data should be processed on equipment surrounded by equipment placed in all the 'wrong' places (by the window, on metal furniture, near the radiator pipes, and so on) processing non-sensitive data, so that any classified compromising emanations are swamped.

16.4   TEMPEST-proofed equipment

Despite the possible precautions described so far to counter compromising emanations, it may be decided to purchase TEMPEST-proofed equipment. Such a decision could arise for justifiable reasons, but more likely because the virtues of such devices have been expounded for so long now that some will simply feel naked without them.

Reputable TEMPEST-proofed equipment is difficult to procure and its cost will be much higher than that of standard equipment. It works by creating a copper shield around the entire peripheral, and if properly installed and operated it will eradicate the problems of compromising emanations almost entirely. Some points to remember are:

● You do not have to fit TEMPEST-proofed equipment throughout the system. Only the most leaky, exposed or sensitive devices (say a printer, or VDUs at remote sites where the physical and other security measures are not so reliable, or those handling the most sensitive data) will need to be so fitted.

- Treat the TEMPEST-proofed equipment with respect. It may look tough, but it can be damaged by rough handling or misuse. The regular and unnecessary opening and closing of the encasements, for example, can cause breaks in their seals; a small leakage in an otherwise leakproof cabinet will cause compromising emanations to be literally squirted out like a jet, all the power of the caged transmissions concentrated into one single beam. In such a case, you will be worse off than with no screening at all.
- Most companies which opt for the purchase of TEMPEST-proofed equipment will have no ability to check its effectiveness either on its installation or during its operational life. Sophisticated equipment and highly specialized knowledge will be needed to perform such a technical task, and it is vital that the supplier is able to perform this service and back-up.
- Mainframes, or entire computer centres, can be placed within a copper-lined room—a Faraday cage—but this is an extremely expensive option. Great care must be taken and extensive independent specialist advice sought before this path is followed. Apart from any security considerations, such cages are necessarily restricted in size and will contain no windows, and computer staff find such a work environment claustrophobic and oppressive. In one case encountered by the author, the operations manager had moved out of the cage into the adjacent room, leaving the CPU protected and screened but bringing with her the control terminal to broadcast to the world, simply because she could bear no more to work in what she called the 'coffin'.

16.5   Technical eavesdropping

All these above precautions are for nothing if some hidden device is transmitting data to the outside world. Modern radio transmitters, miniaturized to the size and shape of pen tops, or pencil sharpeners, or playing cards and many more, can be hidden to retransmit any weak compromising emanations contained within the premises to far outside the establishment to the ears and tape recorder of an unauthorized outsider. Such attacks are not common, but if the stakes are high enough then there will always be some unscrupulous individual willing and able to carry out such questionable activities for a price. Certainly, for computer equipment handling classified data, or at particularly sensitive times such as during the lead up to a take-over bid, precautions must be taken to prevent such attacks, or at least to detect any planted devices as soon as possible after their illicit arrival.

In addition to the attack against electronic equipment, simple microphones and transmitters can be placed to pick up conversations in, say, the boardroom or over the telephone, both at work and in the homes and cars of senior company staff likely to discuss sensitive matters.

Devices to tap communications lines are considered in the chapter on network security, but their principles and their detection are very much the same as for other technical eavesdropping devices and can be considered in this context.

16.5.1 Defences aimed at prevention

Once again we can call upon traditional security measures to help prevent the planting of these technical eavesdropping devices:

Physical security In order to plant a device, access to the site and equipment must be gained. Good physical security measures, effective access control and close supervision of all visitors is essential, and to all parts of the system including user terminals, remote sites and cabling.

Personnel security Insiders may be subverted to plant devices at will. They will be allowed access to the installation, and will have knowledge of the system, its uses, its importance, its vulnerabilities, and the best places to strike.

- Good supervision of staff, proper vetting procedures and sound personnel security measures will identify potentially disaffected employees.
- Good staff management will improve morale and group identity, thereby reducing the motivation of staff to hurt the enterprise in this and other ways.
- New staff members should be especially watched; they may have sought and gained employment with you simply to gain the necessary access and trust. Staff recruited from competitors, although probably entirely trustworthy, just might have been sent as 'secret agents' into the sensitive heart of the establishment, and care should be taken again, especially in the lead up to any sensitive times or new company projects.
- Do not forget access by ancillary workers, such as cleaners, builders and others.

Hardware security All items of hardware should be protected as appropriate to prevent the insertion of some unauthorized device.

- Cabinets should be sealed and locked. Seals must be checked regularly for tampering.
- Regular inspection of the insides of the equipment should be carried out by someone who knows what he or she is looking at and who will recognize any interference.
- Maintenance engineers must be supervised and their work checked—remember the telephone engineer as well.
- Inspect telephone equipment for listening and monitoring devices, especially those within sensitive areas or those used at home or work by senior staff members likely to discuss sensitive data on the phone—a cardinal sin anyway, but something that will happen.

TEMPEST Those precautions taken against inadvertent radiation of electronic signals will, if applied conscientiously, at the same time help prevent or at least reduce the strength of the transmissions of the listening bug. For example, if the CPU has been placed at the heart of the site within the centre of a building, the signals from any device planted in it will have this to overcome before they even get to the perimeter fence, reducing their strength.

The environment A rural site will allow any unauthorized listeners to be more easily identified and observed. Beware sites with overlooking countryside or buildings which could be used to site powerful directional radio receivers, or even audio microphones to pick up speech.

- Encourage your staff to be alert when travelling in the area of your establishment, say to and from work, for suspicious cars parked.
- Task your guard force with mobile patrols of the local area at random but frequent intervals.
- Good liaison with the local civil police force, and a candid explanation of your fears and worries in this respect, especially if they are prompted by such as a take-over bid, will often elicit their help.

16.5.2 *Defences aimed at detection*

'Look for things that are missing, look for things that shouldn't be there.' It is desirable, from time to time, to carry out sweeps of the sensitive areas in order to discover any listening devices planted within the equipment or room/building/site in question. Such sweeps should be carried out if it is in any way suspected that a bug may have been planted; on the completion of any new building work; after the introduction of any new equipment (of whatever type); prior to any particularly sensitive processing periods, or before classified meetings or conferences; and on a regular but random basis (say six-monthly). Such sweeps fall into two categories:

- *Non-technical sweeps* These involve close physical inspection of the site. They are best carried out by the staff, who will be most familiar with what should be present and who will be most likely to spot anything out of place. They are time-consuming if carried out properly, and are best performed during quiet times, such as night shifts or weekends/bank holidays. Searchers should be provided with building and services plans, and careful study should be made of them. The site should then be swept methodically, and all possible hiding places searched. Common sense will suggest where to look. Place yourself in the shoes of the enemy and imagine where you would plant a listening device. In telephones, behind power sockets, under desk and table tops, behind pictures and notices on the wall, under rugs, inside lampshades—the list could go on. The devices will be designed to be undetectable, but one component that will often give them away are their aerials, usually lengths of wire. These sweeps will not guarantee that a device will be unearthed, but for relatively little effort and cost they will reduce considerably the chances of one remaining undetected. Whole buildings can be searched, and this method can be thought of as 'quick and dirty'.

- *Technical sweeps* For localized areas (such as the boardroom or the computer suite) more thorough sweeps can be performed, involving the use of electronic surveillance devices to detect the presence and transmissions of hidden bugs, combined with very careful examination of the fabric of the building. It may be necessary to lift floorboards, remove skirting boards or crawl around in roof spaces. They are understandably more time-consuming and expensive than non-technical sweeps, and the services of a specialist to assist local staff should be sought. Technical sweeps could be performed immediately prior to the sensitive event, and strict control of entry to the swept area must be enforced from then on or the effort will have been wasted. Once such follow-up security is relaxed, the area must be considered once more vulnerable. Even with these methods, the area cannot be considered completely clear—some technical eavesdropping devices are externally, or time-, or voice-activated, and may not be transmitting at the time of surveillance. Their perpetrators will have been unbelievably imaginative in their placing of the device and you may not be clever enough to find it during your search. However, this represents the best shot possible. Remember to select the specialists you employ carefully; it would be ironic if they were the ones to plant the device.

Sweeps should be performed silently—if a surveillance device has been secreted and can be discovered without the enemy realizing, then false information can be fed to one's advantage instead. To activate any sound-activated devices to allow electronic detection, use normal conversation which does not reveal one's motives. As a process of elimination, repeat technical sweeps with a combination of electrical equipment in the room switched on and off—some devices draw their power like parasites from the equipment they are tapping, and only operate while it is operating.

17
Communications and network security

Computers store and process their electronic data, but increasingly they now also share that data with other computers. Indeed, most modern systems would be almost worthless without the ability to communicate with others, either within the immediate area and within the confines of the enterprise (Local Area Networks or LANs), or further afield to outside enterprises or over great distances (Wide Area Networks or WANs). These three essential elements of computing—data storage, handling and now communicating—are becoming increasingly interrelated. In addition, and not a new feature, the various components and peripherals which go to make up a particular computer system will usually be spread about the immediate place of work and possibly over great distances to remote sites, and these all need to be connected. However, there is a steady trend away from the central host computer driving reliant peripherals and exercising firm control over them and the data interchanged between them, to more distributed resources with their own processing capabilities. The former tight discipline is being significantly eroded.

A variety of direct communications channels will need to be established for these various needs, and such data links represent possibly the most vulnerable aspect of any computing system. They may employ private connections/communications links, either wholly under the ownership and control of the enterprise (in-house) or leased by the enterprise. More likely, though, the public systems (telephones or satellite links) will be used, when access by unauthorized persons cannot be prevented. The links may be over short or long distances. Certainly those qualities demanded of a modern IT communications network and especially a LAN—namely openness and ease of access, flexibility and user friendliness—are those very same things which create an insecure computing environment. As ever, a balance is needed between the business function and the security effort, with some risk accepted in the name of overall efficiency and growth.

In this chapter the various methods of data transmission will be considered, together with the vulnerabilities of data while it is being transmitted and the measures which can be used to counter these risks.

17.1   Methods of data transmission

Data transmission can be effected through a number of media, the most common being electrical connections, but fibre optic cables, radio waves, microwaves and optical links are also used. The speed at which a channel operates is termed its 'bit rate', and is usually expressed in terms of bits per second. Signal power loss as it travels along or through the medium, termed attentuation, increases as the signal frequency increases, distance increases, or the diameter of the copper wire decreases.

The quality of transmission depends on, and is limited by, the noise level of the medium—those undesirable electrical signals caused by the nature of, and imperfections within, the transmission medium:

- *White noise*   Identified, for example, as a hiss on an audio line, and caused by thermal agitation of electrons.
- *Impulsive noise*   A form of interference commonly known as spiking, caused by electrical activity around the transmission medium, giving rise, for example, to clicking sounds on telephone lines. Spikes are a common cause of data error.
- *Crosstalk*   The interference between adjacent lines in which the signal in one is passed to the other by electromagnetic induction—those same compromising emanations as described in Chapter 16.

'Fixed' media can be grouped into the following:

- *Twisted wire pairs*   Most commonly used in telephone wiring, it comprises two copper wires twisted together. While in this way the effects of crosstalk are reduced, the pairs have limited frequency range and speed, they are susceptible to noise and can be easily tapped.
- *Multi-core cables*   Several lines run together in the same casing. There is poor resistance to noise unless shielded, and they are expensive. However, a single wire is thus well hidden among a number of others, and an attacker will have more trouble in isolating the one he or she wants.
- *Coaxial cable*   Most commonly seen as television aerial wire. It is robust, lightweight and has a good frequency range. It can produce high data communications rates.
- *Fibre optic cables*   Made up of a bundle of continuous glass rods, very thin and very flexible. The information to be transmitted is converted into pulses of light which are then bounced down the glass rods; at the other end the light pulses are turned back into an electrical signal. High transmission rates are possible, there is no electrical interference or crosstalk, and it is virtually impossible to tap. Costs are now comparable to traditional cabling.

17.2   Transmission characteristics

17.2.1 Bandwidth

The bandwidth of a communications channel defines the range of frequencies that can be safely and satisfactorily conveyed by the channel; outside these frequencies, the data is likely to be distorted or lost.

Narrow band

Operating at the relatively slow speed of up to 110 bits/second within telegraphic circuits, this band is usually transmitting at frequencies between 20 Hz and 20 kHz.

Voice band

The voice band employs telephone circuits and operates between 200 and 2400 bits/second at between 0.3 and 3.4 kHz.

Broad band

The broad band employs special high-grade circuits, and radio and microwave links. It operates at speeds greater than 2400 bits/second and at 48 kHz and above and between 2 and 11 GHz.

17.2.2 Modulation and modems

When communicating data, except for very short distances (less than 4000 m) or within the narrow band, it is necessary to employ a carrier signal, and to modulate this with the data in its binary code (i.e. 1s and 0s). The carrier wave frequency should be suitable for conveyance within the chosen medium and bandwidth, and on reaching the other end it should be demodulated to reveal the data in transit. This method is employed with television sets, where the signal is modulated at the TV station and demodulated in the TV set at home. This MOdulation/DEModulation process is performed by a modem (one at each end) (Fig. 17.1)

Figure 17.1.   Modems.

17.2.3 Types of transmission

There are two types of data transmission within computers:

1 *Asynchronous transmission* A low-speed method of transmission in which
   units of data (characters, words, or blocks) are preceded and concluded by
   check pulses or bits (start and stop signals). The start bit triggers a timing
   mechanism in the receiving terminal which counts off the succeeding bits or
   characters as a series of fixed time intervals. The stop bit re-sets the receiver
   ready for the next character. This stream is similar to lorries on a motorway,
   all driving along independently to the same destination, and traffic is not
   continuous.
2 *Synchronous transmission* A high-speed method of transmission in which
   data is transferred as a continuous sequence of bits, and there are no gaps or
   start and stop bits mixed in. The receiver establishes synchronization with the
   first bit of any sequence of bits and maintains synchronization with a
   clocking mechanism. In this way, the modems at each end of the communications link are initially set up and then a stream of characters is sent. This
   stream is like a train of freight trucks moving along a railway line.

17.2.4 Modes of data transmission

There are three modes of data transmission used for communications purposes:

1 *Simplex* A simplex line is capable only of transmitting data in one direction.
   There would be a transmitter at one end and a receiver at the other. This
   method is rarely used within the computing function since there is then no
   way for the receiver to acknowledge receipt of the message. Radio and
   television broadcasts are examples of simplex transmissions; a one-way street
   is another.
2 *Half-duplex* A half-duplex line can send data in both directions, but not both
   at once. At any one time, one modem is the receiver and the other the
   transmitter. Typically, A sends data to B, who then acknowledges in a return
   message that the data was received successfully, or not as the case may be when
   A would re-transmit. These conversations between ends is referred to as the
   network's 'protocol'. A single lane track is an example of a half-duplex channel.
3 *Full-duplex* A full-duplex channel can send and receive data in both directions at once—a normal two-way road.

17.2.5 Multiplexing

A number of messages can be interleaved into a communications channel,
thereby improving its efficiency and reducing overhead costs. Separation of the
signals can be achieved by frequency or time.

17.2.6 Private (leased) lines

Private (leased) lines are links between two points used exclusively by one party. However, although called private, they will often be owned by the telephone company and leased to the party.

17.2.7 Public/packet switching network

Since private wires are expensive, and sometimes lie redundant for much of the time, many enterprises send their data along the public telephone network. The links may be direct, in effect along lines made private for the duration of the 'call'. More likely these days the message will be split up into separately addressed and sequentially numbered packets. These packets are sent independently of one another along a number of different routes via various exchanges within the Packet Switching Network (PSN), to be reassembled as an entire message by the receiver. Not only is this method quicker, more reliable and more resource efficient, security is (incidentally) improved since the information *en route* is only in small chunks. Any interception will disclose only a small part of the entire message.

17.3   Networks

A group of interconnected computers capable of sharing each other's data is called a network. They may be broadly classed as wide area or local area.

17.3.1 Local area networks

Usually a local area network (LAN) is restricted to within a single enterprise, and then often within a single site under the control of that enterprise. An automated office system is an example of such an arrangement, with a number of desktop computers and shared resources (printers etc.) contained within one office block. The network can allow the selective transfer of data between the various devices on it, and can be arranged in a number of ways:

1 *Star* Originally, a single host computer ran a number of terminals, and had, say, a shared printing facility. In such a star arrangement, the host was able to control the activities of the other components by individually addressing them (Fig. 17.2). This arrangement is becoming less common with the advent of distributed resources and modern computer technology.
2 *Ring* The computers and other hardware devices are all on a shared ring. A message passes round the ring, through all the computers and devices in turn until it reaches the one to which it is addressed (Fig. 17.3).
3 *Bus* The computers and peripherals are connected to a common bus. Mes-

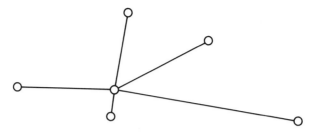

Figure 17.2.   Star LAN.

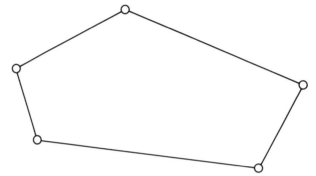

Figure 17.3.   Ring LAN.

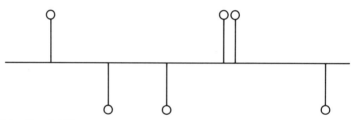

Figure 17.4.   Bus LAN.

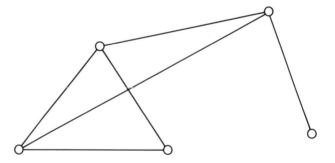

Figure 17.5.   Unconstrained connections.

sages pass up and down the bus, and are received by all the devices that are
connected (Fig. 17.4).

4   *Unconstrained connections*   Connections exist in no ordered way. Often such
a network emerges as a system develops and grows (Fig. 17.5).

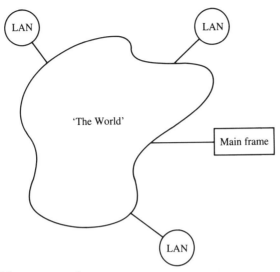

Figure 17.6.   Wide area networks.

17.3.2   Wide area networks

LANs can be interconnected to other LANs, or computers can be connected to other computers over wide areas and great distances (Fig. 17.6). Such wide area networks (WANs) may cross not only between sites, but also between organizations, countries and even continents. Ultimately, WANs which use the public telephone system have a potential public of some 600 million.

As a useful security guideline, a LAN can be considered as becoming a WAN once *physical* custody over any part of the LAN, including communications media, is forfeited.

17.3.3   Metropolitan area networks

Metropolitan Area Networks (MANs) have emerged recently as a further category of networking (Fig. 17.7). MANs are simply WANs restricted geographically within the confines of, say, a city or conurbation.

17.4   Aims of communications and network security

We must aim to preserve the confidentiality of data passing through any communication channel. We must ensure that the message is unaltered during its transmission, retaining the integrity of the data being passed. We must have reliable and effective communications at all times—continuity must be maintained. These requirements have been a common theme throughout this book. With communications security, though, we must also be certain that we are actually connected with whom we believe we are connected, and they in turn must be certain that we are who we have said we are, and there is in this context,

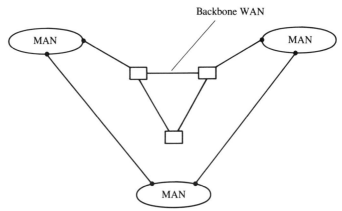

Figure 17.7.   Metropolitan area networks.

therefore, a fourth quality to the information being passed, its authenticity. Finally, there must be ways of proving both that a transmitted message has been successfully received at the other end, so that such receipt cannot be repudiated by the other party, and who sent it, a 'digital signature'.

Any network security measures employed within a computer system must be designed to counter those of the threats relevant to and ranged against the system and its parent enterprise. In summary, though, they must aim to:

- make sure the message is received at its intended destination(s), and nowhere else;
- make sure that the contents of the message are exactly the same at receipt as at transmission, and that they have not been altered or deleted in any way for any reason;
- make sure that only authorized users have access to the network, by controlling access to the component parts—terminals, modems, multiplexers, switches, transmission lines and so on—and to the necessary passwords and/or access tokens. Any attacker should thus be physically barred from the network;
- make sure that a sender of information can verify its receipt by (and only by) the authorized recipient;
- make sure that a recipient of a message can verify that the sender is indeed the person from whom the message appears to come;
- make sure that information in transit cannot be observed, altered or extracted from the network by some unauthorized person or device;
- make sure that any attempts to tamper with data in transit, or with any communications link, will be revealed and that appropriate remedial action can be taken;
- make sure that alternative routes are available within the network to provide for failure or deliberate destruction of any network component. Prompt back-up service should be available to restore normal facilities as quickly as possible;

- make sure that if both primary and back-up communications links are simultaneously disabled, there exists some other means of communicating, and that this emergency procedure actually works and has been tested and practised by those who will have to enforce it.

These, then, are the aims. What are the threats against achieving them, and how can the link be attacked?

17.5   Threats to communications and networks

17.5.1 Passive attacks

Passive attacks on a communications link are characterized by the interception of data without detection:

- *Eavesdropping*   The unauthorized capture of transmitted data either by some form of line tapping, or from the compromising emanations broadcast by the electrical signals in the line. Radio, optical and microwave signals can be similarly intercepted covertly.
- *Traffic analysis*   Even if the message has been protected by enciphering, an analysis of the traffic down the line can, in many circumstances, reveal much to an outsider. The number, size, frequency and times of messages sent, their sources and their destination can indicate, for example, an impending take-over bid, or the launch of a new product.

17.5.2 Active attacks

As the name suggests, the attacker takes active steps to interfere with the data being transmitted down a communications channel:

- *Modification*   The message contents can be deliberately changed.
- *Re-routing*   The message is diverted to elsewhere than its intended destination. One ploy is to divert to a PC, gather the password, and then break the link with a 'line out of order—try again' instruction. After a while all the passwords can be collected from an entirely unsuspecting enterprise.
- *Injection of false messages*   A bogus message is sent.
- *Re-play*   The attacker causes the message to be repeated over again, perhaps many times. Since the original message was found by the recipient as entirely acceptable, so too will any re-plays of it.
- *Deletion*   The message is deleted, and thus never reaches its destination.
- *Delay*   The message is deliberately delayed.
- *Masquerade*   An attacker masquerades as an authorized user of the communications channel, and by this impersonation obtains use of the system as normally befitting only an authorized user.

- *Piggy-in-the-middle*   The attacker cuts into the link between two communicating parties, and conducts two conversations, one with each party, while convincing each they are talking to the other.
- *Between lines*   Penetration is made on legitimate user's communications channel when the valid user is not using it, such as when he or she has remained logged on during the lunch break.
- *Jamming*   Radio, optical and microwave links can be interfered with by signal jamming—the creation of a stronger signal to drown the intended transmissions. (Optical links can be physically interrupted, either deliberately or accidentally by atmospheric pollution/cloud, but they are usually only over short distances and often within a single site, and so the threats against them are reduced.)

17.5.3   Accidental interference

There are a number of accidental threats to the data being transmitted and the communications channel in use which can be as damaging as any of the deliberate attacks:

- *Message loss*   The message just disappears after being sent, never to be seen again.
- *Message duplication*   The message is accidentally duplicated, or perhaps repeated many times.
- *Sequence errors*   The message is jumbled up, especially if it has been split into packets around the Packet Switching Network. Text will be obviously corrupted, but errors in numerical messages may not be so obvious.
- *Message re-routing*   The message ends up at the wrong destination, or is seen during its journey by an authorized user without the need to know.
- *Message corruption*   The message is received in a corrupt or garbled fashion.

How, then, do we protect ourselves from these threats in order to achieve those aims we have defined for network security?

17.6   Methods of protection—cryptology

The most useful of all techniques to improve the security of transmitted data is encryption. The study of data encryption and its applications is referred to as cryptology. It is a highly specialist subject and only the principles are discussed in this book. There are a number of specialist firms in the market today which are able to provide effective, cheap, easy to install and easy to use encoding equipment. What is necessary, though, is an overview of the methods of achieving satisfactory security by cryptology.

Data encryption is the performance of complex mathematical transformations that make any data unintelligible to an outside party. These transformations are made using an algorithm—the mathematical formula—and a cryptographic key, which is a special data item, usually kept secret, used as input into the algorithm along with the data itself. To recover the data (plain text) from the encrypted version (cipher-text) it is necessary to know both the algorithm and the secret key.

The design of secure systems using encryption techniques focuses mainly on the protection of the secret keys. Key management is the term used to describe the generation, distribution, storage, entry, use and destruction of cryptographic keys. Keys are protected either by encrypting them under other keys, or by protecting them physically.

The principles of modern cryptology can be summarized as follows:

1 Security should not depend on the secrecy of the encryption method, only the secrecy of the keys.
2 The secret key must not be deduced from matching plain text and ciphertext.
3 No human being should have knowledge of the secret key.

17.6.1 Encryption algorithms—DES

There are many algorithms available, but by far the most important is the Data Encryption Standard (DES), developed by IBM for the US Government back in the 1970s. It is symmetric, in that it uses the same secret key to encrypt and decrypt the data. It is used extensively within the financial services sector (banks etc.). Despite the imminent withdrawal of US Government support for it on the grounds of its age, it is likely that it will continue to be the standard for the international financial institutions for many years to come, since its replacement (involving a number of ciphers incorporated into chips and never published) will be of little worth to the world of commerce. DES is widely available on special silicon chips, although the use and distribution of these in the United Kingdom is subject to licensing by the British Government and the export of this technology is carefully controlled by the Department of Trade and Industry.

17.6.2 Encryption algorithms—non-DES

For those organizations not permitted to use DES there are many suitable proprietary algorithms marketed by, for example, British Telecom and other specialist companies. They are usually conveniently packaged into efficient, cheap and easy-to-use encryption devices which readily 'bolt on' to most computer systems.

17.6.3 Encryption algorithms—public key systems

The RSA algorithm—named after its inventors Rivest, Shamir and Adleman—is the other main contender in the algorithm stakes. It is a public key encryption system using two keys, one public and one secret. One key is used to encrypt, the other to decrypt, and the algorithm is therefore termed asymmetric.

When a device generates its pair of keys, one is publicly distributed to all other elements of the system and its users, while the other is kept completely secret. A message is encrypted using the public key; only the device which holds the matching secret key can decrypt that message, and therefore no secret keys need to be moved about or shared. Conversely, if a sender wishes to sign a message with some form of digital signature, the encrypt operation should be performed on the data he or she wishes to 'sign', using the secret key. All other users on the system have the public key, and can therefore verify the 'signature' by performing the decrypt operation. The 'signature' is unique since only one user possesses the secret key with which it was generated. Non-repudiation of signature is therefore achieved—a receiver can be certain who sent the message, and can prove it—which is an important advantage over DES-type algorithms. At the same time, this non-repudiation gives protection against forgery by the receiver, allows authentication of the source by many receivers without loss of security, and key management is simplified. In a practical system, certification of public keys is also required to prevent them being substituted by an opponent. This involves a trusted third party putting a digital signature on every public key.

RSA does have the disadvantage that it requires a great deal of processing power to perform the decrypt process, and is thus unsuitable for the bulk encryption of data. It is most useful in establishing confirmed links between users before sending unencrypted messages—so-called 'handshaking' processes—and for signing longer messages.

Another asymmetric algorithm which is becoming increasingly important is known as 'El Gamel'. This provides another way to construct and verify digital signatures and is currently proposed by the US Government for a digital signature standard (CDSS), the signature equivalent of DES.

17.6.4 Message authentication

Many computers in the financial services industry are concerned with the transfer of money (electronic funds transfer or EFT), in which payment instruction messages are transmitted from one computer to another, and not necessarily within the same enterprise. Trust is an important factor here, on both sides, and it is vital that these 'paperless' transactions are secured in such a way that they cannot be altered without such alteration being detected. While many government systems require high levels of confidentiality, in the financial environment the data's integrity is paramount. While we can never hope to guarantee that a message has not been corrupted either accidentally or deliberately, we can take steps to ensure that any such changes are detected at once and automatically.

This is done by the generation at the source of the message of a special data field—a label, in fact—called the Message Authentication Code (MAC). This MAC is produced by processing the entire message through a DES machine. Each 64-bit block of the message is processed using the secret key; the resulting ciphertext controls the encryption of the next 64-bit block, and is then discarded (the message is eventually sent plain text or encrypted separately, this is not a message encryption process as such). Eventually, at the end of the message the ciphertext output from the last 64-bit block encryption will be related to every single bit of the entire message—it is in fact a checksum, but one which can only be generated with knowledge of the secret key. Anyone altering the message in any way, even by one digit or letter, will not be able to alter this MAC unless in possession of the secret key.

When the message is received at the other end, the MAC which was generated at its source is received with it. The receiving machine performs the same MAC-generation process on the entire message, and compares its result with the received MAC. A successful match is regarded as a verification that the message has not been changed one jot. Naturally, and as with all other aspects of cryptology, protection of the secret keys is paramount.

17.6.5   Data encryption for privacy

The most obvious use of encryption is the transformation of data into a form unreadable to an unauthorized third party who has not been given the encryption key—the enforcement of confidentiality over the data while it is being transmitted. (Incidentally, data can be encrypted for storage, for example password files or other extremely sensitive material, so that any outsider, browser, or indeed authorized user stumbling across the data, will not be able to read it.) This encryption of data obviously makes any attacker's task much more difficult, but it also solves the problem of message replay, where an attacker causes a successful message to be repeated to personal advantage—for example the transfer of funds can be caused to happen perhaps many times over on the strength of the single original transaction. While time stamping and serialization of transactions is designed to counter this, weaknesses may be left which could be used for successful attacks. If, however, the entire data-stream is encrypted, an attacker can see no message structure and is therefore unable to perceive message boundaries or message contents, thus eliminating entirely the message replay problem. To a degree, also, traffic analysis is defeated, but not entirely since the message is still noted as having been passed, unless dummy traffic is encrypted and transmitted. Encryption of entire messages, for encryption's sake and with no refinements such as MACs, is easy and cheap to achieve with a number of encryption devices available on the market, which 'bolt on' to the system, and which are entirely unnoticeable—transparent, to use the up-market term!

17.6.6   Data encryption—methods of transmission

A message can be transmitted between users in a variety of ways:

1   *Private leased line*   Where the users are talking to each other along a private leased line, when the link is fixed, then the encryption/decryption devices can

be set up—initialized—with each other, one at each end, and left to chatter happily. This is the easiest and cheapest method, except that the link will be expensive to maintain.

2 *Dial-up systems* With dial-up systems, each time a link is made it can be between a new pair of users. The call can come in on any one of a number of lines from any of the possible remote locations, and so there will be many possible combinations of encryptors/decryptors that can find themselves in need of establishing a conversation; this problem will increase as the size of the network grows. But there are special products which have been developed for this sort of environment and which can be easily installed. However, the need for proper and well-administered key management schemes is even more important in this arrangement, one of the most common in commercial sectors. Fast 'handshaking' routines are the most common features of any solution, where RSA signatures are exchanged to establish an authentic contact before the exchange of data even begins.

3 *Packet switching* The final complication comes when the link between two users is through a packet switching network. In-line encryption/decryption devices are needed which can deal with messages which have been chopped up into small packets, sent off in all directions and which only come together again at the destination to be re-sequenced and reassembled/decoded to the original form. In the end, the solution has been to encrypt only the message itself, and the label on each packet is left alone to allow its safe delivery; once again, though, bolt-on devices are readily available and the user will be unaware of them.

17.6.7 Key management

The security of any encryption process depends entirely on the manner in which the secret keys are protected from unauthorized disclosure. These keys must be generated, distributed, stored, entered, used and destroyed without their values being disclosed to hostile parties, and ideally without disclosure to any human being. The most secure systems are those that hide the keys totally, even from the system's designers. The security of the computer and its network will only be as good as this weakest point. Key management involves the careful combination of a number of techniques:

- A key used to operate on data, either to encrypt it or to produce a MAC, is called a data key, or session key.
- A key used to encrypt other keys is called a key encrypting key, or master key. Such a key is greater in importance than the data key; a hierarchy of keys can thus be created, usually of a number of layers.
- A data key, generated by a sender who wishes to encrypt data, must be transmitted to the receiver who is to decrypt the data. Moreover, the data key must be changed regularly, at least once a day, to overcome the threat posed

by someone attempting an exhaustive key search. A mechanism for regularly sending new data keys is therefore required. The usual way is to have a key that is used only to encrypt data keys—the master key—whose exposure to attack by search is limited because of its restricted use and the fact that it is used only to encrypt random numbers. It can have a life of several months.

- Periodically, the master key needs to be moved from sender to receiver in a most secure manner. This can be done either manually or it can be automated using RSA encryption.

- Keys that are stored within a unit, and keys that are in use, cannot be protected under higher level key-encrypting keys. They must be stored within a tamper-resistant environment, usually in a chip alarmed to detect attempts to penetrate the hardware and read the key. If the alarm is triggered, the keys are immediately wiped from the memory. The hardware can be designed to detect attack from a range of threats, from the simple removal of the lid by unscrewing through to more sophisticated attacks such as drilling, grinding, chemical solvents and X-rays.

17.6.8 International standards

Standards are important to all aspects of security, but especially computer security. They provide assurance that the design of the system's security is sound and tested to prescribed limits, that there are no gaps in the defences, and perhaps most importantly in today's market they allow interoperability.

In the context of computer communications, perhaps more than anywhere else in the computing world, this ability to talk with machines anywhere is vital if we are to get the most from our investments. With network security it is important that data that has been encrypted on one computer system can be decrypted on another authorized system. Compliance with international standards is the mechanism for helping to ensure this happy state of affairs.

The most important standards-making bodies are ISO (International Organization for Standardization), ANSI (American National Standards Institute), and CCITT (International Telegraph and Telephone Consultative Committee). While their various standards cover a very wide range of technical subjects, some of them are specifically related to telecommunications and network security.

The foundation stone for security in open systems interconnection (OSI), which is ISO-speak for computer networking, is the international standard ISO 7498–2: *Information Processing Systems—Open Systems Interconnection—Basic Reference Model Part 2: Security Architecture*. This document gives a general description of security services and mechanisms for OSI, describes the relationship between services, mechanisms and layers, and details the placement of security services and mechanisms. It also discusses in broad terms security management in OSI networks.

To be able to implement the services and mechanisms described in outline in ISO 7498–2, some detailed standards are required for each. Much work is under way in this area, but much also remains to be done. Current standards and draft standards include:

> CCITT X.402 Section 10 (1988)—MHS (Message handling system) Security Model
>
> ISO 9594–8 (1990) (identical to CCITT X.509 (1988)—The Directory Part 8: Authentication framework
>
> ISO 9796 (1991)—Information Technology—Security Techniques—Digital signature scheme giving message recovery
>
> ISO 9798–1 (1991)—Information Technology—Security Techniques—Entity Authentication mechanisms—Part 1: General Model
>
> ISO DP 9798–2 (1991)—Information Technology—Security Techniques—Entity Authentication Mechanisms—Part 2: Entity authentication using symmetric techniques
>
> ISO DIS 9798–3 (1990)—Information Technology—Security Techniques—Entity Authentication Mechanisms—Part 3: Entity authentication using a public key algorithm
>
> ISO DP 10118–1 (1990)—Information Technology—Security Techniques—Hash functions for digital signatures—Part 1: General
>
> ISO DP 10118–2 (1990)—Information Technology—Security Techniques—Hash functions for digital signatures—Part 2: (not yet published)
>
> ISO/CD 11166—Key management by means of asymmetric algorithms
>
> Recommendations for UN/EDIFACT Security from the Security Joint Working Group
>
> RFC 1113, 1114 and 1115—Privacy Enhanced Mail (PEM), Internet Activities Board

When one starts to investigate what standards are currently available to implement an open distributed system such as that required for EDI (electronic data interchange), it soon becomes clear that this impressive list of standards currently hides some serious omissions. For example, there is as yet no clear standard definition of all the syntax rules for cryptographic variables such as keys, signatures and certificates. The entire issue of how to run a certification (notarization) service is as yet not addressed by any of these standards, and without this it becomes very difficult to implement a truly 'open' system, since the cornerstone of open systems is the existence of open standards.

17.7   Methods of protection—physical and procedural security

The physical security of all components of a computer system, but especially those parts connecting the various elements or to other computer systems (networks), is vital to the overall security effort. Communication links, though, are often the unseen and therefore forgotten parts. They usually travel outside the immediate area of the data centre and thus beyond the secure physical environment that should exist around the computer itself. The cabling can travel along routes shared by a host of unknown outsiders, or even along the same channel within the public telephone network or a satellite link. Usually, the physical defences around a site extend understandably only to the perimeter fence, just beyond which will be the telephone company's junction box open to attack and which contains all the communications links to the outside world. Any communications line is especially attractive to an attacker, since often the data is available in its entirety during the period of transmission in these vulnerable places.

Considering their frailty, it seems surprising that communications links are as reliable as they are. Clearly, physical and procedural precautions need to be taken to protect these links, and countermeasures drawn up in case of their failure. These precautions should assume that a communications link cannot be satisfactorily protected throughout its length, and the defences must be concentrated in the main on the protection of each end in addition where appropriate to the cryptographic detection of any attacks during the actual transmission.

Physical communications links—cables—follow predictable routes. They can usually be seen coming overhead into any site, or through the known underground ducts. Further afield, they cross barriers in predictable ways—river crossings will be slung under bridges, for example. There is little effort involved in tracing these lines, and attacks upon them—active or passive—can be achieved with only a fraction of the effort and risk involved in attacking the more secure site itself. There are many natural and accidental hazards to these vulnerable communications links. Cars run into telegraph poles, trees fall across lines, water gets into underground ducts, or into junction boxes. Workmen and their mechanical diggers seem attracted to any underground cabling (see Murphy's Law). Satellites go out of place, or the atmosphere becomes unsuitable for reliable radio links. Simply, two systems may be unable to talk to each other because they are incompatible.

1   For systems to be compatible, there must be:

   (a) *Physical compatibility* It must be possible, for example, for magnetic media written on one system to be physically mounted and read on another.
   (b) *Electrical compatibility* For example electrical voltages must be the same.
   (c) *Logical compatibility* A format in which information is displayed on one system must be recognized by the other.

Such compatibility can be achieved either by planning for the standardization of all equipment in use throughout the network—the obvious and in the long term cheapest solution—or failing that devising some form of 'conversion unit'. This may be an electronic device or it could involve the dumping of the data on to paper tape, to be read by a tape reader fitted to the other otherwise incompatible device; this is an attractive option since there are none of the problems of file and directory structures associated with magnetic media, and the character codes and formats are standardized already and are widely understood. Optical character readers are another simple solution, with the second system 'reading' the printed output of the first.

2   Special care must be taken when two systems are communicating but which operate at different levels of classification, even within the same enterprise. It is important that the lower system cannot read the classified data on the higher system and that the higher system cannot write data down to the lower system. This 'No Read Up, No Write Down' rule is an important principle of any computer security policy and should be an important factor when devising the communications security countermeasures. It may be particularly relevant when one intends, for example, to link to the systems belonging to a rival or potentially hostile partner. Data flow regulators, which automatically perform this control, are not yet widely available, and so it is better to arrange the system so that:

(a) 'Push Only' data transfer occurs, in that the lower system sends its data to the higher system, rather than is requested for it. In this way, only control information is passed from the higher to the lower, in a virtually one-way flow.
(b) If it is necessary to send data from a higher to a lower system, the information to be released must first be inspected to ensure it contains no information classified higher than allowed on the receiving system. Then, only the data that has been approved should actually be transmitted to the lower system.

If doubt exists, create a physical break in the link, supervised by a pair of human eyes to watch for potential or actual security breaches. The tape reader, or optical character reader, described above is ideal, though for greater volumes of data magnetic tapes may need to be considered.

3   Access, both physical and logical, to all components of a computer system must be strictly controlled; this aspect has been considered elsewhere in the book at length.
4   Any communications links within the site should travel along known routes, within sealed trunking. Such trunking should be transparent, and visible along its entire length so that staff can see immediately if the cabling within has been tampered with. Regular inspections of the trunking should be

carried out by staff technically qualified to recognize any signs of interference. Junction boxes should be physically secured, and access to them restricted.

5   Lines into the site should if possible come along underground routes; on-site manhole covers and ducts should, wherever possible, be sealed. Overhead cables should drop to the site along visible routes, and be inspected regularly for signs of tampering.

6   Wires must not be labelled with their role, especially sensitive circuits. References should be made to maps and circuit diagrams held under appropriately secure conditions.

7   To reduce compromising emanations and the resulting crosstalk between cabling, fibre optic cable should be used whenever possible. In the event that copper wire is to be used, separate runs should be separated by at least one metre along their entire length, and should cross at right angles. Special shielded cabling can be used to reduce leakage, and at the same time it will detect any attempts to penetrate the cable jacket to gain access to the inner cores. As would be expected, the expense is significant and use of such cabling should be restricted to the most sensitive of circuits.

8   When a network is installed within a building or site, it is inevitably intended that the LAN will expand with time. Spare ports are therefore installed, often in currently unused offices and store rooms. Control over these ports is essential, since they provide an immediate entry into the network to an unauthorized user. Similarly, all terminals are potential workstations for an unauthorized person; access to them must be strictly controlled.

9   Traffic on a communications link, especially outside the enterprise, can be padded with 'rubbish' to hide the real data and to make traffic analysis more difficult.

10   Careful control must be exercised over the routing of data transmissions. Some routes will be inherently more secure, and others will have had a greater security effort applied to them. Likewise, some will be inherently insecure. It is sensible to direct the more sensitive or valuable traffic along the more sensitive routes.

11   Where appropriate, make the routing 'one way'.

12   A fixed communications link, such as an on-site fibre optic or copper cable run, or a private wire link to a remote site, can on installation be tested with a special device which reads the link's 'signature' to produce a unique signal spectrum. Any physical interference with the link, such as re-routing into a tapping device, or cutting or bending, will change the signature; regular re-tests and comparisons with the original spectrum will show up any such interferences, either deliberate or accidental.

13   Similarly, fixed links can carry a continuous signal in addition to any data transmissions. Any break to the link, even for an instant as, for example, some eavesdropping device is inserted, will be detected as a break in this carrier signal, and alarms will be sounded.

14   Radio and microwave transmissions should hop frequencies randomly but

to a prescribed and private routine, and call-signs should be changed at regular intervals and kept secret.

15 Make system and network users re-authenticate at regular intervals.

16 Take care with remote diagnostic facilities and enforce strict control over maintenance procedures (see Chapter 13 on hardware security). Take particular guard over the telephone engineer, and over the use of 'datascope' equipment.

17 Service can be assured by diverse routings—physically separated cable runs to, say, separate telephone exchanges. A disaster at one point would not then disable the entire communications system, since a second one can be brought into use. However, two separate connections will cost something like twice as much; furthermore, a telephone company will sometimes claim two links to be separate when in fact they may share a common path, perhaps only to the junction box on the main road but nevertheless prone to danger as a single point of failure. Ideally, dual cable runs to the outside world should emerge either side of the site and never meet.

18 All maintenance work on communications links must be authorized in advance by the system manager, and inspected afterwards. No excavation work should be permitted until the proposed area has been inspected for buried cabling.

19 Employ dial-back devices. An outsider contacts the installation requesting access to the system. Demand the contact telephone number, and then break the link. Call back the outsider to re-establish and then allow the link, providing the caller's identification matches the place he or she purports to be calling from, and that that number matches a master list within the system. In this way, at least we are sure that the link is to a terminal we are happy with—'I know who you say you are, and I agree that you are phoning from where you should be phoning from'—thereby reducing the possible places of attack. But:

(a) Most automatic dial-back facilities depend on the caller breaking the link. It is possible to fool the dial-back facility into thinking the link has been broken when it has not, thus allowing unauthorized access to the system. Insist on a device that breaks the link for you. Better still, dial-in lines should all be operator controlled. All lines should automatically cut off after the caller has finished his or her business.

(b) Insist on a dual-line device that calls back on a separate line to the one the caller comes in on. Again this will help prevent the device being fooled.

(c) Watch out for return numbers to a local telephone exchange (PABX) where no guarantee can be made about exactly who on the exchange will be gaining access. As a more secure alternative to dial-back, there are a number of system products on the market which offer authentication of a dial-up by means of a one-time password.

20 British Telecom offers a guaranteed response time to fix data links—it may

be worth your while buying this extra service. Fallback lines can also be provided as an extra. Other special agreements to guarantee the maintenance of data links, including mobile satellite dishes, which turn up on the back of a lorry, can be negotiated. The extra costs involved must be considered against the importance of the link in question and the nature of the threats against it.

21 Contingency plans must be devised to counter any long-term failures in electrical/electronic links. These may include the use of another's lines, the physical transportation of data on tape or disk and so on, but the detailed measures will be system specific.

All these specific counters to the dangers ranged against communications and network security must be in the context of the sound defence in depth applied to the other aspects of the computer system. In many respects, those security countermeasures employed to protect other aspects and components of the system—regular inspection of security logs to recognize trends and sustained attacks, for example—are applicable to network security. The problem of network and communications security must not be viewed in isolation, but within the overall security policy for the system.

17.8 Security for EFT and EDI networks

Computer networks have many applications, including file transfer, message handling, client/server access to central databases, integrated corporate management information systems, electronic funds transfer (EFT) and electronic data interchange (EDI). While all of these applications have business requirements for network security, the last two are worthy of special mention, since they are both concerned with the transfer of value from one computer system to another, and as such are attractive targets for criminals and other opponents.

An EFT network is always controlled by a bank or group of banks; indeed, EFT is a banking service in its own right, offered to the corporate customers of the banks. Corporate electronic banking services include cash management, foreign exchange netting, treasury management, and office banking. The equivalent services in retail banking are called EFTPoS (electronic funds transfer at the point of sale) and ATM networks—those networks which control the automatic teller machines or 'hole in the wall' cash dispensers.

The control by the banking community allows these networks to utilize DES encryption (under Government regulations), both for authenticating the contents of the EFT messages and for providing entity authentication to prove the identity of the user. This latter requirement is met by use of special passwords and PINs (personal identification numbers) which are cryptographically generated and verified, and which are also encrypted to protect their secrecy during transfer across the network. Some of the most important international standards which are relevant to EFT are as follows:

ANSI X9.9	Financial Institution Message Authentication (Wholesale)
ISO 8732	Banking—Key Management (Wholesale)
ISO 8730	Banking Requirements for Message Authentication (Wholesale)
ISO 8731	Banking—Approved Algorithms for Message Authentication
	Part 1: DEA
	Part 2: Message Authentication Algorithm (MAA)
ISO 9564	PIN Management and Security
ISO 9807	Banking—Retail Message Authentication
ISO 11166	Banking—Key Management by means of Asymmetric Algorithms

Key management is critical to the security, and must be matched carefully to the perceived business requirements. For example, if two banks exchange funds between them, they do not want to give each other complete access to all their systems, only to the parts of the systems which support this function. This is usually achieved by using different encryption keys for different 'domains' of the network (sometimes called 'zones'). Each bank or organization designs the key management arrangements to allow access by others only on a 'need to use' basis.

EDI is rather different, because here we have a corporate-to-corporate exchange of messages, and often there is no bank participation (unless an electronic payment is being made to settle an electronic invoice). This rules out DES, since only bona fide banking systems are allowed to use it.

EDI means transfer of electronic business documents directly from one computer to another, with no human intervention, and certainly no re-keying of information. The information is structured according to agreed syntax rules (defined in a standard such as UN/EDIFACT), so that the receiving computer can parse a message to discover what it says. These messages are exchanged between trading partners, and cover a wide range of documents, such as purchase orders, invoices, acknowledgements, dispatch notes, shipping orders and instructions, bills of lading, product specifications, parts lists, price lists, catalogues, CAD/CAM design data, and of course, EFT payments for settlement of invoices. The major benefits to business which derive from this automation of document exchange are reduced lead times, speeding up the trading cycle; improved customer service; cost savings on printing, mailing and re-keying; reduced errors from keyboard input; improved cash flow by enabling lower stock levels to be maintained; and improved trust for JIT (just-in-time) supplier relationships.

Current developments in EDI security are more concerned with proving the origin of a message and authenticating its contents, rather than providing confidentiality, and so digital signature schemes are being introduced to meet these requirements. Once again, the specific techniques used and the key management schemes employed must be carefully matched to the business requirements for the system. However, current developments in both the UN/EDIFACT and ISO standards are being addressed specifically at these areas of application, and will provide the framework within which future systems are designed and implemented.

17.9   Hacking

A popular aspect of computer security, and one that springs to the lay person's mind as soon as the whole subject is raised, is that of hacking. A hacker is simply someone who breaches the communications and network security in order to gain unauthorized access to a computer system or its associated network. Hackers are characterized by that supposedly special quality of non-malignancy, in that there is supposed to be no criminal intent in the activity. Hackers do it for fun, they say, for the intellectual challenge, to prove it can be done. They can be outsiders, or they may work within the enterprise and perhaps already have authorized access to part of the system. There is a thin line, therefore, between the browser and the hacker, and an even thinner one between the hacker and the criminal. At what stage, for example, does the actual hacking become a criminal activity, and what happens when perhaps innocently and accidentally the hackers stumble across something they could exploit to their own advantage? Every person has a price, and we must suppose the hacker is no different.

The attractions of hacking include the risk of capture. The rush of adrenalin it is supposed to excite is another bonus, and new challenges can be met every time the hacker logs on. Hacking, it has been said, is the best computer game going. But for criminals too, the hacking process is attractive; there may be high gains at stake, there is a low risk of detection and a low probability of conviction even if caught, and the law as it stands at present has no real teeth to deal effectively with offenders. Competitors see the opportunity through hacking of perhaps corrupting a rival's data or to steal covertly the knowledge held on the system under attack. Knowledge of, for example, a competitor's customer list, or sales figures for the past year, would be very advantageous.

Hackers can be mere opportunists employing passive means of attack: the majority of hackers fall into this category. But hackers can employ active means of attack—they will be more motivated, organized and determined, and therefore a greater threat.

Hackers use a variety of means to gain access to the system, or at least information about how to do so. They can stumble across your system, or they can phone on some pretext. A common ploy is to ring some unsuspecting secretary, claiming to be an authorized user who has 'lost his (or her) password'. They often claim to be students performing a survey, or sales persons offering to sell some security product—an unguarded answer to the question 'do you need some form of encryption device?' will tell the caller if you encrypt your transmissions. Determined attackers can use bribery, extortion, or theft to obtain clues about accessing the system. They headhunt key employees—programmers, communications engineers and so on—and target their efforts on them, especially those with weaknesses or who are disgruntled. They can intercept the communications links in the ways described earlier in this chapter. They can search the rubbish in the bins left outside in the backyard awaiting collection. They listen in at conferences and in the pubs near the office for bar talk. They can pick up valuable tips during unguarded conversations either with employees or from crossed telephone calls. Hackers display seemingly unconnected snippets of information on subversive 'bulletin boards' run by hackers for the use of other hackers. They read newspapers and the popular periodicals, which will tell them when a company installs a particular system, and can narrow down and modify their attack accordingly. They can plan their attacks at leisure on their own PCs, devising the programs necessary to break your software security measures. They can use 'demon diallers', devices that work through thousands of telephone numbers until they find the one that allows them into your system. They will best-guess passwords. They are ingenious and devious. They can be very clever, sometimes more so than those who designed your computer!

All hackers, whatever their background or motives, require in order to do their dirty deeds a way into the system. Once this barrier has been breached then they are often free to manipulate and then use the database at will. This way in, though, is the easiest to bar, and sound access control enforced with passwords, identification devices and other physical and procedural controls described in this chapter will go a long way towards keeping hackers out.

There are some golden rules:

1 Do not view hackers benevolently. They are potential criminals, who could do your company real harm.
2 Any defence which makes your system harder to hack than another's will send the hacker elsewhere.
3 Supposedly 'friendly' agents such as contractors or engineers are often the greatest danger since they have access to the system anyway.
4 Do not have links to the outside world unless you have to. Isolated stand alone systems are impervious to the outsider.
5 Help screens must not be available until after successful log-on. Do not welcome any user to the system; a hacker in the USA mounted a successful defence in a court of law by claiming that the logo 'Welcome to the XYZ system' was an invitation to log on to the system. Always display a warning that all unauthorized users are liable to prosecution and that only authorized users are permitted access.
6 Change telephone numbers of outside lines into the system at regular intervals.
7 If you are under attack and detect this, play the hackers' game and feed them what *you* want. Try to hold hackers in controlled conversation: they may enjoy it and it will give you time and clues to track them down. To intimidate them or treat them with contempt, or simply to block them out, will cause

them to find another way in and could cause them to seek revenge at the intellectual slight. You may even consider enlisting their help to identify system weaknesses, but this is a dangerous game and needs to be played with great caution—hackers may not be innocent, and could be criminals or disturbed persons.

8 Never underestimate the skill and determination of the hackers. They do not necessarily view the world with the same perception or degree of reason we perhaps employ. They may not be emotionally stable.

Finally, if you want to read an excellent case study on hacking, I recommend Clifford Stoll's ripping yarn *The Cuckoo's Egg*, the true story of how he tracked down an international hacking gang because of a tiny discrepancy in his company's phone bill. This is a book everyone should read.

18
Business continuity planning and disaster recovery

Plan on ways to keep the business going.

There is no such thing as total security. Even if there were, no security programme could ever be introduced cost-effectively to achieve it. Computer security, as with all other forms of security, involves the acceptance of a certain level of risk, so that a reasonable effort—in terms of time, money and reduced efficiency—is applied to the protection of the valuable assets, in this case the computer's data.

The security effort applied will, of course, depend on the value and sensitivity of that data and the importance of retaining the availability of the computer's services. The nature and extent of the security measures will be dictated by the nature of the system, its role, and the specific threats directed against it. But ultimately, no matter what it is we are protecting, there will be a limit to how well we can defend, and in the case of a computer how effectively we can prevent data loss, compromise or unavailability. While our main efforts must be directed against the prevention of such harmful events we should recognize that there is no risk that we cannot completely eliminate. We must devise ways to anticipate and thus mitigate the effects of the disaster or other unforeseen occurrence, which results in loss or disruption of computer services (Business Continuity Planning) and in the worst case to recover the situation (Disaster Recovery). Whatever, we must keep the *business*'s lifeblood flowing, if necessary forgetting, at least for a while, our wonderful computer and returning to alternative manual processing.

Disasters may be catastrophic, immediate and obvious, such as a fire, or they may be more insidious, hurting gradually over a longer period. They are certainly inevitable; the probability of a computer installation suffering a serious disruption in any one year is typically about 1 in 750—or within the United Kingdom at current estimates some 20 large installations will suffer a major disaster in any one year. That could be you!

18.1   The need for business continuity planning and disaster recovery

Historically, like other aspects of computer security, business continuity planning and disaster recovery have received scant attention. Even then they were addressed by the computer personnel who are probably least able to recognize the immediate or unlikely threats, or judge independently and dispassionately either the critical computer functions for the survival of the business or the minimum necessary features of a recovery plan.

Enterprises of all sizes are becoming computer-dependent, and loss of, or reduction in, computing facilities and the associated access to data can cripple a company in as little as a few hours, and certainly within a matter of a few days. The preparation and testing of plans to avoid or recover from such a circumstance, however, has in the great majority of cases received little or no attention, and then at an organizational level inappropriate to its importance. Selling the concept of, and need for, business continuity and disaster recovery plans is, to the security and computer personnel, as important an aspect of its introduction as the actual preparation of the detailed plans.

18.2   Business continuity planning

In this book we have been concerned exclusively with the safety and security of the data processing facilities within any enterprise. The computers will probably be one of the most critical support resources for business survival and it is essential that disaster recovery plans are prepared and practised for them. At the same time, though, it is necessary to undertake broader and more fundamental planning to ensure the continuity of the whole of the business in the event of a disaster, not just the data processing function. There will be other critical functions, and the recovery of the computing facility in isolation may not be sufficient.

18.2.1   Objectives of business continuity planning

Business continuity planning should aim to achieve a number of objectives.

Protect life and limb

The protection of life is paramount in any emergency. Not only has an enterprise the social and ethical responsibility for protecting its staff, they are its most valuable asset. Selfishly, an enterprise must protect its players if it is to have any chance of restarting the game.

Throughout the premises, safety leaders should be appointed who are trained in first aid and emergency rescue techniques. They should be thoroughly familiar with all emergency and evacuation plans and procedures. They should be available to take charge in an emergency. Since such safety leaders will need to respond effectively and imaginatively under stress and display authority, they should be drawn from the ranks of senior managers to whom staff would naturally turn for leadership. The importance of this role must be recognized and not relegated as a minor duty to a low-ranking individual.

The premises must be rendered as safe as possible and kept so at all times. In particular, fire detection and suppression systems must be maintained properly and tested regularly. First aid points should be located throughout and kept properly equipped and maintained.

Have an identified emergency control centre—this need not be dedicated; it could be any convenient and safe location. Store copies of the emergency plans here. Install dedicated ex-directory phone lines to allow contact with the outside world during an emergency. Normal lines will become clogged with incoming and outgoing panic calls, making it impossible for those in charge to talk even to the emergency services.

Establish a chain of command

The norms of everyday life will quickly disappear during emergencies and disasters, but at no other times will there be such a dire need for firm leadership, rapid communications and a thorough knowledge of the priorities for business survival. It may become necessary to make urgent decisions that would normally require high-level approval. Individual executives may not be available at the time of the crisis, or might even have been part of it. It is vital that there is devised a clear chain of emergency command and a management succession plan. In addition, emergency powers of authority should be drawn up.

Identify critical business functions

A conscientious analysis of the impact upon the business of all products and services should be carried out to identify those that are critical to business survival. While it is important not to miss any such function, the more there are then the less effective will be any resultant business continuity plan.

Business impact analysis must not consider only direct losses. A host of other less apparent but nonetheless important factors need to be considered as well. Loss of customer confidence, loss of face in the market place, legal and contractual penalties and costly business decisions made on the basis of poor or inadequate information can all occur as a result of any disaster.

Some products or services may need to be restored before others, either because they are more important or because the recovery of some functions can depend on other functions; plans should take sequence of recovery into account as well.

Business impact analysis must receive approval from the highest levels of management, who have both the ultimate responsibility for such major corporate decisions and who are the only ones properly competent to allocate such fundamental business priorities. They will be the ones, too, to ensure the completion of subsequent business resumption planning and to authorize the necessary funding.

Identify critical support functions

Alongside the critical business functions will be a range of associated support functions which should be identified. Data processing will normally fall into this category, along with, for example, communications, component supply lines, production facilities and transportation.

Minimize immediate damage and losses

Business continuity plans should, in the first place, aim to contain any disaster and prevent or minimize its harmful effects upon the enterprise. Subsequent disaster recovery actions should be secondary to this preventative element.

Resume critical business functions

The identified critical business functions should be restored as quickly as necessary, using alternative facilities and invoking disaster recovery plans as appropriate.

Recover the situation to normal

The disaster has not ended until normal business activity has been resumed, but even this process can be eased and hastened by careful forethought within the business continuity plan.

18.3 Developing a computer disaster recovery plan

We return now to our main concern, the computer. Let us consider the preparation of a suitable disaster recovery plan as part of our business continuity plan. Company policy must include a commitment to all the facets of computer security—to an appropriate degree—and the recovery plan is a vital element of such a security programme. Sufficient time and resources must be applied to the development of a suitable plan, and then to its testing and maintenance.

   The following points are equally relevant to gaining support for, and completion of, the business continuity plan.

18.3.1 *Getting going*

The recovery plan will depend on the nature of the enterprise and the role of the computer, but it will incur, inevitably, a cost. The preparation of a realistic and cost-effective plan, and the resources such a plan will demand, will have a finite monetary penalty. Staff will need to be established to maintain the currency of the plan as the company and computing facilities evolve. The plan must be regularly and realistically tested. As with all forms of 'insurance', disaster recovery planning needs to be sold. High-level support will be required if the necessary time and money are to be committed and there are several ways computer and security staff can achieve such support.

Questions

With the risks to a computer system assessed and the proposed countermeasures merged into a cost-effective security policy, there must be asked of senior management a series of simple questions which, in themselves, will point to the need for a computer disaster recovery plan:

- 'Is our security total?' We know that the answer to this is no.
- 'In that case, could we lose our computing facilities, particularly those elements critical to the functioning of our business?' The answer to this, no matter how remote the chance, must be yes.
- 'If we lose such critical computing capacity, can we carry on without it?' We know from surveys that this answer depends on the nature of the business and the extent to which the business has committed itself to the computer. In the main, though, the vast majority of 'computerized' businesses, especially those with their systems established for more than a year, will suffer serious effects on performance within a very short time should such critical facilities be lost or degraded. Those that suffer a major disaster are often out of business within 12 months.

Thus the need for a disaster recovery plan can justify itself. Remember, it is not how often disasters occur which is the basis for the preparation of a recovery plan, but the effect of such a disaster, no matter how remote the chance, on the well-being of the business. Disaster planning, in it simplest sense, is the insurance against the worst case happening.

Explain the consequences

Without a satisfactory disaster recovery plan, a major disaster which destroys or reduces the computing facility will impact negatively upon the company's performance in a number of ways. These effects should be explained carefully to management:

1 *Financial loss* Computers are essential to those businesses that have become 'computerized', and they influence all parts of the enterprise. Loss of this computing facility will result, inevitably, in financial loss, or even ruin.
2 *Legal responsibility* Any management has a legal responsibility to protect its employees, assets and information, and the absence of a suitable disaster

recovery plan, which in itself causes further harm, could lead to legal action against the company.

3 *Market share* Any disruption in customer service will lead to loss of goodwill. Protracted or serious disruption will, in the end, result in customers going elsewhere. Once service is resumed, public confidence in the company will have been badly affected. A sound disaster recovery plan will reduce and limit the disruption and consequential losses, and allow a more speedy return to normal.

Direct assault

If senior management remains unconvinced of the need for disaster planning, then the security manager may have to resort to dramatic methods if the concept is to be sold and thus the final element of the task of creating defence in depth is to be discharged. Clearly, no matter how tempting, the security manager should not cause a real disaster to prove the point. However, at a suitable opportunity— a board meeting, for example—the security manager could, without warning, present a well-planned scenario which involves the loss of part or all of the computer system(s) as a result of some natural or manufactured disaster. Alternatively, principal staff could be asked in advance to spend a few hours (one weekend?) to play-act a disaster situation—major fire, unforeseen flooding, unexpected industrial action either by employees or by outside suppliers of some essential resource or service. Such examples must be introduced with good humour and with clearly demonstrated enthusiasm for the exercise. Senior management should be encouraged to consider the implications on business performance, and the immediate steps to be taken in order to overcome the unexpected. Such brainstorming sessions are virtually guaranteed to expose the dangers and inadequacies of crisis management, and highlight the merits of advance planning. Guidelines for the drawing up of a disaster recovery plan will emerge, alongside both an outline version of the company's recovery strategy and an identification of the critical elements of the company and the computing facilities. At the end, the security manager should have convinced management of the need for a disaster recovery plan, and be armed with much useful information for the subsequent preparation of a documented and feasible first version. Such an exercise can be used to test any existing plans and to reveal any (inevitable) inherent weaknesses and limitations. To the discerning reader, though, the dangers of this method need not be pointed out—an unconvinced board, or one whose own failings and limitations have been unsubtly and embarrassingly revealed, rejecting the security manager's efforts to initiate such an exercise, or worse, failing to accept the results of such an event, will be counter-productive to computer security. It is also vital that the exercise is well planned, or its credibility and that of its instigator will be undermined.

Direct example

The misfortunes of competitors are best used to highlight one's own enterprise's vulnerabilities: 'What if that had happened to us ... ?', or 'How would we have coped with that ... ?' The security manager should never miss such an opportunity, if only to improve the company's own security programme and disaster recovery plan. Minor misfortunes to one's own system, which are bound to happen from time to time, can be used as springboards for further discussion: 'What if we hadn't noticed that leaking pipe ... ?' or 'What if the short circuit had not been detected and the small fire extinguished early, before it had time to take hold ... ?' Chilling thoughts can be used to spur others into action.

Do not be reluctant to hold miscreants up to public scrutiny. Hanging them by the neck from a tall tree outside the main gate might be a little extreme. However those who have in some way caused a security mishap, especially where this led to an adverse event or even disaster, should expect to be exposed to the harsh light of the security education campaign. Any punishments meted out should also be publicized as a deterrent to others in the future.

Reaction to events

As a last resort, reaction to a major disaster at home may prove to be the necessary medium for inspiring the preparation of a disaster recovery plan. This bolting of the stable door after the disaster would illustrate a profound failure by all concerned to recognize the need for a suitable recovery plan and the preparation of appropriate contingencies. It only remains to be hoped that none of our readers finds themself in such a dilemma, drawing up such a plan in the wake of a major disaster. For want of a pre-planned course of action, the business may indeed have died with the fire.

18.3.2   Where to start?

Having achieved agreement and sufficient resources for the preparation of a disaster recovery plan, its broad aims and its essential characteristics need next to be clarified in outline terms for subsequent expansion, refinement and testing.

Any disaster recovery plan must be current, comprehensive, achievable, and must be properly and regularly tested. It must also be properly documented.

Current

No enterprise remains static. Its aims, methods and composition evolve continually, and its computing needs will also change. Any plan, no matter what its purpose, will quickly become out of date and must be amended to remain current at all times. Responsibility for the updating of the plan must be given to a named individual. There must be feedback from computer users and developers alike, to ensure the plan is appropriate and accurate. The plan must be current.

Comprehensive

It is too easy to produce a face-saving and cosmetically satisfactory disaster recovery plan, but in fact the preparation, maintenance and testing of such a plan will, if it is to be of any real worth, be time-consuming and with a real cost. A poor plan is worse than no plan at all, since it masks the company's vulnerability in this crucial area. Any plan must be comprehensive and of a good quality. There is no easy path to the creation of a good disaster recovery plan.

Achievable

It is easy to forget the constraints of everyday living, and devise grandiose schemes which can quickly lose contact with reality and crumble when invoked as human and organizational frailties occur. The best plans are the simplest, since they are easiest to achieve and have less to go wrong. Any plan must be workable, or else it is useless, and its design and preparation must always have this in mind. Consultation with all departments is essential as the plans are drawn up. Sufficient resources must be made available for a satisfactory plan to be established. That most essential resource of all—money—must be provided in sufficient quantities and then not from within the operating budget of the data processing department but from central management resources. Only then can the plan be developed to maturity, and maintained and practised to make it workable at any time and under the worst possible conditions. Staff must be properly trained so that they can react in the desired way to the disaster; essential staff members must be duplicated and contactable at all times. The plan must be achievable.

Tested

Testing of the plan on a regular basis will ensure its currency and prove its achievability. Testing will highlight any flaws in the plan. Testing will provide staff training on the proposed courses of action leading up to and following a disaster, and will enhance the awareness of all staff—including top management—of the need for, and nature of, the recovery plan. Testing may be as simple as careful examination and review of the plan's documentation, or it may be as complex as simulating a disaster. Whatever, though, the plan must be regularly and realistically tested.

Documented

The disaster plan must be formalized into a written document so that whatever the event and whosoever is required to operate the plan, clear, concise and consistent orders will be available. The disaster itself may prevent those members of the staff who had designed the plan from masterminding its implementation—

they may have been injured, or cut off from getting into work, or with the passage of time have moved on to another company or retired. All staff members should study the written plan, sign as having read the plan, and be aware of, and capable of, achieving their personal tasks in the recovery process. The plan must be formally documented.

Any disaster recovery plan must assume the worst case of total destruction of the computer resources, but allow a controlled response to lesser disasters. Nevertheless, the recovery by whatever means—manual or electronically—of the data processing ability remains the primary aim of any such plan.

18.3.3 How to start

There are discrete steps in the development of a disaster recovery plan:

Stage 1: Develop a disaster recovery policy

Critical analysis   In terms of the overall security policy, including the protection of the computing facilities and the electronically stored information, the value of each item of equipment or information should have been defined, and the appropriate classification (level of value) labelled clearly on it. However, for disaster recovery, while this value is of course important, the crucial aspect is an item's criticality to corporate survival. Those that must be recovered above all else should be listed in order of importance, with the impact on business performance of their loss or unavailability for varying periods of time. (Those items which are highly desirable to company recovery should also be identified for attention as and when recovery resources become available.) This list of critical functions is the basis of the recovery plan; it must be entirely accurate, realistic, up to date, and brutal in its exclusion of all non-critical functions. There are those departmental heads who would wish their function to be included for the supposed status it infers.

Losses of computing facilities will affect different departments in differing ways:

- loss of sales
- loss of revenue
- reduced operating capability
- reduced decision-making and forecasting capability
- legal implications
- increased operating costs
- increased stock holdings

The time-scale of such losses can be expressed in terms of the time to recover to normal and the damage incurred:

- *Limited impact*   Recovery to normal within one working day. No significant damage incurred.

- *Severe impact* Recovery to normal within one working week. Significant damage incurred.
- *Major impact* Recovery to normal will take more than one working week and will require considerable resources and effort. Serious harm will be inflicted on the company's well-being.
- *Critical impact* Recovery to normal unlikely. Grave harm to the company's survival prospects will occur.

Other expressions of impact could be subjective assessments of percentage reduction in overall performance, or any other expression which is understood by both user departments and the senior managers who must make their decisions on this information. Remember to include those assets not normally considered in the context of computing functions, and remember too that the computer department itself will suffer impact as the result of a disaster, in terms of reduced development activity.

Such measures of impact will to a considerable degree indicate the nature of the recovery plan, and the resources that can be justified and made available. If, for example, a function will only cause limited damage if lost, or could be dispensed with for some weeks, then it may be possible to ignore the loss and simply buy in replacement hardware, thus making any plans for the hiring of temporary facilities inappropriate.

The decisions about this listing of priorities are entirely the responsibility of the most senior levels of management, since company survival may depend upon such decisions. This is one job which must certainly not be delegated to the computer, audit or security personnel who may not fully appreciate company aims and strategy and will not therefore be totally competent in judging the worth of all items (including those areas not immediately connected with the computer but which would be affected or lost alongside the loss of the computer). However, users must be consulted for the detailed information on many of the lower level computer assets and functions—there may be some absolutely critical but little known resource or function that could be overlooked by higher management.

Integration with others plans and policies The disaster recovery policy should be part of both the business continuity plan and the overall computer security policy.

Stage 2: Appoint a disaster recovery manager

In line with the principle of always assigning duties to named individuals or appointments, the responsibility for disaster recovery and its associated planning must be vested in a particular member of staff. This appointee may be the security manager, already involved actively in the enforcement of other security and safety measures, but it could as easily be passed to computer operations staff or someone within the general management staff.

Unambiguous terms of reference must be drawn up which describe the aim of the appointment—'the design, maintenance and testing of a disaster recovery plan which reduces to an acceptable level the loss of data processing power by transferring the critical processing functions elsewhere (electronic alternative) or by performing those functions by other means (manual option)'.

The appointee should receive appropriate training to carry out the task, and previous experience is especially useful. The appointee should be well versed in the overall aims and methods of the company; have a broad technical knowledge, not least so that the difficulties of computer personnel, to be expected during the post-disaster trauma, may be appreciated; and be able to react under pressure in an intelligent and innovative way, under possibly unpredictable and adverse conditions.

It may well prove necessary, especially for the smaller business, to call upon the services of specialist consultants, where there is available (at a cost) experience of past projects and the associated comparison with like enterprises, and a completely objective viewpoint. However, such outside help will bring with it no intimate knowledge of the company and, once the tasking is complete, there will be no retention of their knowledge. A combined approach, with consultants advising on the preparation of the plan by company staff, is often to be preferred.

Stage 3: Design a disaster recovery plan

With critical and highly desirable computing functions—hardware, software, staff, other resources and the important parts of the data—identified, and the time determined after which loss of each of these critical functions will cause damage to the business, the detailed plan can now begin to be drawn up. It will fall naturally into four phases.

Phase 1: Emergency response In the very early stages of any disaster, protection of life and limb must take priority over all else. At this stage, the standard emergency response plan will probably satisfy the requirements of the computer security disaster recovery plan, with perhaps some amendments and additions to contend with the special qualities and problems of computers.

Phase 2: Immediate back-up The ability to continue critical computing functions with as short a break as possible (hours, minutes, or even seconds), even if such functions are much reduced in capacity or speed, may be vital to the survival of the enterprise or its customers. The air traffic control computer must have an immediate back-up, or lives may be put in danger. The large financial institution active on the computerized stock exchange can incur massive losses after a few minutes if it is unable either to match the performance of its rivals or to keep exactly abreast of the market state. Immediate back-up is expensive, but its cost may be a fraction of the costs incurred by not having such support.

Phase 3: Longer term back-up Having survived the first few hours after a major disaster, and with an eye on continuing operations while replacement facilities are installed, provision must be made for longer term back-up processing capacity for firstly the critical, then the highly desirable, and finally any other computer functions. Such plans could include the use of other computer resources within the enterprise, the leasing of alternative facilities, the hiring of on-site or transportable facilities or the sharing of facilities with another company's data centre on a mutual agreement basis. (Stand-by facilities are described later in this chapter.)

Phase 4: Replacement of computing facilities   With the alligators tamed, it is now time to consider draining the swamp. Having restored, albeit on a temporary and possibly reduced basis, the enterprise's ability to process its data, the replacement of the original facilities and capacity can now be addressed. The unexpected opportunity to refurbish or enhance the computer facility should not be lost.

The difficulty in achieving the final phase of the exercise will, to an extent, dictate the Phase 3 (longer term back-up) strategy. In the same way, the nature of the enterprise, its role and the function of the data processing facility within the corporate structure will dictate the details within the four-phase disaster recovery strategy. It may well be that the computing facility, after careful analysis, will reveal itself to be dispensable, at least in the short/medium term. The selection of immediate back-up sites and expensive stand-by contracts may not be necessary. On the other hand, a function may be so critical—the air traffic control computer—as to justify a complete replication of the computer facility, including hardware, software and operations staff, away from the original site, warmed up and primed with up-to-date data, and ready to take over within a few seconds.

18.4   Stand-by facilities

Disaster recovery plans will usually involve the use of stand-by computer facilities, in the short-to long-term recovery phases pending the replacement/repair of the original computer system. There are several types of stand-by facility.

18.4.1 *Commercial facilities*

Service bureau

A large computer already used by a number of organizations for their routine processing, but with capacity reserved for leasing by a stricken company. Immediate processing is available, especially if pre-planning, pre-testing and pre-positioning of latest versions of software and of the database have been conscientiously carried out. Such a solution is ideal for straightforward processes which must be carried out on time, such as payroll. Security may be difficult to enforce, since it depends on the security standards at the bureau.

Vendor agreement

The seller of the computer equipment promises to provide a compatible replacement system in the event of a disaster. Better suited to the smaller computer, this solution may be long on promises but short on results, since the word of the sales person is notoriously fictional. Security may be less strict than required.

Relocatable units

A portable computer room complete with hardware, brought to a prearranged location in the event of a disaster and simply plugged in. Best suited to non-critical functions where a delay of some days can be accepted, this solution is cheap insurance against the worst case, with most of the costs incurred when the service is called upon. Security can be as good as the existing standards, but pre-planning with the providers of the relocatable units will be required.

Cold starts

An empty shell of office accommodation some distance away from the main site, ready wired and with all necessary services, and which can be fitted out with the required hardware if disaster strikes. Again, a cheap solution but with a significant delay period before service is resumed. If immediate back-up is necessary, look elsewhere.

Warm starts

A fully equipped computer centre with complete and compatible hardware and software available immediately, together with appropriate office accommodation and contracted testing of the back-up plan on a regular basis.

- Data security is usually guaranteed to the required standard.
- If immediate resumption of critical computer services is necessary, this option should be considered. Even so, since such a facility will be shared by a number of organizations on a first-come first-served basis, it may not always be available.
- There will be a time limit of 6–12 weeks on post-disaster occupancy, which could be extended if no other contractees require its use. Other plans are therefore essential if replacement times after total loss of the original facilities are likely to be longer than this.
- The cost will be high, both in terms of contracting fees and charges once the service is invoked. There will be a standing charge, an invocation charge and possibly a fee for the use of the equipment once in use.
- The need for prompt invocation of the facility is vital, especially if the disaster is one likely to affect other companies contracted to the facility.

Widespread storms or flooding, or a major fire in a crowded area such as the City of London could result in several of the customers clamouring for the warm start; the first in gets the computer. However, incorrect invocation results in wasted fees.

18.4.2 Cooperative facilities

Reciprocal arrangements

These arrangements are made between enterprises to accept the critical computing functions of another on a temporary basis if and when disaster strikes. The costs for such an arrangement will be negligible, but the contracts will probably be informal and may be abdicated if assistance will adversely affect the donor's own performance. Gentlemen's agreements quite often lead to gentlemen's disagreements.

Cooperative recovery centre

In effect, this is a private warm start, funded by, and shared between, a number of companies, especially if they are engaged in similar business. This is an effective option if immediate back-up is required, though again concurrent disasters (less likely than with the greater numbers sharing a warm start) are a real threat to its effectiveness.

18.4.3 Internal recovery facilities

A private warm start, dedicated to a single user, gives ideal back-up providing, of course, it is not co-located with the primary system and thus possibly damaged in the same disaster. The expense will be enormous and only justifiable if the primary processing facility is critical—the air traffic control computer once again springs to mind. Larger enterprises with a number of dispersed and compatible computer sites have, in effect, their own warm starts for free, providing suitable plans have been drawn up in advance and spare capacity exists at sites earmarked to take on critical computer functions.

A combination of commercial, cooperative and internal recovery facilities will probably be required by most companies for their disaster recovery plan to be cost effective. The chosen strategy must be laid down clearly in the recovery plan, together with methods for transferring processing capacity to stand-by facilities in a smooth, efficient and pre-ordained manner—and back again once the disaster has been overcome.

18.5   Contents of the plan

No two disaster recovery plans will be the same. The detailed contents of the plan will depend on the nature and importance of the system, the value and sensitivity of its data, and the scale and nature of the threats directed against it. The strategy adopted will be dictated by the urgency for recovery and the resources made available. Whatever its form and content, though, the plan should provide a complete, consistent and practical statement of all actions to be taken, and by whom, prior to, during and after a disaster in order to:

● ensure minimum disruption to company performance—keep the business going at all cost; then
● reinstate critical computer facilities in the order and within the time limits specified by top management.

There is no easy way to produce a good disaster recovery plan. However, since total security is not attainable, the disaster recovery plan remains an essential element of the overall computer security programme and the final stage of defence in depth.

18.6   Invoking the disaster recovery plan

Some disasters are clear to see. A massive fire, or an aircraft falling out of the sky on to the computer building, leaves little room for the imagination and the necessary response will be decided by events. But a communications breakdown, or a hardware failure where the manufacturer's engineer is on site, head buried in the back of a hardware cabinet, muttering in a desperate voice 'any minute now and I'll have it fixed . . .', is a more insidious problem which can suddenly erupt into a fully blown disaster. Events outside one's control are especially frustrating and unpredictable; the discovery of an unexploded wartime bomb in the street outside will mean the evacuation of the computer centre, or police investigation into, say, a major company fraud will cause the assets to be frozen as evidence. Any recovery plan must describe such potential problems and emphasize the need to recognize them as early as possible, with a time limit on specifically how long they should be allowed to develop before appropriate recovery action is initiated. Unless this is done, such a situation is almost certain to drift on until serious harm is inevitable, simply because no one was prepared to make the unusual and somewhat brave decision to invoke the plan.

Any action is often better than no action at all. There must be no doubt about who should do what and when—time and reaction are the vital elements.

19
Computer insurance

. . . transferring the risk . . .

Insurance is not an alternative to either safety or security. Insurance is merely the process of transferring certain identified risks to another party—the insurer—but it can never fully compensate for all losses or disasters. The home which burns down can be physically rebuilt, but the lifetime of personal possessions cannot be recovered. The heartache of having one's home burgled and ransacked can never be balanced by a cheque in the post from the friendly insurance company, no matter how quickly it arrives! Family photographs, for example, are worth in material terms only a few pence, but are priceless to their owners.

19.1   Problems with insurance

Any insurance policy is notoriously limited and patchy, and this is especially true for the complicated area of computer insurance. Most computer insurance policies still refer to the computers of twenty or more years ago, relating to the risks of the fortress mainframe rather than those of open accessibility. They base their cover on the now-false assumptions that hardware costs are the most significant problem, and show their authors' belief that computers have moving parts that require regular oiling and servicing and use punched cards that are batch processed at night. Cover to protect against computer crime is even more confused, having developed in gradual steps from pre-computer concepts into its present unsatisfactory state.

To depend on insurance as the strategy for recovery is unsound. Insurance has an important part to play in any company computer security policy, and to be uninsured in those areas where monetary recompense or physical replacement is possible, satisfactory, and likely to be required would be foolish. But the use of insurance as a substitute for countering recognized failings in the system will produce a false sense of security, and is unsatisfactory for this and a number of other reasons:

1   Insurance can never undo an event, but merely offers compensation in the

form of financial reimbursement to pre-agreed levels. It will not prevent computer disasters happening, nor erase the consequences of those disasters and the associated disruption which can, and often does, ultimately kill the enterprises affected.

2   Insurance companies are not yet expert in this field and do not yet possess the detailed statistics and case histories of claimable computer incidents, upon which they would normally base their premium calculations and from which they would refine their policies.

3   The traditional structure of the insurance market requires risks to be simply labelled—physical dangers, the risks from fraud and other criminal or negligent activities of staff, and so on—but the technical nature of the data processing function and the many and obscure risks associated with it cannot be shoe-horned in such a way.

4   Policy wording is often confused as insurers grapple with the new language of the computer specialist.

5   Obscure risks often remain unimagined until they occur. They cannot be covered in advance by insurance.

6   Insurance cannot prevent loss of opportunities while the computer service is unavailable, or the loss of essential staff either as a result of the actual disaster or the unpleasant circumstances of post-disaster operations. These consequential effects of a disaster—long-term customer loss, loss of market confidence, loss of market share and others—are more insidious than the actual disaster and potentially fatal to the survival of an enterprise.

7   Certain risks are currently (1993) uninsurable, such as the effects of industrial action (either direct or indirect), computer intrusion or misuse, operator or programmer errors, software errors (either deliberate bugs or accidental), industrial espionage or 'hacking'. The threat of damage is similarly impossible to cover, as is damage to reputation.

8   Cover requires limits and parameters. How much will one be insured for? What will one insure against? For how long will back-up facilities be required? What maximum repayment per incident will be set? The nature of potential computer disasters—their type, scale and frequency—is virtually endless, often obscure and their effects not accurately definable. The chance of hitting the right cover for the right event at the right cost is thus remote.

9   The organization of many companies further complicates this difficulty in accurately assessing the type and amount of cover required. The computer personnel, who in any case are notoriously insular and independent, are divorced from the administrative staff responsible for arranging the company's insurance cover and who are probably computer illiterate. Unable to gather or even understand the basic facts, the administrator thus 'best-guesses' the computer insurance cover, and this inevitably inaccurate assessment will be further degraded as the administrator is then kept ignorant of subsequent enhancements and associated increases in values of the computer system. Indeed, in some enterprises, the responsibility for information

technology rests with the engineering and maintenance department, as yet another industrial machine!

10 If material facts—that information upon which a wise and prudent insurer would base any acceptance of risk, and set the associated terms and conditions of a subsequent legal agreement—given to insurers are false or inaccurate, even if provided in good faith, any subsequent claim on the policy can legitimately be refused by the insurers. Since the administrators are probably not qualified to provide the material facts, and those who would be (the computer personnel) are unlikely to be consulted, then the chances of inaccurate or misleading information being given to the insurers is high and subsequent claims would be in jeopardy.

11 Any insurance cover requires the insured to take reasonable care of the assets under cover. Since many enterprises are ignorant of the dangers to their computers and the reasonable countermeasures available, it is very likely that an insurer will be reasonably able to avoid any claim for a loss caused by a risk where care was not taken in the first place to prevent it.

Computer insurance, then, is never likely to be satisfactory, and while a company may feel safe in the knowledge that it possesses ample cover, there will likely be massive loopholes and a number of important risks will not be covered. The policy is unlikely to be appropriate for the needs of the enterprise, and it should never be regarded as an alternative for sound preventative security measures. Furthermore, whatever amounts are agreed between the client and insurer will not prevent the inevitable disaster happening, probably caused, such is the way of life, in the most subtle, trivial, unforeseen and uncontrollable way imaginable.

19.2   Risks that can be covered

Most modern computer insurance policies will cover the following:

1 Damage to, or breakdown of, computer and ancillary equipment (such as air conditioning plant or data preparation facilities) as a result of the physical risks of fire, flood, etc. The cover should be equal to the replacement costs of the equipment, including such factors as clearance of the site and all associated rebuilding costs.

2 Accidental failure or fluctuation of public electricity supplies. Usually, deliberate acts (such as strikes by the electricity workers) are excluded except for those acts which disrupt the supply for reasons of equipment safety or the preservation of human life.

3 Failure of external communications links, such as land lines or satellite links. Again, deliberate actions are excluded.

4 Prevention of access to the computer:

   (a) following damage in the vicinity of the premises

(b) as the result of any actions to safeguard lives by any public/police authority, such as evacuation of an area as the result of the discovery of an unexploded wartime bomb.

5   The immediate effects of data loss or corruption, primarily the cost of recompiling data.
6   The costs of preventing or minimizing the effects of the disaster (emergency repairs to roofing, for example, to keep the elements out).
7   Fines, penalties and damages incurred as a result of the disaster.
8   Loss or accidental corruption of software.
9   The effects of fraudulent activity by staff, and possibly third parties (contract programmers, etc.).
10 Cover can be arranged to some degree against business interruption, consequential losses, extra expenses (overtime at the time of the disaster, cost of stand-by facilities, hotel accommodation for staff at stand-by sites away from home etc.), and increased cost of working. But such losses are difficult to identify and quantify, the possible effects of them on company performance or survival so profound, and the necessary cover so large that the premiums would be prohibitive.

Exclusions abound, and the knock-on effect of any incident can rarely be accepted within the terms of a policy. Extreme care must be taken in the selection of the cover, not because of any intent by either side to mislead but because of the novelty and complexity of the whole area and the understandable caution of the insurance companies when accepting the many and imprecise computer risks. The data processing field has unique vulnerabilities, and any insurance cover must recognize the new perils within this innovative and technical environment, and be designed to incorporate them properly and deal sensibly and fairly with any subsequent claims.

19.3   Types of cover

A company should insure itself for the rarer but more significant computer risks—the catastrophe, the incapacitation of all key staff at once, long-term industrial action—and self-insure to take regular but smaller losses 'on the chin'. Often, however, it is these smaller risks that are covered, with the policy automatically excluding the very things that can really hurt. In a china shop it is no good ignoring the occasional bull while ridding the premises of mice!

19.4   Disaster recovery plans

Comprehensive, effective, well-documented and regularly tested disaster recovery plans are not only essential to the well-being of the company, but will probably be the minimum evidence of forward planning required by the insurance company. Remember that an insurance company may possibly not recognize a good disaster recovery plan even if it fell over one, but a company that does appreciate your well-researched and workable plan is the one with which it is a better bet to insure.

19.5   Where to buy your policy

There are few specialists in the area of computer insurance. Cheapest premiums are unlikely to be the best; more importantly, the insurers should understand computer technology, and should recognize the special qualities, constraints and vulnerabilities of computers and their operations. (Some well-placed questions from the client will quickly reveal the depth of the insurer's appreciation of the topic.) If possible, you should deal with one known and competent loss adjuster, and you should agree the post-disaster procedures to be adopted in order to avoid the costly delays and confusion which surround the settlement of most traditional claims and the effects of which are magnified many times after a computer disaster. The time to arrange cover, and the time to sort out predictable problems, is in advance and not in the middle of a crisis.

The cover selected must depend on a full appreciation of the system assets, role and vulnerabilities, be integrated into the overall company and computer security policies, and be based on a risk assessment agreed by all relevant staff from the management, computer operations and security staff with the guidance and assistance of your reputable and expert insurance broker.

19.6   Dos and don'ts of computer insurance

1 Do take reasonable cover for the material assets and the predictable and measurable risks.
2 Do include insurance as an element of the overall computer security policy, but base it on an accurate assessment made by all involved staffs of all possible risks and dangers to the system, overt and covert, likely or remote. Insurance cover should be used as the cement between the bricks that are the extensive security measures in force at the installation, but as a filler of the gaps and not the main support.
3 Do obtain your cover from one of the few insurers who have expertise in this new field. Do not go for the cheapest premiums.
4 Do recognize that any insurance, but especially computer insurance, can never be comprehensive, cannot prevent the disaster in the first place, can never fully compensate for the losses incurred, and will not protect your company from the profound, long-lasting and possibly fatal effects that inevitably accompany any major disruption to computer services.

Computer insurance has its place, but its effectiveness is far more limited than most suppose. It must never be used as an alternative to, or as an excuse for not introducing, effective computer security measures.

20
Security of personal computers

The march of technology is relentless. What was regarded only a few years ago as state-of-the-art computer hardware and software today is seen as outdated and ridiculously slow and oversized. A mainframe, which only 20 years ago would have cost £3 million, is matched today by a desk-top personal computer costing only £2000, which is more flexible and powerful, and which is capable of vastly refined functions. These PCs are found everywhere, as if the old mainframe has ripened and burst its seeds throughout the enterprise.

This dramatic evolution from expensive, cumbersome, slow and limited mainframes to powerful, cheap and sophisticated PCs is, in almost all respects, advantageous. Those very essences of the computer—speed, accuracy and memory—have been brought to an individual's place of work and placed under that person's direct control, with the added bonus of cheapness. Productivity, efficiency and ease of communication have all improved. Software development has been simplified and made more flexible, and can be carried out by the relatively unskilled programmer. The user-friendly modern PCs have, however, all those vulnerabilities and threats associated with their mainframe ancestry and more, so that indeed they have also become enemy-friendly. The need to consider appropriate and effective countermeasures to secure these small systems and their data is even more pressing.

20.1   History of the personal computer

The microcomputer appeared in 1974, but it was not until 1981 that the first business system was introduced into Europe. There was, then, no talk about networking, and the PC had no capability for the storage of significant amounts of data. The early models were little more than elaborate calculators, designed to work in isolation and to deal with, as the name suggests, personal data; they were certainly not meant to be shared. They were not originally considered as part of the corporate computer strategy.

Their numbers have grown rapidly. With three or four users per system, there are now millions of small system users most of whom understand only the keyboard instructions, have little comprehension of the principles of computing, and are totally unaware of any security implications.

Research and development continue apace in response to the clamour from the customer for greater performance. PCs have become an integral and essential part of many business operations, with often total and blind faith being placed in them by staff and management. Networking has connected large numbers of PCs throughout and between enterprises. PCs can now link directly into the company's mainframe, to take from or alter the central database with the associated implications to its integrity, confidentiality and continuity. The PC can store large amounts of sensitive or valuable data, either of its own or from other sources, manipulate that data, distribute it to other PCs and release it, via printouts, from its electronic form.

The modern PC has considerable processing power of its own, and can act on its own, independent of the mainframe and free from any constraints of company computer security policies and procedures (if any exist). Even now, a new generation of small systems with improved operating systems and advanced hardware is being introduced, which will be even more powerful and useful. By the end of the century, industry and all other sectors of the community and economy, both private and public, will revolve around the PC. Unless the security of such small systems is addressed with the same vigour and commitment as for the large mainframe, they will become a fatal weakness which, like Frankenstein's monster, may destroy those they have been created to help.

20.2   Uses of the personal computer

The PC has done for business what the jet engine did for aviation: spirited us into a whole new chapter of development and achievement. There are a number of major uses to which the PC has adapted itself commendably.

20.2.1 Planning

The database and spreadsheet facilities of the PC can be used to plot and record corporate planning, including:

- decision making
- financial management
- product development
- marketing strategy
- forecasts and modelling
- long-term business strategy

The value and sensitivity of such information is clear to see, and it must be protected at all costs if the survival of the enterprise is not to be put at grave risk.

20.2.2 *Operations*

The company's daily operations can be centred around the PC, to the extent that loss of computing facilities can bring the enterprise to its knees in a very short time. New applications for the PC and its associated network to other PCs, other organizations and even other countries are emerging all the time, including such as desk-top publishing, cashless transactions, and automatic stock control and reordering.

20.2.3 *Administration*

There is a mass of information which is acquired during the running of a business, and which is essential to its continued success, such as:

- personnel records
- salaries
- holiday entitlements
- allowances and expenses
- sales records
- client records and listings
- lists of debtors and creditors
- company accounts
- stock records
- production figures

The PC absorbs this data into its electronic filing system, can subsequently manipulate it and present it in a number of ways, and stores it in a compact and easily retrievable form. Each item of data could be essential to the smooth operation of the enterprise, or be highly sensitive or valuable; aggregated in this way, these facts and figures become both extremely valuable to competitors and potentially very damaging to the company if released into the wrong hands or if corrupted or lost, entirely or in part.

20.2.4 *Word processing*

The traditional pencil-and-paper draft has been killed by the word processor. Speed and efficiency are vastly improved. Authors can have direct control over their correspondence, and when practised can type as quickly, even with two fingers, as they can write a finished draft. The final format can be seen as it is written. The same letter can be personalized to any number of addressees. Corrections and additions are simply achieved, thus avoiding much frustrating effort in rewriting. Typing speeds for secretaries are quickened. Copies of correspondence can be stored in large amounts on small floppy disks. But valuable records and sensitive information so gathered in this way are vulnerable to all those threats against any electronic information, and care must be taken to protect them.

20.2.5 *Communications and networking*

No longer is communication limited to the media of the telephone and the envelope. The modern PC, linked in to a network of other PCs, can swap data at the user's will, and there is an increasing use of electronic mail. Then the individual PC databases can, when combined on a network, create a massive and highly sensitive database worth more than its constituent parts, used by many, and of great attractiveness.

20.3   Weaknesses and vulnerabilities of personal computers

In addition to most of the weaknesses and vulnerabilities of larger systems, the PC, rather than being safer, has a number of other hazards to contend with:

1 PCs are designed to be user-friendly. They are simple to operate, and as a result almost anyone can be taught to operate them. Often such staff will be junior, or they may be plain incompetent or careless, and as a result the following problems are caused:

   (a) Failure to take adequate steps to back up data and protect such back-up copies properly. Often, when back-up copies are taken they are stored in the same room as the PC.
   (b) Failure to control access to the system. Password facilities are not often provided within the operating systems of most PCs, but when they are they may not necessarily be used, or their privacy might not be protected. Passwords are written on the back of the desk calendar, or taped to the underside of the desk.
   (c) Failure to classify data according to its value or sensitivity, so that the more important data is insufficiently identified and thus not protected as well as it should be. Any security measures will be inefficiently deployed.
   (d) Failure to look after computer resources; magnetic disks and tapes are left lying around and open to theft or improper use; PCs are left on and unattended; paper and ribbons are misused and wasted.
   (e) Browsing through the system. Often the most curious of users are those with a newly acquired and limited knowledge of their PC, and their non-malicious but ignorant fumblings can cause serious harm to the data. And beware—not all browsers are innocent!

2 Computers are no longer available only to computer staff, but also to employees who have known no other type of computer. Safe and secure operating practices and security awareness are difficult enough to instil in the professional information technology world; it is even more difficult to educate the clerk or the sales person, especially if any computer staff around are setting a bad example by showing a disregard anyway for computer security.

3   There will have been a total lack of any constraints on PC use since their
    introduction, and poor and insecure user practices will have developed
    which will be difficult to alter. Persuading a workforce to adopt more secure
    methods of PC operations is an awkward and thankless task, especially
    when those methods inevitably include extra work and an apparent reduction
    in speed and efficiency.

4   PCs, being small, portable and easily resaleable, are particularly valuable
    and attractive items. They are usually located in the normal office environ-
    ment, not secured within air conditioned and permanently staffed computer
    centres. They are more likely to be stolen than their larger cousins, to
    subsequently fall from the back of the mythical lorry.

5   The office is an informal place, often the busy heart of the company's daily
    life. The strict standards of housekeeping and orderliness, and the inherent
    security of the more traditional computer rooms, tend to be missing. As a
    result:

    (a) documentation about the system, its software and its operation is often
        poor;
    (b) the loss of the PC's key users can render the PC unusable;
    (c) software development will be unrecorded and haphazard;
    (d) passwords will not be recorded;
    (e) previous manual records will fall into disuse without proper care being
        taken to retain the ability to resort to these in an emergency;
    (f) floppy disks and printouts will be left lying around, leaving them and
        the data contained open to compromise or theft.

6   Criminal acts, not possible with previous manual methods, may become easy
    if the memory and manipulative power of the PC are harnessed by a
    dishonest employee.

7   PCs have often merged the work of several members of staff, and criminal
    misuse of the data and applications, previously impossible without the
    connivance of more than one person, is now possible.

8   These several people, who may have been working entirely separately on the
    previous manual system and who now share the PC's database, will have
    contact with a wider field of company knowledge which they might not have
    a need to know.

9   On a large disk pack, any sensitive or valuable data will be diluted and
    hidden by the vast amounts of relatively unimportant data. On the smaller
    floppy disk of the PC the important data will be less well hidden, and
    therefore more easily sorted from the chaff.

10 PC operating systems, unlike those of bigger systems, do not carry extensive
    software security features.

11 Poor security associated with informal and unsophisticated PC network
    communications may allow unauthorized access to the system.

12 Data can be taken into the PC from the network, or from the mainframe,

and subsequently removed easily from site, either in printed form or on floppy disks.

13 Local software development tools can be used by the PC user to attack the mainframe or network.

14 PCs are prone to physical damage, and their small size and flexibility mean that they are moved around more and thus suffer. The smoking, eating and coffee drinking that go on in most offices are also dangerous to the PC.

15 PCs are just as vulnerable to power supply fluctuations, but usually take power from the unfiltered domestic supply with its spikes, reduced voltage and cuts. Static electricity created in the office will be transferred to the PC by the users, since anti-static mats are rarely provided.

20.4 Countermeasures to protect the personal computer

As with larger computers, certain PCs and particular databases have greater values and thus attract greater threats. Some will perform low-level administrative tasks while others will be vital to the enterprise's function or will be packed with sensitive or valuable data. All will have some worth to the company, but the implications of the loss, corruption or unavailability of each will differ. The nature and cost-effectiveness of possible countermeasures will also vary. A balanced approach to PC security is, as ever, the order of the day, and there are several issues that can be addressed.

20.4.1 Management

The technical solutions available to enforce security on a PC are fewer than for larger systems. Management, supervision and procedures take a more dominant role.

Formalized policies

The majority of enterprises will not have formalized policies for the procurement and use of small computer systems. They will be bought at department level or lower, and even the use of privately owned PCs brought in by staff for use at the office will be sanctioned. In such a chaotic situation the chance of there being any sort of formalized PC security policy is slim. Yet with the large and increasing numbers of PC users with widening access through networking, working more or less autonomously, and with responsibility for the security of those PCs delegated to their users, it is even more vital that a clear and concise PC security policy is laid down by top management and relayed to all staff. Responsibilities at all levels must be clearly identified and advertised, with a named individual responsible for the security of each PC. However, this is most unlikely to be achieved until senior management recognizes the importance of the PC to the corporate survival and performance.

Awareness

The dangers to the PC and its data must be explained to all users, whose poor security standards are usually caused by ignorance, incompetence and lack of care rather than dishonesty. Most employees want to do a job and are willing to cooperate with the requirements of the company, and will respond positively to guidance about how to ensure their data's integrity, confidentiality and continuity. A computer security awareness program should be introduced for PC users as well as for the users of larger systems, and in particular each staff member should be reminded of:

- the need to remain conversant with any regulations and security operating procedures in force;
- the importance of correctly classifying information, and clearly marking that value on all displays of that data;
- the requirement to report all suspicions to security staff, and to challenge all strangers in order to establish their identity and authority to be in a particular place.

Supervision

Associated with an increased personal contact with, and responsibility for, the computing function, which comes with the introduction of PCs, is an increased need to supervise the users. The simplicity and availability of the PC tend to induce a relaxed and hence careless attitude, and this must be countered. Firm guidelines about PC procurement, use and security must be rigorously enforced.

Training

Security will be improved if staff are properly trained in the use of their PC. As car drivers are safer if they understand how the vehicles work and have been taught properly how to drive them, then users of the PC will make fewer errors and take better care of their system and its data if they have been properly trained in the fundamentals of computing and in the correct usage of their particular machine. Throwing a still-boxed PC and its instruction manual at a middle-aged office clerk, or installing a sophisticated word processor and handing it over to a junior secretary with no guidance about its use, will court disaster and insecurity. Similarly, to rely on the word of others as a training strategy will be ineffective except to breed poor practices and bad habits; training should be formalized and should be included as a factor in any calculations and bids for staffing levels. Often, manufacturers will provide introductory training at a price, and there are numerous firms providing such a service too. The issue of a 'User's Handbook' containing the elements of PC use and security would be useful to all users, to be kept by the side of the machine for easy and regular reference.

Posters should be displayed which emphasize the importance of PC security. Finally, continuation and refresher training should not be forgotten.

Inspections and surveys

A regular inspection and surveying programme of PCs in use throughout the enterprise, carried out by company security staff or specialist consultants, will:

- review existing security policies to determine if they are relevant and actually working;
- enforce the security regulations;
- monitor staff performance standards;
- validate training to ensure that it is relevant and effective;
- perform on-the-job training and specialist security advice for staff;
- identify and rectify any incorrect or insecure procedures.

Clearly the most important systems would attract greater priority. New problems will be identified early, and gaps in the current security policy should reveal themselves.

Security operating procedures

Clear and concise security operating procedures must be in force for each PC (see Chapter 6). For standalone machines of limited importance these may extend to only a page or two, and include such things as:

- a description of the system and its location;
- who is responsible for the system;
- its authorized use and authorized users;
- the maximum classification of data to be held or processed on it;
- start-up and shut-down procedures, including any logging in and out routines;
- procedures for the backing-up and storage of magnetic media.

For more valuable PCs, those with a number of users, and those connected to a network of other PCs, such orders will be more comprehensive, and may even be as detailed as those for a mainframe. The relative low value of the PC's software and hardware should not cause the need for proper orders to be overlooked; it is the importance of that PC's role and the value of its data which should be the driving criteria.

Logs

It is unlikely that the small PC system will support adequate audit trials and automatic logs. The maintenance of comprehensive manual logs is therefore even more important. There should be accurate records of system accesses and usage, maintenance, incidents and security violations.

20.4.2 Defence in depth

Imagine the PC and its floppy disks as pound notes, or pieces of paper with highly sensitive company information written on them; apply the same defensive measures in depth to achieve at least the same standards of protection you would afford to those more obviously valuable and attractive items.

Physical security

Good physical security standards should be imposed. In particular:

- Exercise proper control over the equipment by the keeping of accurate inventories and the registration of all computers and peripherals.
- Lock premises properly, especially those offices where PCs are used. Control entry to office areas, or to whole buildings, if appropriate.
- When available, choose and use passwords sensibly. They should not be shared by users, and they should be changed regularly.
- Restrict access to, and use of, PCs to authorized persons only.
- Discourage the movement of PC equipment in order to reduce physical damage.
- Clean disk drives regularly in the approved manner.
- Seal all items of hardware where possible to prevent tampering.
- Fit 'ignition' keys to terminals; control issue and use of these keys; do not leave keys in unattended terminals. Such keys can be traditional, magnetic stripe card (credit card type) readers, or other uniquely magnetic tokens placed into a suitable reading point.
- Fit electric points with lockable covers; use them.
- Fit power surge suppressors to the electricity supply, and use non-static mats or grounding devices to prevent static build-up.
- Locate PCs sensibly to reduce the opportunities for overlooking of VDUs or printers and the chances of inadvertent electronic radiation.
- Local programming should be strictly controlled and supervised, as should the use of software development tools.
- Beware of PCs with fixed disks. These will retain any classified data processed, and will require physical protection appropriate for the highest value of data ever stored. Machines with removable fixed disks, which can be stored separately in appropriate containers, should be purchased for more sensitive functions.
- Take appropriate and sensible measures to protect against the hazards of fire and flood.

Document security

Protect and secure all documents associated with the PC:

- Store floppy disks in their envelopes, within a disk holder, in an upright position. Do not bend or fold disks. Do not expose them to sunlight, or extremes of temperature, or to magnetic fields of any kind, no matter how weak. Always use a felt pen when marking the disks' labels.
- Lock all floppy disks, other magnetic media and system documentation in appropriate containers when not in use. Take proper care of all unused magnetic media to prevent its theft or improper use. All such portable media should be accountable, and no personal media should be allowed on site.
- Strictly enforce the regular backing up of all software and data, and store away from the PC, certainly in another building or preferably at another site. The procedure for taking back-ups must be laid down clearly in orders. Frequently updated database files should be backed up most conscientiously. Records of all changes between back-ups should be maintained, if only as draft printouts to be discarded after backing up. Provide a fireproof safe at some central location for the use of all PC users for temporary safe storage of in-use media (disks, documents etc.), and make sure its door is always shut.
- Positively overwrite during deletion if possible. In any event, destroy floppy disks when their data is no longer needed; do not use them again, they are not expensive.
- Printers should not be co-located with terminals if they are able to produce classified printout; they should be under the control of security or registry staff independent of the PC user, and proper records should be kept of all printing issued.
- Treat PC software as carefully as you would the software within a mainframe environment; it should be written, tested, documented, maintained and physically protected (with copies held elsewhere) to the same exacting standards. Take special care about importing floppy disks from elsewhere other than a reputable supplier; pirate or private disks can be used to introduce software viruses.

Personnel security

Consider the security reliability of each PC user, bearing in mind the impact that his or her actions on the PC and any connected network could have on the company's performance. For the more sensitive PCs, formal screening of users may be necessary. The proper recruitment of staff, their training, security education, supervision and formal arrival/termination procedures should be adopted as for the staff of a mainframe. Consider the sensible allocation of duties so that no one individual is vested with unchallenged authority, or with an unwise level of knowledge or trust; such a situation is dangerous if a key staff member is subverted or run over by a bus.

Network security

Even though a particular PC may hold unclassified data or may be relatively unimportant in function, once networked it could be used surreptitiously for dishonest acts, or if mishandled could cause damage to other PC databases. Likewise, an apparently secure PC could be attacked and damaged by a PC elsewhere on its network. Network security measures should be strictly enforced throughout all parts of the network, which will be only as secure as its weakest component.

Business continuity planning

The same pressures, constraints and responsibilities fall upon the shoulders of PC users as on those of the operators of mainframe systems. There is the same requirement to take care in every way possible of the all-important data; the effect on profitability and survivability of its loss can be dramatic. Thought must be applied in advance to the recovery actions necessary in the event of the PC suffering at the hands of a disaster, for whatever reason, and a disaster recovery plan should be developed. While the mainframe is unlikely to go missing as the result of light fingers among the workforce, such a thing is more than possible with an attractive and highly mobile PC:

- While hardware and standard software is usually easily available from suppliers, the data and specialized software unique to the PC's function will not be obtained elsewhere, nor easily re-created. Back-up copies, stored away from the PC and regularly updated, of all software and data are essential.
- If possible, retain the ability to return to previous manual methods, at least for the period during which replacement hardware/software is being obtained.
- Any disaster recovery plan should, as for a mainframe, be appropriate, achievable, comprehensive, regularly tested and properly documented. Someone other than the normal user should, if necessary, be able to recreate the database on a duplicate machine and continue operating the PC's function with as little disruption as possible.
- If central control over the procurement of PCs throughout the company can be achieved, and standardized hardware and software is used, then spare capacity will be available on other compatible PCs in the event of the loss of one; internal recovery facilities will thus have automatically been installed.
- Consider the selective use of insurance, for replacement costs of the hardware and standard software and for any identifiable consequential losses, but remember that insurance can never be an alternative to a sound security policy.

Software security

The software security measures incorporated in the operating systems of most PCs are extremely limited. There may be the ability to invoke a simple password access control if it is required, but there is only minimal privacy available to users' files (to hide them from other users who share the PC or who are connected to it through a network). Audit trails are rarely found, and encryption of passwords or data held on the system is usually not possible.

The more sophisticated software security features found in the operating systems of the larger computers and mainframes use up only a fraction of the power available, but on a PC would use up a considerable portion of the system's strength. Access control, audit and monitoring, separation of users, and encryption are, in the main, sacrificed on a PC.

The mainframe's software security programs are hidden in vast amounts of other data, or housed in hardware separate from the main areas of data storage and processing; in the PC, any software security programs will have to reside alongside the rest of the data in the active areas of the database—the tree not so well hidden in a smaller jungle—and therefore more easily traced and attacked.

Despite these failings, a PC which has, say, a number of users working unsupervised and uncontrolled, or which is networked throughout a large area, or which has an important role in the operations of the enterprise, or which contains valuable or sensitive data, should have effective software security features. These can be achieved in a number of ways:

1 *Operating system enhancements* High security options are available for some of the more popular operating systems. These are effective as far as they go, but costly in processing power and can reduce the efficiency and speed of the machine. Furthermore, they are developments of previous operating systems, and as security, to be most effective, has to be incorporated during the earliest design stages of any project, such options can never be totally flexible or effective. With a new generation of more powerful PCs and operating systems, though, where security has been considered throughout, software security will be increasingly effectively achieved within the operating system itself.

2 *Embedded hardware* By inserting into the construction of the PC an extra microchip containing software security programs, most of the necessary controls can be imposed on the PC's operations without using up valuable computer processing and storage capacity. Such accessories are being seen increasingly as an effective and reliable method of achieving enhanced software security on a small computer system:

   (a) They are all but transparent to users, who work the PC in the same unrestricted manner they have become used to, unless of course they step outside the rules laid down by the security device.
   (b) They are cheap, easily installed, and provide a wide range of security features such as:

   (i) Password control (including enforced changes after a fixed time, restricted number of log-on attempts, minimum number of characters).
   (ii) Extensive audit trails which can record as little or as much information as considered necessary.
   (iii) Positive overwriting of files during deletion.
   (iv) Encryption of data.
   (v) Improved privacy controls over user files.

 (c) They cannot be subverted without physical access and alteration. Normal physical security measures, such as use of, and regular inspection of, seals, will reduce this risk.

By the use of these devices within all the company's PCs, or at least the more important or sensitive ones, management can recover central control over all PCs; the embedded hardware would be configured and monitored by the security officer, under the policy direction of senior management. The PC users should be allowed no contact with the embedded hardware; their access privileges (read/write/delete/execute) and device privileges (drives, printers, modems etc.) will be pre-selected by the security officer, even down to the time and day access is allowed.

20.4.3 Portable ('lap-top') computers

Portable computers are emerging as powerful mobile working tools with all the sophistication and flexibility of the desk-bound PC. They can be taken on business trips, even abroad, or used back in the office. Often they come with their own built-in modems so that data can be swapped with, say, the mainframe back at headquarters, or a network can be accessed and used for sending electronic mail (if necessary throughout the world, even using a car-phone). If the security of static PCs is considered a headache, it must be recognized that those problems are increased many times over with lap-tops. Strict procedural controls need to be enforced over their procurement and use, with clear orders issued to all users. They should not be used for sensitive data.

21
Computer viruses

There has been much talk recently about computer software viruses. These are only the latest in a series of mischievous coding problems causing concern within the computing world.

Originally, bugs in the software were probably caused by scraps of unwanted code left in the system and reactivated accidentally by a certain set of circumstances and stimuli. The term is reputed to have originated in the days of mechanical relays and switches before the modern solid state technology, and an infamous fault in an important system which was eventually traced to an insect caught between a set of crucial electrical contacts. Bugs were then introduced deliberately as irritating but harmless amusements; on the system manager's birthday, perhaps, all terminals would display greetings from the staff. Then they became increasingly sophisticated, and more sinister uses were made of them until now collectively they represent a real threat to the computer's security:

- *Trojan horses* Computer programs with apparently or actually useful functions but which contain additional (hidden) functions that surreptitiously exploit the system, such as making blind copies of sensitive files.
- *Sleepers* Areas of code within programs which will be activated at a later date to result in compromise, denial or loss of data.
- *Trapdoors* Hidden software mechanisms that permit security features within the software to be circumvented. They may be activated in some non-apparent manner such as a special random key sequence at a terminal.
- *Logic bombs* These spring into action with devastating results, such as the wiping of entire storage disks or the destruction of programs.
- *Cancers* The corrupt coding grows and spreads throughout the database.

Such deliberately damaging pieces of programming are no longer termed bugs; the word is now reserved for unintentional software errors.

Viruses may be distinguished from bugs and other dangerous types of software in that they are self-replicating, making copies of themselves to escape and affect other systems. Their actual effects are otherwise similar in many cases. They can move rapidly and exponentially around networks. They can persist for very long times, hidden in storage media or lying dormant. Their examples are growing in number and their viciousness is increasing. Defence against viruses is essential, but is not easy or guaranteed. Viruses are difficult to trace and their perpetrators are free to experiment and repeat their mischief. Prevention is the best, and some say the only, defence:

- Gone are the days when computer users could swap programs at will, downloading from hackers' 'bulletin boards' or passing disks between friends and enterprises. Such permissiveness is no longer prudent, and behaviour has to become more conservative.
- Only software from a known and guaranteed source should be introduced into the system. For example, demonstration disks, even from computer security firms, must be ignored, since they could contain viruses. Certainly, the latest 'bright idea' disk created by one of the programmers in his or her own time should be treated very carefully.
- Physical barriers must be erected wherever possible to stop the virus spreading. Make full use of write-protect tabs on floppy disks.
- Good standards of programming control must be employed at all times.

Even then, no system is entirely immune. With every care in the world taken, one can still be infected by a virus during normal contact with another and trusted system. Precautions can fail, too—it is notoriously difficult, for example, to supervise programmers effectively. A sense of proportion is needed, though. With sensible precautions, and use of sound defence in depth, all but the most pernicious of viruses can be avoided and then the effects of any infection reduced.

21.1   The virus threat is real

Accurate statistics about virus attacks are difficult to come by, but this is not especially important. The issue is not what sort of virus has attacked or when, but whether it has caused some business impact.

Many viruses originate abroad, from countries with little or no legislation to protect software or to categorize hacking and virus writing as a criminal offence. In the absence of any national quarantine arrangements (such as those which control rabies) the business community must protect itself from infection. Viruses are a public health issue not confined to one sector or group within the information technology community. We must all help in keeping each other virus-free.

There is still much misinformation surrounding viruses. Many product vendors and security consultants naturally blacken the air with overstatements of the incidence of infection and cause our toes to curl with gruesome disaster stories. Nevertheless the threat is real and growing.

Although there are more than a thousand different viruses recorded internationally, many of these are not found in the 'wild' and many are minor variations of others. In truth, there are probably only 25 to 30 active viruses in the UK at present (1993) of which a mere 8 to 10 are regularly reported. They mostly infect personal computers, since such environments are much more prone to their invasion than mainframe communities.

21.2   Routes of infection

Viruses may enter a computer system in a variety of ways:

- on a floppy disk (usually from a source which should not have been trusted);
- on a tape (for example carelessly re-infecting a system from a back-up);
- over local or wide area networks (for example by shared use of a file server or downloading from a bulletin board);
- by direct PC-to-PC links;
- through the computer keyboard—the original virus writer probably typed in a source program to create the virus, and others may have modified it in the same way.

   One of the main potential infection routes is the use or installation of un-authorized software. Only authorized software should be installed and run on IT equipment to reduce the threat of importation of a virus infection (or other bug) via:

- unsolicited demonstration disks received through the post or included with PC magazines;
- otherwise trusted suppliers sending demonstration software;
- shrink-wrapped software which already carried a virus;
- contract staff using their own software. Many contractors would prefer to use their own 'tools of the trade' and must be educated to use only company approved software;
- use of non-company portable PCs and home-owned PCs which themselves have become infected—typically from a computer game, shareware or a bulletin board;
- company portable PCs which are used at non-company locations.

   Another infection route is that of deliberate attack. An attacker wishing to introduce a virus deliberately is unlikely to be deterred by rules forbidding unauthorized software. Deliberate attack, especially from people who already have legitimate access to the computer systems, will always be difficult to prevent.

   More likely, however, is accidental infection. Possible sources include:

- visiting engineers, loading files or attempting to reinstate data/software which has been infected at another site;
- unauthorized users. Systems which have inadequate physical and/or logical access control may be used by unauthorized personnel.

21.3   Impact of viruses

Viruses can cause:

- the reformatting of disks;
- the destruction of data and programs;
- the deletion of files from disk when triggered;
- the corruption of the directory on a disk, making files inaccessible;
- the slowing down of the system;
- redefinition of the keyboard, and subsequent confusion to typists;
- strange things to happen to the screen display, such as letters falling down the screen;
- the corruption of programs, data files or printed reports;
- the system disk to become unbootable;
- the prevention of files or programs so that the user cannot recover them.

There are many variations on these themes with some viruses deliberately randomizing their behaviour so that they are less predictable (or detectable). It is easy to imagine further destructive things that a virus could do.

Ironically, viruses with some of the most destructive properties above (e.g. reformatting disks) have so far posed less of a threat than their more timid relatives. To use a medical analogy, an infection which kills its host rapidly may get less chance to spread.

21.4   Developing an anti-virus strategy

It is important to develop a strategy for countering the threat of viruses, but the cost and inconvenience of their prevention and cure have to be weighed against their potential impact. While the virus threat must be kept in perspective, their potential to destroy data or make it unavailable warrants caution and an appropriate, measured response.

One extremely effective anti-virus strategy within one large enterprise stated simply that 'anyone reporting a computer virus, even if that person was responsible for introducing it, will not be punished. Anyone not reporting a virus, even if that person was not responsible for introducing it, will be liable for dismissal.' While its direct approach might be criticized by some, its intent was to identify viruses as quickly as possible. However, a more comprehensive policy will normally be preferred, to deal with prevention, detection and cure.

21.4.1 Centralized expertise and facilities

The overwhelming majority of system users do not need to know the name of a virus, let alone its characteristics. All they want is not to catch one in the first place, and if they are unlucky enough to do so, for someone to remove it as soon as possible with no loss to themselves. Only a few specialized personnel need therefore to have the detailed knowledge of viruses, but these people must be available at short notice and with the correct tools. The departmental security officer should act as the focal point for any incident or security breach, and maintain overall management responsibility in terms of identification, containment and resolution of any virus attack.

21.4.2 Quarantine facilities

Quarantine facilities should be established within secure areas. Strict access and procedural controls over the use of these facilities should be implemented. This equipment will provide a clean environment in which to dissect viruses and a 'gateway' facility which can examine disks on receipt into the enterprise and before use elsewhere.

21.4.3 Reporting viruses

Viruses might be discovered at any time. It is essential that support is available at short notice in order both to quickly confirm the presence of a virus (many false alarms will occur) and then to protect the enterprise from further damage. Speed is essential to limit damage already caused and to identify who to alert and what action is necessary while investigations progress.

An emergency cascade system (ECS) should be established for rapid notification of a virus attack in progress to all departments, system managers and users.

21.4.4 Education and awareness

A key element necessary to any plans for preventing virus attack is the education of all personnel involved with computers about the nature and characteristics of viruses, actions to prevent their attack, and actions to take in the event of their occurrence. For example, instructions, warnings, reminders and formal training courses will highlight the issues. Specialist videos are available and should be used. It is important that security, including protection against virus attack, becomes part of the culture of the enterprise. Commitment and good example must stem from the top of any enterprise and awareness training must also be directed to senior and executive management.

21.4.5 Anti-virus software

Anti-virus software falls into three main categories:

1 *Virus-specific detection software*, which detects and identifies known viruses. At present such software dominates and has proved successful. It works by searching files and disks for known patterns of bytes which indicate the presence of a known virus. While there are moves towards 'intelligent'

scanners which detect virus types or the likelihood of a virus presence, such software must have a basic knowledge of what it is looking for and therefore requires frequent updating on the known viruses. While industry experts vary in their estimates, and some claim to have systems which will cope with many thousands of viruses, there must be a limit somewhere before the overheads of running detection software become unacceptable. In skilled hands, for example PC support groups, it provides a valuable 'aid' to diagnosis and recovery. It is also valuable for areas which regularly have to receive and/or distribute executable code.

2   *Virus non-specific detection software*, which operates by detecting the system changes which are symptomatic of virus activity. However, detection is possible only after the virus has gained entry. The advantage is that it is potentially 'future proof' in that even previously unknown viruses will be detected. False alarms are to be expected when legitimate changes to executable code have been made, since the software will be unable to distinguish between legitimate change and that due to virus infection. While operational areas should not expect regular changes to executable code, this is not true of development and research areas; virus non-specific software is therefore of limited benefit.

3   *Virus recovery software*, which is used to repair systems after identification of a known virus. It is available for some common viruses where the infection can be easily removed and the software returned to its normal state. As viruses become more sophisticated, though, the usefulness of virus recovery software will be reduced. It is perhaps best to incorporate recovery software for selected virus into the armoury of investigative tools and defensive measures.

21.4.6 General software security

Software security controlling access, audit and separation is available for most computer systems, including PCs. Such software will prevent the transfer of highly classified data to lower levels of authorization. However, there are no compulsory measures to stop data and programs from lower levels migrating upwards. This leaves open the obvious route for inserting a virus-infected program at lower levels which can then be executed by higher level users who will unwittingly spread the infection. Such software security does, however, reduce the threat of deliberate virus attack by reducing the ability of unauthorized personnel to access the system. Even so, some viruses loaded from floppy disk could spread.

21.4.7 Responsibilities

As ever, anti-virus responsibilities must be allocated to named individuals. Specific responsibility for producing policy and guidance must rest with the corporate security officer. The notification, investigation and recovery processes must be allocated to those specific individuals or departments with the necessary technical and administrative skills and resources. Each PC user should be made responsible for:

- back-up;
- checking incoming and outgoing disks;
- checking executable software sent or received through email;
- reporting any signs of virus infection.

21.4.8 Good housekeeping and security practices

Many of the good security practices which should already be in place will assist in the prevention and/or detection of virus attack. It is important to recognize the part the following play in either preventing or detecting virus penetration, or assisting in recovery.

1 *Software certification* to ensure that all installed software does what it is supposed to do and no more. Clearly this will include a check for known viruses and will form part of the 'authorized' software base of the enterprise.
2 *Release procedures* which will ensure that formal testing of software has taken place and that no tampering is possible between testing and the release into the live environment.
3 *Back-up copies* of all software (and data) should regularly be taken and stored at a remote location. The complexity of this operation must not be underestimated but it is an essential undertaking for all IT users.

Do not take chances. If you receive software from somewhere, check it is not infected. Games should not be played on company computers or PCs.

21.5 High-risk systems

There will be systems and PCs which deserve more protection than that afforded by the baseline controls so far described. Such systems will vary from enterprise to enterprise, but would obviously include such as financial systems, safety-critical functions and live operational systems. The following are examples of the controls and techniques that should be considered for such sensitive systems; it is not intended to be an exhaustive list.

1 *Sophisticated virus non-specific software* which uses a more certain technique for detecting virus activity by examining program code directly for alteration. Indeed, such direct examination is the only way (apart from its possible misbehaviour) to detect a boot sector virus, since it will not have associated file attributes. This is widely considered the most powerful current technique for detecting virus activity, since it is actually capable of detecting unknown new viruses as well as the ones already catalogued. The main technique used

is checksum calculation, with the sequence of bytes within the program producing a short 'checksum'. With careful algorithm design there is a high probability that any change to the program code will cause a change in the checksum value. Thus if program checksums are initially calculated when the system is known to be free of viruses, they can be rechecked at a later date to discover changes.

2 *Software controls*   Other software packages or routines can materially assist in the fight against viruses. The following are some of the better methodologies.

(a) *Authenticated disks*   These may be required for all computers in a particular area. This is achieved by placing an authentication code on each disk which is read by the software installed on each protected computer. Failure to validate the authentication code results in rejection of the disk. The disk may be read by an unprotected computer, but any attempt to write to the disk results in the authentication code being destroyed. Thus it requires re-authentication (by a 'gateway' system) before it can be used by protected computers. This technique requires the authorization process to pronounce a disk and computer 'virus free' in the first instance, but affords significant advantages thereafter.

(b) *Memory-resident virus monitors*   This technique imitates the action of a memory-resident virus. The virus monitor program is loaded into memory when the system is booted and remains resident in memory thereafter. The exact actions taken vary between products, but may include scanning memory and any disks inserted during operation, preventing copying of files and/or detecting attempts to write to program files or the boot sector. The main drawback of memory-resident software is the overhead imposed in memory and (to a lesser extent) performance. The advantage is that the virus check happens continually, rather than once a day or once a week.

(c) *Recovery software*   When a virus infection has been found, any sensible user will want to remove it and prevent its return. The major tool for doing this must be the security back-up taken at a date before infection (including the write-protected original release disks for much commercial software). The safest procedure is to reformat the infected disks (including a 'low-level' format of any hard disk), and copy the original programs from the backups. It is essential that the back-up programs are virus-free if this is to work. Problems may arise if the virus has been present for several months before detection, since back-ups may be infected too, and so regular virus checks are desirable. All other media associated with the infected machine should be virus-checked at the time of recovery to ensure the virus does not re-infect the system shortly afterwards.

21.5.1   *The overheads of anti-virus procedures and precautions*

1   *Implementation costs* must not be underestimated. For large enterprises it may involve visits to many different sites. While the establishment of local area networks can ease the workload, the whole process of implementing the anti-virus action plan will require significant time and effort.

2   *Continuing administrative costs* will largely depend upon the protection systems chosen, but must be taken into account in cost-justifying any protection measure. Specifically, it is worthwhile remembering that any virus specific detection software will require regular updates and that change detection software may require attention after system upgrades.

3   *Monitoring*   All systems require regular monitoring and auditing. It is essential to provide executive management with the reassurance that all is well. Anti-virus measures are no exception and require this constant reassurance, which must cover all aspects of operation and use.

4   *Review*   No enterprise exists in isolation—we are all subject to occurrences outside our control, there will always be changes which we cannot influence. Incidents and security breaches will happen and new threats will emerge. There will always be the malicious person trying to gain entry by the back door, there will always be ignorance (irrespective of the amount of training given), and newcomers cannot be expected to understand immediately all the rules. For all these reasons and many more we must be ever vigilant and constantly review all our strategies and policies.

21.5.2   *Contingency plans*

In case any of the outside influences impact on our strategy we need a good contingency plan if it goes wrong. Good, efficient, and quick communication is essential in any 'disaster' situation, and part of that communication must be knowing what to do.

The essential elements include:

- incident identification and containment; problem escalation; alert and emergency cascade procedure;
- investigative and recovery action guidelines; monitoring and post event review activity.

21.6   The future

Viruses are not going to disappear. Over time, virus-specific detection may not be practical nor adequate. Change detection routines may be over-complicated, time-consuming and may actually spread a virus. Newer operating systems may offer partial solutions, as may the more intelligent scanning programs now being developed which attempt to detect the likelihood of virus presence. Hardware redesign, however difficult, remains the most likely 'permanent' solution.

While there remain people who harbour malicious intent or relish in the 'intellectual challenge' there will always be threats to our IT systems. These threats will continue to include viruses. Nevertheless, effective protection will still be available using the commonsense structured approach used to combat other security threats.

22
Training and awareness

. . . the food and drink of security . . .

Surveys consistently reveal in all sectors—industry, commerce and government—that there remains widespread ignorance among management and workforces alike of even the basic concepts of computer security. There is little perception of the scale and variety of the risks ranged against enterprises' computing functions, and even less insight into the available countermeasures. Few managers even concede the vital importance of computer systems and associated networks to the growth, or even survival, of their enterprises.

There is now a very real need for improved awareness before general standards of computer security can improve significantly among the general user population. The urgency for structured computer security training and awareness campaigns grows daily as we are driven towards greater networking, more distributed resources, and massive computing power pushed downwards to the desks of the lowliest workers with, perhaps, no IT training of any sort.

The need to raise security awareness among a wide range of personnel to greatly differing depths will require flexible and comprehensive education programmes understandable by all. Admittedly such programmes can represent a weighty and continuing overhead within, especially, the larger enterprises. What is certain, however, from the evidence of those enterprises that are committed to such programmes, is that raising awareness and educating a wide audience in the basics of computer security will achieve, pound for pound, a far more profound and longer lasting improvement in computer security than any purely technical solution could ever hope to achieve.

This chapter is intended to assist managers in the preparation, targeting and implementation of effective computer security training and awareness programmes, so that the wealth of cooperation and honesty that exists in any workforce can be harnessed towards strengthening the security of the IT systems. It does not attempt to describe in-depth training courses, but emphasizes those ways in which good security practice and conscientiousness may be fostered and encouraged throughout an enterprise.

22.1   The importance of security awareness among staff

Almost every piece of written work, or every lecture, on the subject of computer security starts with a pronouncement about the growing importance of computers to the wealth and success of any business and the dangers that lie in wait for the unwary, unwise or careless. Like Peter and the wolf, though, the message can become tired and the listener bored. Moreover, examples of disaster and tragedy are still not abundant, and do not necessarily receive, for a variety of reasons, the widespread publicity needed to drive home the point that there is a real computer security risk.

It is thus all too easy for managers and workers alike to ignore the warnings, and bury their heads in the sand. 'It won't happen here' is still too common an attitude. Precious little still seems to have been done to introduce practical computer security, while the risks are growing all the time. Perhaps this is caused to some degree by the computer security industry itself, which has tended to concentrate on the exotic threats and technical solutions to the exclusion of the more obvious dangers and the mundane ways of improving security standards. Unfortunately, the evidence is now clear that the greatest threat lies not from the sophisticated attack, but from low-tech insider crime and operator error made possible by poor procedures, a lack of work discipline, and most importantly a lack of awareness of either the risks or the basic countermeasures.

While, on the one hand, those people who surround our computer systems and networks are the greatest danger to safety and security, if we can educate those same staff in the basics of computer security, and make them want to be safer and more secure in their operations, then they become our greatest security asset. It is this attitude change which is of immense importance. There is a saying that security breaches and disasters should be more likened to being 'nibbled to death by ducks than being eaten by an alligator'. Almost every such incident is caused not by some massive mistake but by a series of trivial occurrences which combine to form a chain. Break any link in that chain, and you prevent the incident. The staff will break that chain, but only if they are alert to the dangers and committed to conscientious operations.

There is nothing to suggest that the vast majority of those working within the computing world are anything but honest and hardworking. Nearly all of us, in whatever field we work, want to do a good day's work for a good day's pay, and be thanked in return for our efforts. Most of us are highly motivated, at least at first, to our particular callings. If we fail in any way, it is unlikely to be with malice aforethought, but because we are ignorant, or careless, or in a rush. It is probable, therefore, that security and safety standards will improve dramatically if only the awareness among staff can be raised. There are a growing number of case histories which show this to be true.

Computer security is not simply a technical matter. There is, of course, a highly technical element, but not all the answers lie with the equipment. Computer security is as much a management problem, and as ever it is people who are the greatest issue. The technical solution must become increasingly difficult, expensive and cumbersome either to achieve or to enforce. Involving staff at all levels and encouraging them to discharge their personal responsibilities towards computer and network security is increasingly being recognized as the area of greatest importance and reward.

In 1960, following his study of security in government departments, Lord Radcliffe stated that then 'the single biggest risk to security is probably a general lack of conviction that any threat exists'. Nearly 30 years on, this has become so true of computer security today, but as noted in the Radcliffe Commission report, this attitude of mind can be overcome by a sustained and skilfully directed educational effort in the right quarters. History suggests to us a way forward.

22.2   Key issues

The need to alert a wide range of personnel about computer security to greatly differing depths will require a flexible and comprehensive awareness programme, understandable by all. In the latest (1990) Audit Commission Survey of Computer Fraud within a variety of UK government departments, there are a number of assertions which point us in the direction of what is needed:

- 'As in 1987, most frauds were made possible by the absence of basic controls and safeguards';
- 'The adage that "prevention is better than cure" is particularly relevant as there is little doubt that the installation of adequate control and security measures would have prevented most of the reported incidents';
- 'Keep it simple. Basic controls implemented successfully could reduce the exposure to risk';
- 'What is now apparent is that many organizations are simply not aware of the risks they run'.

There is nothing to suggest that the UK government departments involved in the survey were any better or worse than enterprises elsewhere. So, what are the key issues that all such security awareness campaigns, no matter their detailed contents, must embrace?

> *Make people want to be secure*   Above all else, any security awareness campaign must make people *want* to be secure. There is no real gain from bullying staff, or threatening them or bribing them. Lasting and effective security will only be maintained once staff are properly motivated towards such a regime, and it is this motivation which is the critical factor in any security education programme.

> *Display high-level support*   Security will always fail unless it has total commitment and support from the highest levels. Such support must not be concealed, it must be visible to staff. Senior management must also be seen to be following the rules themselves, or the rules will be debased.

Teach people what to do   Unless staff know what to do, and how to do it, how can they be expected to perform to the required standards? There is the true story of the young secretary who was told to make back-up copies of her floppy disks at the end of each working day. When her office automation system inevitably fell over, she produced a folder with diligently filed photocopies of her disks. Who was to blame? She had done what was asked of her to the best of her knowledge and skill.

Encourage people to be alert   For every security manager or systems supervisor, there may be dozens or even hundreds of other staff. By galvanizing them through an awareness campaign, this whole workforce, rather than just a few of its members, can be employed to police and care for the systems and networks. It is important that the enterprise's culture both enables and encourages staff to report disgruntled or dishonest colleagues, to challenge strangers, and to highlight potential or actual security loopholes and weaknesses.

Point out the risks   The starting point for any computer security effort must be an understanding of the risks to the enterprise and its IT systems and networks. Unless staff are aware of the dangers they face, they cannot be expected to take appropriate precautions. It is rather like a doctor reaching for a bottle of tablets for a patient without any diagnosis of the illness. There is little chance of so choosing the right treatment, and even less chance of the patient keeping it up. The awareness campaign must at least outline the risks, especially the everyday ones the staff will face.

Prevent   Prevention must always be preferable to cure. Awareness campaigns must teach avoidance of security incidents in the first place, though of course there must also be instruction about follow-up actions should the worst ever happen.

Be comprehensive   Awareness programmes need to address all aspects of security by considering the complete triad of confidentiality, integrity and continuity.

Be simple   Computer security, for most users of most systems, need not be expensive, complicated or overly technical. Many of the countermeasures are straightforward, involving in the first instance proper organization and the strict enforcement of codes of good practice. To use the medical simile again, we need to encourage healthy living. Unfortunately, most computer security effort continues to be directed towards brain surgery while the patient inexorably dies from the common cold.

Address the widest possible audience   The more staff at all levels who can be included in awareness campaigns, the greater the proportion of our workforce pulling in favour of the security effort. Of this range though, it is most important to win the support of top management, for without their total commitment there is little chance of any security effort succeeding. All staff are equal when it comes to an awareness campaign, except some are more equal than others.

Allocate responsibilities Unless you give a security task to someone, then it simply will not get done. It is essential that everyone is made aware of their individual responsibilities towards security so that they may place themselves in the overall picture and identify their parts to play.

Be positive and persistent The awareness campaign must state clearly what it expects of everyone, and then it must repeat its message. The more important that message, then the more often it should be repeated, and wherever possible in a different way each time. The effort should never be relaxed.

Be current, relevant and up-to-date Keep the awareness fully up-to-date and relevant. Make sure any changes to company policy, especially where they affect computer security practices and procedures, are incorporated into the campaign and brought to the attention of staff. New systems may require extra or different protection and staff must be told of this.

Never assume Do not assume any individuals to have security knowledge. Tell them.

Be two-way There must be a proactive element, since staff are bound to have great contributions to make to the security issues. Potential or actual security weaknesses will best be identified by those staff members dealing with the systems every day. Furthermore, a listening attitude by management, especially when things actually happen as a result of suggestions from the floor, will encourage even more that positive attitude towards safety and security which we seek above all else.

Be targeted Direct specific awareness issues at specific audiences and in specific ways. The needs of senior management, for example, will differ from those of input clerks, and a course designed for all will end up as a success for none. This does not exclude the need for an awareness framework, though, from which we may pluck the parts we need; indeed, it makes the need for that framework even greater.

Be entertaining and amusing Security will never be the most riveting of topics, but it is important that staff are made aware of the issues. Thus, a lively, entertaining and amusing campaign will stand a better chance of being remembered than the usual dull recitations of the rule book. There is no method too outrageous, no medium out of bounds. A single cartoon can be worth a thousand words. And as for one of the best places for a poster; well, where do most of us spend a few minutes of each working day in private contemplation? However, do not confuse entertaining and amusing with frivolous and silly.

Be measurable   There must be built into any campaign a method for monitoring and testing its effectiveness.

22.3   Motivating staff

Above all else, any security awareness campaign must make people want to be secure. It may be necessary to provide incentives for staff to follow the rules. There must be rewards—real or abstract, reinforcing good behaviour—and there must be penalties for those who fail their security responsibilities. Since we are trying to change behaviour, and since such change is bound to be painful for most staff members, we must keep those staff motivated towards security.

Motivating staff towards security is always going to be difficult, since the subject does not naturally lend itself to excitement. Such motivation is nevertheless vital, and is perhaps the only real way of ensuring that security remains an issue in people's minds after the initial enthusiasm or fear created by a campaign burst has faded in the memory.

> *Basic physical needs*   Each of us has our hierarchy of human needs. Our basic physical needs include food, shelter, warmth and sleep, and we are all strongly motivated to satisfy these. As Murt Daniels of the Bell South organization in the USA has so wonderfully understated '. . . you can get people to do almost anything if you deprive them of their air supply'!

> *The need for certainty*   Beyond our basic needs, we are all then varyingly disposed towards the satisfaction of a further hierarchy of needs. We all need to be free of threats to our physical and emotional safety. We need to know that our jobs are secure and that our salaries will be maintained. We need to feel safe and secure.

> *The need for self-esteem*   Next we attend to requirements which are not essential to our survival but contribute to the quality of our lives. We all need to be loved. We need to feel we belong, to our family, our friends and to our peer group. We seek friendship, affection and acceptance. We look for the respect of those around us, and for recognition of our achievements. Finally, at the highest level we have to be sure of our own self-respect, and we have to feel we have realized our full potential.

It is perfectly valid for those devising and implementing security training and awareness campaigns to play on these emotional and physical needs. More obvious examples are, say, the giving up of cigarettes, or dieting. Individuals will not be able to stop smoking, nor diet, unless they really want to, and it is this attitude change and subsequent behaviour modification that we must first achieve before there can be any lasting success. There are the sorry tales of those who have given up smoking six times this week already, or who have lost three times their actual body weight during abortive diets over the past few years and are still heavier than when they started!

There are negative motives which can also be harnessed. People do not want to get punished, or lose their jobs, or be disgraced in public. More selfishly, for example, they will not want to stay behind for many extra hours rebuilding their database because they failed to do proper back-up copies. There is a place for deterrence in any awareness campaign, and there should be no reluctance to highlight the penalties for not abiding by the rules. There should be no similar hesitation in publicizing any disciplinary action brought against those who transgress, deliberately or by error. Quite simply, point out to staff the advantages to their following the rules and making sure others do too. Make sure at the same time they realize what may happen to them if they don't abide by the rules themselves, and the possible consequences to the health of the enterprise. Make sure everyone understands how the welfare of the business is linked directly to their own employment prospects and financial security.

22.4   A proposed framework for awareness campaigns

With a clear picture in our minds of what IT security awareness programmes should be trying to achieve, let us now consider a framework, addressing the issues of who, how and what we should teach.

22.4.1   Who should we teach?

As information systems move away from the mainframe towards the distributed office resource, and as networking further reduces the control we once had over our electronic data, each person in the enterprise, from managing director to cleaner, must be made aware of, and trained to comply with, his or her individual responsibility towards computer security.

Obviously there will be differing needs among the workforce. However, there are certain appointments, and certain roles, which will consistently require specific skills to certain depths.

> *System manager*   The system manager, the key person for any computer system, is the captain of the ship with responsibility for all aspects of that system's functioning, including its security.

> *System security officer*   The system manager will not be able to give security the attention it deserves. The daily administration of security should be delegated to a system security officer.

System user   While the users of a computer system are perhaps the greatest risk to its safety and security, at the same time they can become its greatest asset if only they are made aware of, and trained in, their daily responsibilities towards security. These are therefore the most important group to receive computer security awareness training. In truth, an individual user's security tasks are often very simple, but if conscientiously executed, will result in an enormous improvement in security at very little cost and with a relatively small effort.

System development/maintenance staff   Those specialist staff responsible for the development and maintenance of the system, its software and its data, have an especially privileged position. Their skills allow them extraordinary power over the well-being and security of the system, and their mistakes, carelessness or dishonesty can have an inordinate effect. It is particularly important that such staff are aware of their role in maintaining the safety and security of the system; they should be chosen for their security reliability and positive attitude, they must be more closely supervised than staff members with less influence, and they must be constantly reminded of the importance of security rules and procedures.

Heads of department   Supervisors and managers with responsibility for computer systems must exercise proper control and supervision over the security of those systems. They must, therefore, be aware of this responsibility. This is especially relevant to the highest levels of management within the enterprise. No longer can the excuse be accepted that it is too difficult, and no longer must senior managers hide behind computer illiteracy as a reason for abdicating their duties. The Human Resources manager will need to be especially aware of his or her security responsibility, since it is likely that any dishonest or careless worker will be noticed in other ways dealt with by this department.

Corporate security manager   At the highest level, the corporate security manager will be responsible for the security of all computer systems within the enterprise.

Network security managers   Responsibility for a network's security is notoriously difficult to assign, and is easily assumed to be someone else's job. Each network must, therefore, have a named network security manager, and each system's security manager on that network should report through to the network security manager for the security of each node.

Auditors   The internal audit department has responsibility for checking all aspects of an enterprise's operations and administration. This department, quite rightly and sensibly, must be conversant with computer security, as it must be conversant with any other discipline, and must therefore be included within the training and awareness programme.

22.4.2   How should we teach?

Each of the groups described above will require different levels and types of computer security awareness and training. In addition there will be a variety of computer systems, from standalone PC to corporate mainframe to networks, each in their turn needing a differing emphasis on security. It is important, therefore, to target each group on each system with an appropriate awareness technique covering the appropriate material. The differing needs mean that no single method, and no single course, presentation or medium, will satisfy everyone.

But this does not mean that there can be no training and awareness framework around which detail is added or deleted as part of a graduated scheme. Indeed, a structured framework is almost essential if the whole range is to be incorporated efficiently and cost effectively. Fortunately, though, the basic principles of computer security apply across the spectrum of system types and sizes, and the greatest training burden by numbers—the users—is perhaps the easiest message to get across.

> *Specialist computer security training*   For those specifically tasked with the enforcement of computer security within an enterprise, at system, department or corporate level, it will be appropriate for them to receive detailed training. It may be best given in a number of stages:

- Firstly, say, for system security managers, to allow them to advise systems staff on the security of their system, monitoring security procedures, and providing a first level of help and advice on site;
- After successful completion of this first stage of specialist training, and perhaps after a period of on-the-job training as a system security manager, the more able and suited could then return for further training for appointment to departmental or corporate security manager posts.

Clearly, specialist computer security training represents a considerable investment in time, staff and money and will probably only be appropriate for the larger enterprises. For those who are able to set up their own in-house training, though, the courses can be tailored to their particular business needs, risks and strengths, and the students will be able to relate to, and thus be more highly motivated to learn from, the training. The investment can also be used to prepare the awareness programme for the lower levels of skill and knowledge required by the following groups with less specific computer security tasks.

> *Security awareness for system managers*   System managers will need a diluted version of the specialist training. They will not need to carry out the detailed work of their security managers, but will need an apprecia-

tion of the risks of their systems, the basic countermeasures that should be applied on a daily basis, and the sources of help and advice they and their security managers are able to turn to.

External training courses   For smaller enterprises without their own training machines, and even for larger organizations for certain training needs, it is often simpler to send students to external training courses. Unfortunately, there are few agencies undertaking such work. System-specific courses, such as training on the software security packages of the larger systems or networks, or courses to train on products such as anti-virus vaccines, are more readily available, but courses designed to equip user staff with the general techniques of basic computer security are still rare. This is perhaps a result of market demand, with the whole issue of computer security still far from the top of the list of management priorities. It must also be because the emphasis within the computer security world so far has been upon the technical solution, with less regard paid to the management issues or the everyday duties of system users.

Conferences and publications   Conferences are another source of external training, with the added advantage that much which is discussed at such events is new and as current as it is possible to be. There are a number of journals and periodicals covering the computer security issue, and these, too, are a source of much valuable and up-to-date information and comment. Remember there are two learning environments at any conference—in the auditorium, and then in the coffee bar and pubs; the auditorium is often less informative and rarely more enjoyable!

Briefings for senior management   On appointment to any senior position, executives should be introduced (probably for the first time) to computer security. It is essential to remove the fear and ignorance which has surrounded computer security so far. Top management should be made to see the importance of their support to the success of the security effort. They should also be convinced of the sense of making as many personnel as possible—including themselves—aware of the risks to the computing function, the possible effects on the welfare of the enterprise should those risks materialize, and the ways in which adherence to codes of good practice will reduce those risks significantly and cost-effectively.

Arrivals briefings   The opportunity should not be lost during any employment inductions to draw the attention of new staff to the security rules in force, and point out the penalties for non-compliance. Insist that staff sign as having read and understood the regulations. Include security requirements in standard job descriptions, and within contracts of employment. Insist on non-disclosure agreements for those leaving the employ of the enterprise.

Special interest training for all staff Management, security staff and systems users should be encouraged to study together and in more detail any computer security issue which affects or interests them. Special interest seminars might be an appropriate method, and it might also be of benefit to link with other enterprises, perhaps in the same line of business, since each might have much both to offer and learn.

General awareness techniques General awareness techniques used in many other areas—health and safety at work, quality assurance, fire safety, and so on—can also be brought to bear on security awareness. Such general advertising of codes of good security and safety practices should continue at all times, and in whatever ways can be devised. Nothing can be too outrageous or innovative, and the main aim of such a general awareness campaign must be to keep the security issue to the forefront of everyone's mind. Each staff member must be urged to remain vigilant at all times, and encouraged to carry out their own duties in a safe and secure manner. The most obvious techniques include:

- Posters, which should be eye-catching, interesting, simple, and limited to a small message. They must be rotated regularly to avoid them being overlooked, and they should be placed in every possible position to catch attention, such as toilets, canteens, waiting rooms and general offices.
- Newsletters and staff bulletins. Include security articles, puzzles, competitions, quizzes, cartoons and case-histories.
- Videos and slide shows with pre-prepared scripts to draw out the main points in discussion. Although expensive to produce in the first instance, they can subsequently be used widely by local security managers to reduce the cost per head and to provide a consistent message throughout the enterprise.
- Prizes and awards. Prizes and awards for good security efforts or ideas will reinforce the positive attitude of the enterprise towards security. To be of greatest value they must be used sparingly, and need not necessarily be of great worth. It is more important that the award is made publicly so that the individual gains both esteem and recognition.
- Competitions are also useful in motivating staff towards good security. Why not try 'the least number of operator errors this month', or 'best security log maintained during the year'? Again, the rewards need not be great; a simple trophy would suffice.
- Trinkets with a security message are always effective. Free pens, pencils and rulers with a suitable catch-phrase, and beer mats with the same slogan, will reinforce the message almost subliminally. Why not send employees a card to celebrate the anniversaries of their joining the firm, with the security slogan prominent and thanking them for their efforts to maintain security over the year?

Security training and awareness are not once-a-year matters: they are a continuing overhead and the effort should never be relaxed. What is certain, however, is that the energy applied will be handsomely rewarded. By harnessing the eyes and ears of all members of staff, and with an alert and competent workforce, any security weaknesses or any attempts to subvert security practices will be revealed and corrected much earlier.

22.4.3 What should we teach?

Computer security must address confidentiality, integrity and continuity of data, and it must include all the various defences in depth, from organization, then physical, document, personnel, hardware, software and network security, compromising emanations and disaster planning, through to insurance. Since there can be no such thing as total security, and since in any case there should never be total reliance placed in a single line of defence, greatest assurance can be achieved by wrapping layers of security around that essential resource of electronic data. Then, where each layer of defence in depth is inevitably inadequate, hopefully each gap will be countered by the barriers provided by other elements of the security policy.

Although there is a wide range of personnel needing differing levels of computer security training and awareness, the essential elements about which they should be taught are consistent throughout. The detail and emphasis might change, but the underlying messages remain the same. In the broadest sense, we must put across certain key themes:

- Computer security is essential to the growth and prosperity of the enterprise. Without it, and should some disaster or breach happen to the computing function, then the very survival of the business might be threatened.
- Computer security is everybody's responsibility. It cannot be ignored, delegated or postponed.
- Computer security need not be intrusive. It does not always have to be overly technical, expensive or complicated, and to most individuals within an enterprise it involves no more than the adherence to a set of commonsense and reasonable good practices. It does require a consistent effort, though, by everyone at all times.
- Computer security has the support of the highest levels of management, and it is expected that everyone will conform.
- Computer security applies equally to all those within the enterprise. None is exempt. Everyone, no matter their role or status, is expected to be alert and vigilant to attacks, to potential weaknesses in the defences, and to carelessness or non-compliance among other staff members.
- Data is the essential asset. Many confuse this with the need to care for the hardware of the system. But is it the paper file's intrinsic value we worry about rather than the words written upon the sheets within it? Likewise,

while the computer system or network will have a capital value, the data contained within it is far more important than the replaceable equipment.

- What the threats are to the enterprise. Unless we know what it is we are defending against, how are we to devise the correct policy? A doctor must examine the patient and determine the illness before there can be any chance of choosing a correct treatment, yet many companies seem happy to apply a lottery of defences that seem a good idea at the time.
- Having emphasized that security is everyone's responsibility, it is then necessary to describe computer security tasks as appropriate so that everyone may place themselves in the overall picture and identify their parts to play.
- Describe in general terms the main elements of computer security.
- Describe the purpose of risk analysis, and the company's chosen methodology.
- Show how to draw together all the elements into the production of a cost-effective, efficient computer security policy, translated then into workable, understandable and achievable security practices and procedures.
- Stress the importance of awareness among systems staff, and instruct systems managers on the various techniques to help keep security to the front of everyone's minds.

22.4.4 Testing the effectiveness of awareness programmes

Any awareness campaign must have built into it a method for testing its effectiveness. This will inevitably comprise a number of essentially subjective measures based on the observations of those both administering and receiving. Quite simply, the measure of success will be how many people follow the procedures they are trained to follow.

Objective measures of security are notoriously difficult to calculate accurately. Indeed, the ultimate test of all security is that there should be nothing to report, which itself must always bring into doubt, in senior management's eyes and among the workforce, the point of it all. Security is an overhead which must be justified continuously, and security managers must always be alert to the need to display their efforts as contributing to the overall performance of the business. Therefore, any evidence of the worth of awareness campaigns, even that derived subjectively, is important to the continued support of all concerned:

- Course assessments should be included, for students to complete at the end of training. Such assessments should comment on the relevance and effectiveness of each element of the awareness programme, and ask for suggestions to improve the teaching.
- Surveys and questionnaires among staff will reveal both the innate level of security awareness, and improvements in that awareness as the programme progresses. They might even, if constructed and administered carefully, show how long the effects of particular awareness modules last. If performed face-

to-face, they will give security managers useful opportunities to talk with staff and glean valuable feedback. In turn, this chance for staff to influence the awareness programme will enhance their positive attitude towards security.

- Monitor the frequency and type of security breaches and incidents. Ideally, the occurrences will reduce as a result of awareness efforts, but they will never cease altogether. Look for patterns, too, by department, or time of day, or value. Compare findings with any publicly published figures to try and determine the enterprise's comparative security performance. Bear in mind, though, that as awareness increases, so too will the number of reported incidents and suspicions, even though this does not reflect an increase in insecurity!

- It can be possible to test security. The extreme example of this is the so-called tiger-testing of software, but on a more mundane level security managers should try to guess user passwords, visit offices during lunchbreaks to see if terminals are logged on but unattended, and in a dozen other ways try and test all aspects of a system's daily security routine. Treat it as a game at first, and the staff will likely respond to the challenge. Only for the most serious offences, or when blatant contempt for the rules is discovered, should disciplinary action be brought to bear. Remember to thank staff when it is discovered that they are complying with the rules; this will be more effective than simply punishing those few who are not.

22.5   Awareness issues for the future

There is no doubt that security awareness remains the poor relation of computer security at the moment. There is still not enough recognition, despite an increasing amount of evidence and a growing number of case histories, that training and motivating staff in the basics of computer security produces an impressive improvement in security standards for relatively little investment. Encouragingly, there are a growing number of initiatives both to improve awareness and to discover and coordinate existing work.

Major studies are currently being sponsored by, among others, the European Commission, to determine exactly what computer security training is available and where, what awareness campaigns have already been tried and are continuing, and the impact of all of these on computer security standards. Government departments, and commercial agents acting on their behalf, are devising awareness campaigns. Many large enterprises, at last realizing the importance of computer security, are designing their own programmes. But all this effort is still too little. Unfortunately, the situation is not helped by the fact that even professionals within the computing industry are mostly ignorant of computer security, mainly because there is virtually no security content within most computer science training. From the earliest days of their associations with the industry, most computer staff are taught to view the security issue as of the lowest importance.

There is now an urgent requirement to improve computer security awareness at all levels. No matter how well laid one's security plans may be, all will be for nothing if staff are untrained and unaware of what to do and how to do it. Since the technical solutions have already progressed far beyond the needs of most companies, it seems that the best way to improve standards might now be the more general dissemination of security awareness among personnel at all levels. Certainly those companies that have performed this exercise can report encouraging results.

With the persisting unsatisfactory standards of computer security throughout all sectors, raising awareness and educating a wide audience in the basics of computer security is one positive way of overcoming the apathy and ignorance which remains today. Everyone in the computer security industry must now attend to this management issue with urgency, and do everything in their power to support and encourage the current research in this area.

22.6 Some final thoughts

Computer security is not simply a technical matter. Most of those working in this field are from a computing background and they tend understandably to rely on, and in fact may be limited by, their own knowledge and skills. The countermeasures do, of course, need to take into account the technical nature of the environment, but the answers lie not with the equipment, but, as ever, with the people who surround it. Computer security, I believe, is not a machine problem, it is a people problem.

Computers are here to stay, and their numbers will continue to escalate at an ever-increasing rate. The trends are towards smaller systems of awe-inspiring power, more distribution of resources to bring computing to the desks of the lowliest workers, networking, and with open systems interconnection to a more open provision of information. The need for computer security will also continue to grow, but I believe the technical solution will become increasingly difficult and cumbersome both to achieve and to enforce. Involving staff at all levels and making them carry out their personal responsibilities towards computer security will, I think, be the area of most importance and reward.

I believe that raising awareness and educating a wide audience in the basics of computer security will achieve, pound for pound, a far more profound and longer lasting result than any technical solution could ever hope to achieve.

Part 4
Crime and legislation

23
Computer crime

It is notoriously difficult to differentiate between computer crime and simple security breaches, and it is even more difficult to define exactly what does constitute such an offence. We have, earlier in this book, identified the criminal as a threat to our systems, and recognized that the scale of the problem has still to be accurately determined. We do know, though, that computer crime is extremely lucrative, presents a low risk of detection to its perpetrators, and is difficult to trace and prove (Fig. 23.1).

Simplistically, and to illustrate my point, in 1960, say, a bank robber might hope to get away with perhaps £20 000 but ran a high risk of capture and faced a lengthy and punitive prison sentence. In 1990, though, the modern computer robber can net millions of pounds with a much more remote chance of apprehension and an even lower chance then of conviction. How much closer to a perfect crime can one ever hope to get?

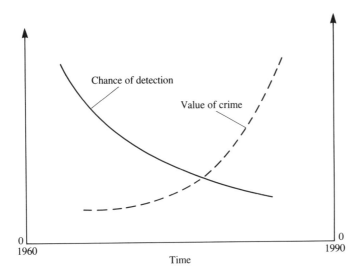

Figure 23.1.   The nature of computer crime.

23.1   What is a computer crime?

For many years now, numerous attempts have been made to identify the nature
and extent of computer crime. Mostly these surveys have proved inadequate and
have shown simply that the nature of computer crime is varied and extremely
difficult to define and prove. What is certain, despite the froth and bubble which
surrounds the whole issue, is that computer crimes are usually straightforward,
play upon human weakness, and target the simplest of deceptions which
abound—and always have done—aplenty. Once again we see that low-tech
insider crimes made possible by poor procedures and lack of work disciplines are
the major threats, not highly sophisticated attacks against the system itself.

Many urban myths have evolved around the computer about the nature and
scale of previous computer crimes. They should all be taken with a massive pinch
of salt. It is possible, though, to allocate recorded computer crimes to certain
categories:

1 *Computer abuse* Computer abuse involves any intentional act where
   knowledge of computer use or technology results in gain by the perpetrators
   and/or loss by the victims.
2 *Computer-related crimes* Computer related crimes are those crimes that
   involve a knowledge of information technology for their execution.
3 *Computer crimes* Computer crimes are those crimes which use information
   technology as their instrument of perpetration. Such crimes can be considered
   a form of white collar crime which involve the abuse of power, position or
   influence for illegal gain, usually committed by individuals in the upper and
   middle social classes and/or certain high-status occupations. They are generally non-violent acts of deception, concealment, misrepresentation, corruption
   and/or breach of trust. They are usually business-based. Computer crimes
   may involve information technology both actively and passively, against
   enterprises or individuals who use or are affected by systems, including those
   about whom data is stored or processed.

23.2   Characteristics of computer crime

There are certain qualities of a computer crime which set it apart from other
types of offence:

• Whatever definition one uses, there is no doubt that a computer crime
  involves computers, and its executor must be armed with new knowledge and
  techniques related to the information technology age.
• Existing legislation is not always applicable to computer crime, and so
  prosecution is not always straightforward. There is no great pressure for
  legislative reform, especially when the public tend to view computer criminals
  as modern-day Robin Hoods.

- The police and other investigative agencies are not always adequately trained to investigate computer crime. The Metropolitan Police, the City of London Police and an increasing number of the provincial forces have or are establishing specialized teams of police officers dedicated to this field, but they can only be deployed once untrained officers have identified an offence as a computer crime and, hopefully but not always correctly, preserved the evidence.
- Computer crime used to be restricted to computer specialists, but increasingly with the advent of the PC the number of those able to dabble is increasing.
- With international communications, there are no limits to the distance at which, nor the times during which, a computer crime can be committed. It is a totally depersonalized form of crime, where the attacker is divorced from the victim and can remain entirely anonymous.
- Computer criminals need not be motivated by money. They may simply be testing their skills against a system, or they may have political incentives or be driven by revenge against enterprises or individuals; they are that much more unpredictable than the thief, and that much more difficult to catch.
- Companies are reluctant to report computer crimes, or even to investigate them, since they then lay themselves open to acute embarrassment and possibly significant consequential losses if public confidence in their computer systems is damaged by adverse publicity which highlights system weaknesses. Prosecutions are thus relatively rare, and there are allegedly cases where criminals have been 'paid off' to keep quiet or even to reveal their methods to the victim.

Computer crimes inevitably display certain discerning characteristics or they fall short of our definitions.

1 *Knowledge* The criminals will have competent knowledge about the illegal act being committed. They will know what they are doing, or at least be reasonably aware of the consequences of their actions.
2 *Purpose* The criminals will have an underlying purpose, a specific intent, behind the illegal act. Without such intent, an act such as hacking and browsing will not in itself entirely constitute a computer crime, but will merely be electronic trespass. Indeed, without knowledge or intent it may even be classed a simple and accidental security breach, perhaps the stumbling of an incompetent user.
3 *Malice* The perpetrator will be motivated by malice and will wish in some way to do harm. Even with knowledge and purpose no real crime will be apparent unless this element of malice is present.

23.3   Computer crime methods

Computer crimes will, ultimately, target the following domains of information
within a computer system:

- Information being entered (inputted) into the system.
- Information being processed by the system.
- Information being stored somewhere within the system, either within the
  hardware or stored on computer documents.
- Information produced (outputted) by the system.
- Information within the operating system of the computer.

Although computer crime statistics are inaccurate and limited, there is sufficient
evidence to identify certain types of computer crime. Prevention and detection of
each type will draw variously on the whole range of countermeasures described
earlier in this book.

1   *Equipment theft*   In its simplest form, computer crime can simply be the
    theft of computer equipment. This is at best irritating and costly, and at
    worst potentially catastrophic if the stolen equipment contained valuable or
    sensitive information. Indeed, the theft could have been directed at that very
    information. PCs are now highly sophisticated, attractive items which are
    portable and often found in that most informal and insecure of environments,
    the modern office. Armed with a white coat and clipboard, a thief is almost
    guaranteed to be able to walk off with whatever takes the fancy.

2   *Data theft*   The straightforward, physical theft of information from premises
    is made that much easier because of the concentrated form of electronic
    documents, their small size and their easy transportability.

3   *Data corruption or destruction*   The destruction or corruption of electronic
    data can have widespread and expensive consequences. Corruption or destruc-
    tion of electronic data can occur at any time—how many of us have not
    altered or deleted files accidentally?—but malicious acts of this nature are
    difficult to prevent or to prove. They can be performed by outsiders from a
    distance if they have (unauthorized) access to a system, or more insidiously
    by disaffected or dishonest employees with authorized access.

4   *Masquerading*   In this type of computer crime, the attacker assumes the
    identity of an authorized user by deceiving any access controls in place. Such
    deception can be technical—by the capture and abuse, or replication of,
    passwords or access tokens—or non-technical, by phoning into an enterprise
    and bluffing information from unsuspecting staff about passwords or other
    sensitive system information. Masquerading is one of the most commonly
    reported forms of illegal access to systems, and perhaps the most difficult to
    prove.

5   *Piggybacking*   With piggybacking, an intruder gains access to a system,
    again either technically or non-technically, on the back of an authorized
    user—non-technically by following them, for example, through physical

access points such as doors or turnstiles, or technically by compromising an authorized communications link either with a covert terminal tapped into the authorized line or by commandeering an improperly logged off or unattended terminal.

6   *Tailgating*   Tailgating involves the incorrect connection of a user to a system under the user-identification of another user.

7   *Data diddling*   Data diddling involving the alteration of data before or during its input, or during or after its output, used to be known in the old days before computers as 'fiddling the books'. As such, data diddling is the modern manifestation of a form of theft as old as accounting itself.

8   *Superzapping*   Superzapping involves the illegal use of Superzap utility programs, best compared to master keys and which are normally held and controlled by system managers to gain emergency access to systems and which circumvent all normal access controls. The powerful Superzap programs, readily available on the open market, can be used illegally to great advantage, giving high-level privileges over the system to unauthorized users which in turn can allow unauthorized system activity.

9   *Scavenging*   Scavenging involves the retrieval of waste information which is discarded by and surrounds any computer system during and after processing. Once again, this crime can be technical (for example, electronically scavenging data inadvertently retained on magnetic media) or non-technical (for example, physically searching any waste bins or scrap paper skips for discarded printout and other hard copy output).

10   *Viruses*   Viruses have been described in Chapter 21. There is no doubt that the extensive coverage afforded to viruses over the years has over-exaggerated their frequency and power. They have been restricted in the main to the PC environment, and then within the more relaxed education sector where controls are notoriously poor, perhaps deliberately so. Elsewhere, they have proved merely irritating rather than damaging.

11   *Worms*   Worms are programs which travel through a computer system or network by copying themselves from one part to another. They differ from viruses in that they act independently of their host, and in that given enough time and motivation their origin can be traced and proven.

12   *Trojan horses*   The presence of Trojan horses—programs which hide their outward appearance by trickery, like the Trojan horse of Greek mythology—especially places computers at risk of abuse since their very essence is to perform unauthorized (illegal?) functions under the cover of authorized activity. The Trojan horse is the most commonly used method for computer program-based crimes; it can be rendered virtually invisible within the complex operating systems of modern computers, and even if discovered will lend no identity to its author.

13   *Salami slicing*   Salami slicing is the technique which involves the taking of very small pickings (salami slices) from a very large treasure chest so that no notice is taken of the gradual but—over time—lucrative theft. Usually, the

pickings would be transferred internally to authorized accounts set up covertly for this purpose, and then transferred out of the system within the confines of the normal system rules (thus finally avoiding any chance of detection). There are numerous legendary examples of this computer crime, most of which have gone down in folklore and which have generated public sympathy for their audacity and because there were never any identifiable victims. Odd half-pennies can be shaved off accounts, large cash balances can be subtly rounded down, all concealed carefully to deceive auditors and never greedy enough to bother the individual victims or even, probably, come to their notice. Unfortunately for that part of the computer security fraternity intent on frightening the user community, there is no proven evidence that this type of crime has ever been committed!

14 *Logic bombs*   The equivalent of the terrorist's bomb, logic bombs destroy data or shut systems down in an explosive attack when triggered by some event such as a date, or a time, or when a memory space is saturated. Such bombs may be used as a revengeful attack, or more likely to destroy the evidence on completion of some other illegal act.

15 *Trapdoors*   There are often areas of program code provided during design to enable programmers subsequently to insert fresh code during system maintenance or development without entering via access controls. If left in place, either inadvertently or deliberately, they can provide a hidden route for an attacker, avoiding the controls on the front door. More insidiously, trapdoors can be inserted covertly and left hidden for later use by skilled attackers including hackers, during authorized use of the system or during even a single authorized session, even if that session has been discovered and passwords subsequently changed. As they say, it only takes once. . . .

16 *Hacking*   Hacking is discussed in Chapter 17. It represents one of the most prolific of unauthorized activities on computer systems, but not all examples may be classified as criminal, since often there is no real purpose to the activity—'it is just for the challenge'—nor any associated malice. Nevertheless, there are many cases where malevolent hackers have deliberately caused real harm, and the advice given earlier in this book, especially never to treat hackers benevolently, should be carefully heeded.

23.4   The investigation of computer crime

A computer crime may come to light in a number of ways—from information from an alert and observant member of staff, from the results of an offence itself, from a system failure, through audit, or as a spin-off from other enquiries. Whatever, and in common with the investigation of any other crime, the very first actions must endeavour to freeze the situation, to preserve the scene of the crime. Ideally, equipment must be physically and electronically isolated, documents (traditional and magnetic) must be seized and secured with evidential continuity, witnesses must be interviewed; at the very least, no harm should be done. But in the modern age of computers, things are never that easy and any investigation will inevitably be pitted against time and operational pressures. It is imperative that enquiries begin as quickly as possible in order simultaneously to:

- prevent further damage
- limit the losses incurred
- find out what went wrong
- identify the perpetrator
- preserve evidence

Investigators must work closely with system and security staff, auditors, personnel staff, legal advisers, the police and senior management. It may be that the investigators delegate for example actions to limit further damage directly to system staff who will best understand the necessary safeguards and procedures, and to senior management who will appreciate the business impact and who will be able to assess consequential losses. Whatever, and in whatever respect, it is essential that all those involved in post-crime clear-up operations are working together and communicating freely if the best result is to be achieved in the shortest possible time.

23.5   Punishment and deterrence

Ideally, an investigation will positively identify an offender, recover all the necessary evidence to ensure a successful legal prosecution under appropriate legislation, and the cowboy wearing the black hat will be marched straight off to gaol. But life is rarely that straightforward. Prudent enterprises will, therefore, have included in their computer security policies clear boundaries of acceptable staff conduct beyond which employees must expect disciplinary action or even dismissal to follow. In this way, deterrent action can be taken even when the heavy proof needed for full legal recourse is not available. Employees should be required to sign, as part of their contract of employment and during annual appraisals or other refresher interviews, an acknowledgement of their understanding of the rules and their acceptance of the possible penalties for any misconduct.

24
Computer security and the law

Until only recently legislation over the use of computers has been relatively immature in:

- enforcing appropriate levels of computer security within the business community;
- properly prosecuting individuals for computer misuse;
- using computer-produced information as admissible evidence in criminal and civil prosecutions.

Legislation enacted prior to 1984 was simply inadequate for information technology. Furthermore, the concept of electronic information as an asset with real value had not been recognized by the legal system. Given the pervasive impact of computers on most aspects of the business world, the need for such legislation to maintain order in business practices became urgent.

24.1   Current legislation in the United Kingdom

24.1.1 Legal enforcement of computer security

Recent legislation has imposed stricter controls and more stringent monitoring of businesses in the United Kingdom.

1 *The UK Data Protection Act, 1984*, established an independent public register of information systems containing information about individuals, and legislation for protection of that information. The Act aims to ensure that personal data is accurate, used appropriately to its declared purpose, and is securely held.

2 *The Financial Services Act, 1986*   The necessity to use computers to perform, record and monitor the business activities of enterprises providing financial services is recognized by the Financial Service Act, 1986, and additional provisions to regulate their use have been included. The requirements are for:
  - an organized systems development methodology;
  - up-to-date documentation of systems;
  - effective change control procedures and adequate testing of system changes;

- effective access control software, including procedures which ensure that passwords are sensibly designed and then issued, used and controlled in a secure manner;
- adequate, up-to-date and well-tested disaster recovery plans.

In addition, the Act set up self-regulatory organizations to monitor compliance. As an example, the Securities Association requires that:

- member firms establish and maintain systems of internal controls, and procedures for the security, privacy and preservation of their records;
- all records are maintained in sufficient detail and with sufficient cross referencing to establish an adequate audit trail.

3 *The Banking Act, 1987*   A Guidance Note was issued by the Banking Supervision Department of the Bank of England in September 1987 to all institutions authorized to trade under the Banking Act, 1987. This Guidance Note, on Accounting and Other Records and Internal Control System (AORICS) covers a wide area, including the following topics:

- disaster recovery
- systems development risks
- data entry errors
- business interruption
- fraud
- access to confidential information
- organization of a bank's computer department
- PC-based applications
- regular monitoring of internal control
- the function of internal audit

4 *The Building Societies Act, 1986*   A Prudential Note circulated by the Building Societies Commission explains the need for a Society to establish and maintain a 'system of control of its business' covering the totality of the business process. Security-related requirements identified in the Note are:

- identification and assessment of risks and the adequacy of controls
- documented security policy and procedures
- disaster recovery
- adequate security measures
- effective internal audit
- assurance of accuracy of records
- assurance of safeguarding of assets

24.1.2 Applicability of existing laws to computer misuse

Before the passage of the Computer Misuse Act, 1990, attempts had been made to apply existing laws to computer misuse. In many cases these laws were held by the courts to be incapable of use in an information technology environment.

1 *The Criminal Damage Act, 1971*, can be interpreted to exclude destruction of
   data or software, which may not be seen by the courts to be tangible damage
   to property. However, an Appeal Court decision in 1991 (R. vs. Whiteley)
   upheld the view that, if an alteration to the contents of a disk 'caused
   impairment of the value of usefulness of the disk to the legitimate operator',
   the necessary damage was established.
2 *Offences under the Theft Act, 1968*, cannot be applied to the copying of
   valuable or sensitive information, since:
   ● the property involved is intangible
   ● the owner is not deprived of anything
   ● a machine cannot be deceived
3 *The Forgery and Counterfeiting Act, 1981*, was held in the House of Lords
   ruling of R. vs. Gold and Schifreen to be inappropriate when considering
   unauthorized use of a password to enter a computer system.
4 *The Data Protection Act, 1984*, will apply to hackers only if:
   ● personal data is accessed;
   ● they are registered data users acting outside the terms of their registration;
     or
   ● they become unregistered data users as a result of their hacking activities.

24.1.3   The Computer Misuse Act, 1990

The Computer Misuse Act, 1990, represents the first successful attempt in the
United Kingdom to designate unauthorized access to a computer system as a
crime. There are three categories of offence:

● unauthorized access to computer programs or data (maximum penalty six
  months' imprisonment and/or £2000 fine);
● unauthorized access with intent to commit or facilitate the commission of a
  serious offence (maximum penalty five years' imprisonment and/or an
  unlimited fine);
● unauthorized modification of computer data or programs (maximum penalty
  five years' imprisonment and/or an unlimited fine).

The offences can apply not only to external hackers, but also to employees who
exceed their access authorizations. The Act does not impose statutory duties on
system owners, but in order to be assured of the full protection of the law they
will need to take certain precautions, such as ensuring that:

● employees and other users fully understand the limits of their authority;
● all instances of misuse are detected and properly logged at an early stage.

In common with many other laws the Act has avoided defining a 'computer' in
order to allow the courts greater flexibility. The Act introduces new rules
governing jurisdiction, allowing UK courts to prosecute cases of computer
misuse directed at computers in the UK, wherever they originate. Similarly, a

misuse originating from the UK which affects computers abroad can be prosecuted in the UK, provided it is an offence in the other country.

24.2   Admissibility of computer evidence

24.2.1 Criminal law

In criminal cases a great deal of time is spent deciding whether evidence is admissible or not. Until 1984 such decisions were based on common law, refined by a number of—sometimes conflicting—judgements. The decisions required answers to the following questions:

- Is it real evidence or hearsay? Was the evidence generated wholly by computer or with human involvement?
- Is it reliable? Computer people may testify as experts, but only if their opinions are based on proper scientific analysis.
- Is it the 'best evidence'? This test has gradually been eroded in respect of business records. The rule rejects 'inferior' evidence such as a copy of a document or a witness's description of an object if the original is obtainable. However, courts on both sides of the Atlantic are now happy to accept copies of original documents where they are not in dispute.

The Police and Criminal Evidence Act, 1984, agreed for the first time that computer output can be considered admissible unless it can be shown that the computer is faulty. Section 69 of the Act governs all computer-generated evidence placed before the English and Welsh criminal courts. It states that such evidence will only be submitted if a certificate is provided by the system manager stating that:

- there are no reasonable grounds for believing that it is inaccurate because of improper use of the computer; and
- that at all material times, the computer was operating reliably, or, if not, that any respect in which it was not operating properly or out of operation could not have affected the production of the printout document or the accuracy of its contents.

It should be noted that the phrase 'no reasonable grounds' features only in the first clause. Its omission from the second clause means that the system manager must be certain that the system could not have acted incorrectly during the period when the relevant information was entered, stored and printed out or, at least, that any such malfunction would not have affected the integrity of that information. Anything less and the evidence will be excluded.

The recent case of R. vs. Spilby made it clear that a Section 69 Certificate is only needed where there has been some human intervention in the computer process. A Section 69 Certificate would be needed to prove an entry in a bank statement relating to a withdrawal by cheque, since at some stage a human being has written the amount on it in magnetic ink. However, this section would not apply to an entry relating to a withdrawal through an Automated Teller Machine (ATM) since there is no human input to the process. R. vs. Spilby concerned printout showing the details of the telephone calls made from certain rooms at a hotel, captured by a private automated branch exchange in the building. The court ruled that, as there had been no human involvement, the printout was 'real' and not 'hearsay' evidence. The court could, therefore, invoke the legal presumption that the equipment was working properly and ignore Section 69.

24.2.2 Civil law

In civil cases exceptions to the hearsay rule are codified in the Civil Evidence Act, 1968. Section 5 was drafted explicitly to cover the admissibility of computer evidence. However, the section is limited in its scope and reflects the state of technology at the time the Act was passed. The section refers to a computer as 'any device for storing and processing information', which covers the hardware but ignores the existence of software.

For a computer printout to be accepted as admissible evidence in a civil case the following conditions must be satisfied:

- the printout must have been produced by the computer during a period over which the computer was used regularly to store and process information for the purpose of any activity regularly carried on over that period;
- over the period there was regularly supplied to the computer, in the ordinary course of those activities, information of the kind contained in the statement or of the kind from which the information so contained is derived;
- throughout the material part of that period the computer must have been operating properly or, if not, that the impairment was not such as to offset the correctness of the result;
- the information contained in the statement reproduces, or is derived from, information supplied to the computer in the ordinary course of those activities.

However, the provisions might exclude output which is not regularly generated, such as *ad hoc* reports produced for internal or external auditors or a print of the system log.

24.3   USA legislation

1   *The Foreign Corrupt Practices Act, 1977*, contains provisions which require all companies to maintain an adequate system of internal accounting controls and records of financial transactions. In the event of bribery being proved on the part of any member of the enterprise, evidence of proper control and recording of transactions would assist in proving that the enterprise had no

corporate responsibility, thereby avoiding or mitigating the severe punishments which can be imposed.

2   *The Counterfeit Access Device and Computer Fraud and Abuse Act, 1984 (PL98–473)*, prohibits unauthorized access to and disclosure of:

   - information protected or restricted from disclosure for national security reasons;
   - financial records kept by financial institutions or consumer reporting agencies;
   - information stored on any 'federal interest computer'.

The law provides for fines of up to US$10 000 or up to ten years' imprisonment for first offenders. Although some computer crimes could be prosecuted under long-standing federal laws against wire fraud and interception of communications offences, this was the first Federal law that specifically targeted computer crimes. Under the law, fraud associated with automated teller machines became a federal crime.

3   *The Computer Fraud and Abuse Act, 1986*, extends federal jurisdiction to cover computer crimes which affect federal interest to major financial institutions and businesses involved in interstate commerce. It extended the 1984 Act's coverage to medical records, examinations, diagnoses, care and treatment; made fraudulent or improper use of passwords illegal; and further defined the term 'financial institution'.

   The Act makes it illegal for an unauthorized person to obtain classified information by a computer 'with the intent or reason to believe that such information so obtained is to be used to the injury of the United States or to the advantage of any foreign nation'. An unauthorized person is defined as one who 'knowingly and intentionally accesses a computer without authorization or exceeds authorized access'. The maximum penalty for a first offence is ten years' imprisonment, with twenty years for any subsequent breaches.

4   *The Electronic Communications Privacy Act, 1986*, broadened the definitions of electronic communications provided by the original 1968 wiretap law, although it added specific exceptions for a variety of uses 'readily accessible to the public'. It allows prosecution of criminals who gain unauthorized access to computers across state lines via telecommunications networks, and encourages communications service providers to take advantage of the Act's protection by scrambling and encrypting their signals. Equally important, the Act authorized, for the first time, recovery of civil damages as well as criminal penalties.

5   *The Computer Security Act, 1987*, gave the National Institute of Standards and Technology (NIST) authority over computer security in non-classified federal interest computers. This covered databases; the responsibility for protection of classified data remained with the National Security Agency. All agencies were required to report to the Institute on their plans to implement security features and develop security awareness training.

6 *The Credit Card Fraud Act, 1984* (Section 102, of Title 18, US Code), used the term 'access device' to define credit, debit cards and ATM cards. The following activities were stated to be felonies:

- to produce, use, or traffic in counterfeit access devices;
- to possess fifteen or more counterfeit or unauthorized access devices;
- to produce illicitly, traffic in, have control of or custody of, or to possess access device making equipment.

The Act also gave authority to the US Secret Service to investigate any activity that affects interstate or foreign commerce in regard to such fraudulent access devices. It also included the use of legitimate account numbers on illicit cards.

7 *State legislation* 48 US states have now passed computer crime or fraud and abuse laws. In many cases the state laws offer more protection than Federal laws, and some allow civil litigation against the perpetrators not only for actual damages, but also for extra damages and costs.

24.4   Other relevant international legislation

24.4.1 Australia

1 *Amendment of 'Summary Offences Act', 1966, by Crimes (Computers) Act, 1988, (Victoria)*   Section 9a: 'A person must not gain access to, or enter, a computer system or part of a computer system without lawful authority to do so'.

2 *Amendment made to 'Crimes Act', 1914, Following Proposals in 'Review of Commonwealth Criminal Law,' Nov 1988* Section 3: '"Data" includes information, computer program or a part of a computer program'.

Section 87B(1): '(1) A person who, without authority, intentionally obtains access to:

(a) data stored in a Commonwealth computer; or
(b) data stored in a computer (not being a Commonwealth computer) on behalf of the Commonwealth or a public authority under the Commonwealth;

is guilty of an offence'.

3 *Proposed Introduction of New Chapter to Tasmanian Criminal Code proposed by Law Reform Commission of Tasmania*   Includes: 'Any person who, without authority, knowingly gains access to a computer, computer network or any part thereof, is guilty of a crime'.

'"Data" includes any information that is capable of being stored or being retrieved by a computer and includes computer programs.'
'"Data" means a representation that has been transcribed by methods, the accuracy of which is verifiable, into the form appropriate to the computer into which it is, or is to be, introduced' (Tasmanian Evidence Act).

'"Access": includes to communicate with a computer.'

24.4.2 Canada

1 *Canadian Criminal Law Amendment Act, 1985* Section 301.2 punishes 'everyone who fraudulently and without colour of right ...

   (b) by means of an electromagnetic, acoustic, mechanical, or other device intercepts or causes to be intercepted, directly or indirectly any functions of a computer system ...'

In this section 'data' means 'representations of information or of concepts that are being prepared or have been prepared in a form suitable for use in a computer system'.

24.4.3 Denmark

1 *Penal Code Amendment Act, June 1985* Section 263(2): 'Anyone who gains unauthorized access to anyone's data or software intended for electronic data processing will be punished'. The penalty of up to six months imprisonment rises to two years if the crime is committed for the purpose of stealing trade secrets.
Section 279 punishes anyone guilty of 'Data Trespass', i.e. anyone who, with the intention of profiting, amends or deletes data or programs or attempts to disrupt computer processing.
2 *The Danish Public Authorities Registers Act, 1988, and Private Registers Act, 1988*, govern the use and registration of personal data in EDP systems. Supervision of compliance with the requirements is the responsibility of the Data Surveillance Authority (DSA), which has produced a set of standards (Recommended Security Measures) for the use of personal computers.
3 *The Danish Supervisory Authority of Financial Affairs* is responsible for the surveillance of banks, insurance companies and other financial institutions. It achieves this by:

- performing regular security reviews;
- issuing instructions to Certified Public Accountants on the audit of the financial sector.

4 *The Bookkeeping Act, 1959* New instructions came into force in 1990 extending the rules of this statute to cover security and auditability of electronic vouchers. These include the following:
- the company should have all necessary updated documentation of systems, files, functions etc. concerning all applications and hardware in use in the last five years;
- the company should be able, irrespective of any changes in hardware or software, to print out all necessary vouchers, transactions, financial output

which might be necessary in order to audit the last five years' bookkeeping;

- all transactions should be filed and be retrievable, including changes in basic files (parameters, variables, etc.);
- all automatically generated vouchers should be auditable through the system documentation;
- there should be a clear transaction trail (from the individual transaction to the financial statement) and a clear audit trail (including documentation, parameters and any algorithms used).

24.4.4 France

Law Relating to Information Fraud, 1988

Article 462-2: 'Whoever, fraudulently, accesses or remains within all or part of a data processing system will be punished'. The offence is punishable by:

- two to twelve months' imprisonment *and* a fine of Fr2000 to Fr50 000; or
- two months' to two years' imprisonment with no fine; or
- a Fr10 000 to Fr100 000 fine.

Access or remaining in the system provides the offence—there is no need to prove intent to commit a further offence.

'Data' is defined as 'representation of a piece of information in an ordered form designed to facilitate its processing.'

Articles 462-3 and 462-5 impose sentences of:

- three months' to three years' imprisonment and fines of Fr10 000 to Fr100 000 for interfering with the operation of a data processing system;
- similar terms of imprisonment, with fines of between Fr2000 and Fr50 000, for interfering with the authenticity and integrity of the data.

Under Articles 462-5 and 462-6 it is illegal to falsify a computerized document to the detriment of any person or to use such a forged document. The punishment for either offence is one to five years' imprisonment and a fine of between Fr20 000 and Fr2 million.

24.4.5 Germany

1 *Second Law for the Prevention of Economic Crimes, 1986* Section 202a: '(1) Any person who obtains without authorization, for himself or another, data which are not meant for him and which are specifically protected against unauthorized access, shall be liable to a penalty of three years imprisonment or a fine. (2) Data within the meaning of subsection (1) are only such as are stored or transmitted electronically or in any other form not directly visible'.

Section 263a prohibits—on pain of up to five years in prison or a fine—causing loss to another, with intent to gain, by influencing the result of a data processing operation by the following means:

- incorrectly configuring a program;
- using incomplete, unauthorized or incorrect data;
- other unauthorized impact on computer operations.

Section 303a creates an offence—punishable by terms of up to two years imprisonment or a fine—to unlawfully delete, suppress, alter data or otherwise render it unserviceable.

Section 303b punishes by imprisonment of up to five years or a fine, conduct which impairs a data processing operation which is of vital importance to an external plant or another enterprise, by any of the offences described in Section 303a. If the same result is achieved by destroying or rendering unserviceable a data processing plant or data carrier, the same penalty applies.

2 *Kreditwesengesetz* (KWG) 1985 The main purpose of KWG is to safeguard and support the functioning of the financial apparatus, strengthening the foundation of the financial system by regulating competition, publicity and bank supervision over loans and liquidity. It subjects all financial institutions to federal bank supervision and also implements a complete licensing system. The security of bank deposits is ensured by the legal requirement to publicize large loans as well as certain types of loans to agencies or authorities, an activity performed by an organization called *Evidenzzentrale*.

3 *Bundesdatenschutzgesetz (BDSG) 1977*   The legal basis of BDSG is to protect the public from misuse of 'personal-related' data. It applies to everybody who handles such data in their work. The protection of personal data from misuse applies during the saving, transferring, changing and deleting processes of data handling. Access to personal data requires the permission of the affected person, or explicit permission given by laws requiring the release of such information. The affected person has a right to request information about what is being done to his personal data, and to request the protection as well as deletion of the data.

24.4.6 The Netherlands

The Franken Commission Proposals, April 1987

Data is described as 'representation of facts, concepts or instructions in an agreed manner, suitable for transfer, interpretation or processing by persons or by automated means'. If Proposal 1 is implemented, anyone damaging or causing a malfunction of a security measure in a computer could be imprisoned for:

- up to six months, or fined if the 'common good' were hindered by the act; or

- up to 15 years if the act caused someone's death.

By Proposal 2, the above actions, if caused negligently, could render the perpetrator liable to up to a year's imprisonment. Proposal 4 recommends that one who deletes data, or makes it useless or inaccessible, should be liable to up to two years' imprisonment or a fine. Proposal 15 lays down that any person who unlawfully intrudes into a computerized device protected against such intrusion, used for the storage or processing of data, or into a protected part thereof, shall be liable to six months' imprisonment or a fine. If that person then sells any information taken during the intrusion, the punishment could be increased under Proposal 16 to three years' imprisonment or a fine.

24.4.7 Norway

Although there are few laws and regulations which directly regulate computer security in general, some current laws apply to specific areas.

1 *Losbladforskriftene, 13 May 1977*   This sets up provisions for documentation of 'business control systems' (primarily relating to record handling in accounting systems) using any other medium than bound ledgers. The regulation states that there should be a description of the accounting system and the accounting functions included in the system and documentation of the control system established to ensure complete, accurate and reliable bookkeeping. There should also be detailed and easily understandable documentation making it possible to trace and control each transaction for processing and presentation (an audit trail). The regulation also sets up certain requirements in relation to the auditability of the cash book, debtors' and creditors' ledgers and the general ledger. Changes in master data files that may affect the transaction processing are to be documented separately.

2 *Regulations Concerning the Use of Computers and Terminals in Commercial and Savings Banks*   Introduced in 1983 by the Banking Inspection Agency (Bankinspeksjonen) it updates the *Public Supervision of Banks and other Financial Institutions Act, 1956*. The regulations are intended to ensure that the development, maintenance and operations of computer systems are orderly and secure. They cover the following areas:

    - *Standards*   There should at all times be standards relating to system development, maintenance, operations and documentation.
    - *Systems*   For purchasing, development and maintenance of systems there must be routines or procedures which ensure correct system specifications and adequate documentation.
    - *Operations*   There must be established routines or procedures to ensure completeness and correctness in electronic data processing.
    - *Information interchange*   Automated information transfers between banks, customers and clearing houses should be regulated by written

agreement in order to ensure that availability of necessary functional and operations documentation.

Documentation should be sufficiently detailed to enable parties other than the original developers to use, maintain, control and perform error recovery and should cover:

- standards, routines and procedures;
- description of technical aspects for development, maintenance and operations;
- description of manual routines relating to data collection, error recovery and handling of system output.

3   *Personvernloven (Individual Protection Act of 9 June 1978, No. 48)*   This Act regulates the storage and processing of individually related information. It covers manual as well as automated systems in both the private and public sectors and applies to information related to any single individual, organization or foundation. The information held should be reasonable with respect to the administration and operation of the organization conducting the registering. Unless it can be shown to be necessary, information should not be held concerning:

- race, political or religious conviction;
- an individual who has been suspected of, charged with, or sentenced for a criminal offence;
- health or alcohol and drug abuse;
- sexual matters;
- family matters other than family relationship and status.

Establishing a 'register' with personal information relating to individuals requires a specific concession. Additional regulations have set up several general concessions serving as exceptions to this requirement, allowing the use of more trivial information without the need for a specific concession. The law also provides for the establishment of Datatilsynet as an oversight agency. It is established to handle questions relating to individual protection and give concessions for establishing registers covered under the law. Datatilsynet will also advise on securing registered data. The Act makes provisions for an individual to gain access to registered information relating to that individual. It also regulates the manner of correcting incorrect information and the transfer of individual-related information to other countries.

4   *Proposed Changes to the Penal Code, 1922, Section 270*   The changes are related to fraud, and make it a criminal offence for anyone to inflict a loss or a possible loss by introducing changes in data or computer programs or in any other illegal way affecting the outcome of electronic data processing. The penalty may be fines or imprisonment for up to three years.

24.4.8 *Sweden*

Swedish Data Act, 1973   Section 21: 'Any person who unlawfully gains access to a recording for automatic data processing or unlawfully alters or obliterates or enters such a recording in a file shall be sentenced for data trespass'. An addition to the penal code in 1985 designated as a fraud the act of altering a program or otherwise, without permission, affecting the results of 'automatic information processing' in a way which involves gain for the offender or loss for others.

Bibliography

Appleby, Colin, Information Technology Security Evaluation Criteria (ITSEC), *Datapro Reports on Information Security*, January 1991.

Beattie, Henry J., Computer security belongs in the security department, *Security Management*, May 1983.

Carroll, John M., *Computer Security*, Butterworths, London, 1977.

Coe, Robert R. and Armstrong, John. W., Computer eavesdropping, the practical approach, *Compsec 87*, Elsevier, London.

Collier, G., Relations between audit and the security function, *Compsec 86*, Elsevier, London.

Commission of the European Communities (DG XIII), *Information Technology Security Evaluation Criteria*, ESCS-EEC-EAEC 91.

Cresson Wood, Charles, Using information security to achieve competitive advantage, *Compsec 91*, Elsevier, London.

Daniel, Murt, Motivation is critical, *Compsec 91* (UK).

Datapro Reports on Information Security, *Data Classification and Ownership: the IBM Approach*, June 1990.

Davies, D., Computer insurance: the strategy, *Compsec 87*, Elsevier, London.

Davies, D., The limitations of insurance, *Compsec 87*, Elsevier, London.

Davies, D., Consequential loss insurance, *Corporate Computer Security 88*, Elsevier, London.

Davies, D., Insuring computer risks, *Computer Fraud and Security Bulletin*, January 1992.

DeMaio, Harry B., *Information Protection and Other Unnatural Acts*, AMACOM, New York, 1992.

De Morgan, B., The system is only as safe as its staff, *Security Gazette*, January 1988.

Department of Defense (USA), *Trusted Computer System Evaluation Criteria*, 5200,28-STD, December 1985.

Dubash, M., A plague on your systems, *Practical Computing*, April 1988.

Forage, G., Systems security, presented to Professional Personal Computer Conference, London, October 1987.

Gordon, John, The security of packet switched systems, *Corporate Computer Security 88*. PLF Communications, Brighton.

Hearnden, K., How can security managers advance their cause?, *Security Gazette*, January 1988.

Helsing, C.W., Corporate Contingency Planning, *Datapro Reports on Information Security*, January 1989.

Hollins, J.D., Implementing computer security within a commercial organisation, *Compsec 91* Elsevier, London.

Jackson, Carl B., How to sell top management on information security, *Datapro Reports on Information Security*, June 1990.

Jackson, Carl B., The need for security, *Datapro Reports on Information Security*, October 1990.

Jackson, Carl B., EDP auditing: Background and issues, *Datapro Reports on Information Security*, September 1991.

Jackson, Hruska and Parker, *Computer Security Reference Book*, Butterworth Heinemann, Oxford, 1992.

Keddie, S., Personal aspects of computer security, *Compsec 86*, Elsevier, London.

Langley, M., The confidential agents, *IBM Computer Today*, August 1987.

Lee, Robin, *Electronic Eavesdropping*, Elsevier Seminars 88, Elsevier, London.

Lindsay, D., Personnel and recruitment policies?, *Corporate Computer Security 88*, PLF Communications, London.

Lowe, S., Data security, *PC Week*, May 1987.

McIntosh, J., Controlled access, *Systems International*, November 1987.

McLean, K., Choosing a security product, *Compsec 87*, Elsevier, London.

McNulty, L., Small systems security, *Compsec 86* (UK).

Martin, J., *Security, Accuracy and Privacy in Computer Systems*, Prentice-Hall, Englewood Cliffs NJ, 1973.

Moffat, J., Protecting the system from the enemy within, *Computing*, 5 May 1988.

National Audit Office, *Computer Security in Government Departments*, HMSO, October 1987.

National Centre for Information Technology, *Survey of IT Security Failures and Breaches*, NCC (UK), 1992.

Parker, Donn B., Computer Crime Methods and Detection, *Datapro Reports on Information Security*, December 1990.

Parkin, R., A practical anti-virus strategy, *Virus Bulletin Conference 92*, Soplios, Edinburgh.

Poindexter, Dennis F., The gap between computer people and security people, *Security Management*, October 1980.

Reed, A., *Computer Risk Manager*, Elsevier, Amsterdam, 1987.

Samocuik, Martin, *Hacking: will you be the next victim?*, Elsevier Seminars 87, Elsevier, London.

Schweitzer, James A., *Computers, Business and Security*, Butterworths, London, 1987.

Serpel, S., *Security Implications in Commercial Networks*, Elsevier Seminars 88, Elsevier, London.

Serpel, S., *Security Implications in wide area networks*, NCC IT Conference 88, NCC, Blackpool.

Shari Mendelson Gallery, *Computer Security*, Butterworths, London, 1987.

Shelton, E., Viruses—a terrorist tool of tomorrow?, *Computing*, 21 April 1988.

Sherwood, John, Network and telecommunications security, *Compsec 87*, Elsevier, London.

Slater, Ken, *Information Security in Financial Services*, Stockton Press, New York, 1991.

Smith, J., *Secure People*, IBC Technical Publications, London, 1989.

Smith, M., How to promote security awareness, *Datapro Reports in Information Security*, March 1992.

Smith, Peter D., Multilevel secure local area networks using trusted workstations. *System Security 88*, Elsevier, London.

Tantam, M., *Computer Abuse Investigator*, Elsevier, Amsterdam, 1990.

Tompkins, Frederick G., Are you computer wise?, *Security Management*, September 1982.

UK Audit Commission, *Survey of Computer Fraud and Abuse*, HMSO, 1990.

Whitley, Duncan M., Physical Security, *Compsec 87*, Elsevier, London.

Wilson, R.D. and Silverman, M.E., Why haven't you done something about EDP security?, *Security Management*, March 1985.

Wong, K., Security aspects of office systems, *Compsec 86*, Elsevier, London.

Index

format of, 42
importance of, 40–41
PC security, 219
reviews of, 45
system security policies, 39
technical security policies, 39
uses for, 47–48
  see also Personal computers, Security
  operating procedure
Portable (laptop) computers, *see* Personal
  computers
Protocols, *see* Network security
Psychometric testing, *see* Personnel
  security
Public key systems, *see* Algorithm
Purging, *see* Document security

Registration of computers, 73–78
  see also Illegal software copying
Relocatable units, *see* Standby facilities
Remote diagnostics, *see* Hardware security
Responsibilities for security, 41, 45, 51–62
  see also Duties
Risk, 19
Risk analysis, 19–21, 31, 37, 40, 45, 71
  policy decisions, 41–42
  techniques, 22–26
  see also Policies, computer security
Risks to computers, 17–21
Rotation of duties *see Personnel security*
RSA, *see* Algorithm

Salami slicing, *see* Computer crime
Scavenging, *see* Computer crime
Screening *see* Personnel security
Security,
  definition of, 5–6
  nature of security features, 26–27
Security inspections, 65, 68, 221
Security operating procedures, 39–40, 65,
  71, 221
  see also Policy, computer security
Security staff, problems with being, 54–56
Separation, *see* Software security
Service bureau, *see* Standby facilities
Smartcards, 137
Software security, 29, 47, 127–144
aims of, 127–128
  audit, 141–142, 148
  assurance, 128, 149, 155, 157–158
  covert channels, 144

general measures, 130–132
limitations of, 128–130
logical access control, 132–137
modes of secure processing, 138–141,
  151–152
passwords, 67, 133–137, 217
PC security, 225–226
programming, 142–143
separation, 137–141
tokens, 137
Sleepers, *see* Viruses
Standby facilities, *see* Disaster recovery
Superzapping, *see* Computer crime
Sweeps, *see* Technical eavesdropping
System high mode of secure processing,
  see Modes of secure processing
System security policy, *see* Policy,
  computer security

Tailgating, *see* Computer crime
TCSEC, *see* Orange Book
Technical eavesdropping, 84, 165–168, 177
  see also Compromising emanations,
  Network security
Technical security policy, *see* Policy,
  computer security
TEMPEST, *see* Comprising emanations
Threats to computers, 10–13
Tokens, *see* Logical access control
Training, *see* Awareness
Trapdoors, *see* Viruses
Trojan horses, *see* Viruses
Trusted computer base, *see* Evaluation
Two person principle, *see* Personnel
  security

Valuing data, *see* Classification
Vendor agreements, *see* Standby facilities
Viruses, 129, 227–236, 259
  anti-virus strategies, 230–233
  future developments, 235–236
  high–risk systems, 233–235
  impact of, 230
  overheads of countermeasures, 235
  routes of infection, 229
  see also Computer crime
Vulnerabilities of computers, 13–15

Warm starts, *see* Standby facilities
Worms, *see* Computer crime